GOD IN THE FOXHOLE

INSPIRING TRUE STORIES OF MIRACLES ON THE BATTLEFIELD

Charles W. Sasser

THRESHOLD EDITIONS

NEW YORK LONDON TORONTO SYDNEY

Threshold Editions
A Division of Simon & Schuster, Inc.
1230 Avenue of the Americas
New York, NY 10020

Copyright © 2008 by Charles W. Sasser

First Threshold Editions hardcover edition November 2008

THRESHOLD EDITIONS and colophon are trademarks of
Simon & Schuster, Inc.

For information about special discounts for bulk purchases,
please contact Simon & Schuster Special Sales at 1-800-456-6798
or business@simonandschuster.com.

Designed by Mary Austin Speaker

Manufactured in the United States of America

10   9   8   7   6   5   4   3   2   1

ISBN-13: 978-1-4165-4137-0
ISBN-10:   1-4165-4137-3

For Pastor Jimmy Layne

CONTENTS

FOREWORD

They say that nothing in this universe happens by accident. That
includes the writing and creation of this book. How the author got
inspired to collect these stories and share them with the world is no more
an accident of fate than are the stories inside this book themselves. It was
almost as if they had a life of their own and were waiting for the author
to gather and harvest them.

When Chuck (author Charles W. Sasser) e-mailed me and then talked
to me on the phone about his project, the timing could not have been
better. I had a similar project in mind and had gathered dozens of stories
for a book about the spiritual experiences of men in combat. I was recovering from a heart attack and it was not certain I would have the time
and energy to complete this holy task. My goal was simply to gift these
stories to the world so they would inspire others. I soon realized that
Chuck's goal and mine were forged of the same intentions; thus a spiritual partnership of sorts was formed. I gave him my blessings and all my
contacts, and access to any of my own personal experiences he chose to
write about. (Some of these accounts appear in Chapters 11 and 14.)

What is inside these pages represents the faith and courage of men
whom both of us knew and learned about. Every one of the stories

presents evidence that God's amazing grace exists in great abundance in those who are open to His loving and protective arms. A simple battlefield prayer, the cry of a wounded or dying soldier is heard and honored more than most realize. I hope that when you read the personal accounts and experiences of these men you will find inspiration in your own life battles and know that miracles continue to happen to those who have faith.

I know many of the men mentioned in this book on some personal level and believe that each of their stories is sacred and holy. They share them for the same reason that Chuck wrote this book—to inspire each of you on your own "spiritual journey" through life.

Reverend Bill McDonald
Author, *A Spiritual Warrior's Journey*

INTRODUCTION

There are, according to an old saying, no atheists in foxholes. Even atheists and freethinkers find compelling reasons to seek spiritual solace whenever bombs start falling and bullets flying. U.S. Marine Sergeant Leland Belknap, who fought in the South Pacific during World War II, didn't believe "there were very many of us who didn't do a lot of praying up there. The only atheist that I knew said he would not pray when he got up front. The first night he came crawling over to the man he had said that to and they prayed together."

The presence of faith is exceptionally strong in the armed forces, especially during wartime when soldiers face the prospect of dying. Hardship and horror, fear, loneliness, and rage have driven warriors over the centuries to reach for their spiritual side. The battlefield, as author Stephen Mansfield notes, is as much a test of faith as it is a test of arms.

In 1991, I was a U.S. Army first sergeant for a military police company preparing to ship overseas for Operation Desert Storm, the first Iraq war. The night before my outfit emplaned, a chaplain conducted services and passed out pocket Bibles and little silver crosses. Virtually every MP in the company wore his cross on his dog tag chain until the war ended. I still have mine.

I served twenty-nine years in the military (active and reserve), including thirteen years as a Special Forces (Green Beret) soldier. I heard hundreds of stories of spirituality, conversion, and, yes, miracles from the battlefield. It finally occurred to me that one important aspect of combat has rarely been explored—that of the spiritual and how soldiers at war turn to it. I began soliciting such tales from warriors old and young. The result is this book, a chronicle about soldiers at war, but a war story with a deeper turn to it.

Many may rationalize or attempt to offer other explanations for spiritual conversions or metaphysical experiences in battle, but to those who lived them they are and will always remain *real*. Here, then, are the incredible war stories of soldiers whose faith has been born, reborn, tested, sustained, verified, or transformed under fire.

I would also like to take this opportunity to thank all the fine men and women who participated in reliving their personal experiences, filling in the gaps of history, and sharing the stories that appear in these pages. Their help in the monumental task of researching and writing this book made a difficult project an enjoyable experience.

Particular thanks also go to longtime editor and friend Kevin Smith at Pocket Books, and to editor Kathy Sagan, who helped launch this project and see it through fruition; to my literary agent and friend Ethan Ellenberg, who has guided and directed my writing career for over twenty years; and, as always, to my wife, Donna Sue, for her patience and understanding.

Actual names are used throughout except in those rare instances where names were lost due to either memory loss or a lack of documentation, where privacy was requested, or where public identification would serve no useful purpose and might cause embarrassment.

In various instances dialogue and scenes have necessarily been re-created. Time has a tendency to erode memory in some areas and selectively enhance it in others. Where this occurs, and where only limited materials were available, I strive to match personalities with the situation and the action while maintaining factual content, using my own extensive military and combat experience as a guide. The recounting of some events, therefore, may not correspond precisely with the memories of everyone involved. In addition, all data has been filtered through the author. I must therefore apologize to anyone omitted, neglected, or somehow slighted in the preparation of this book. I take responsibility for such errors and ask to be forgiven for them.

While I am certain to have made interpretational mistakes, I am just as certain that the content of this book is accurate to the spirit and reality of all the brave people who participated in the events described in this book.

Charles W. Sasser

1

FAITH

For verily I say unto you, If ye have faith as a grain of mustard seed, ye shall say unto this mountain, Remove hence to yonder place; and it shall remove; and nothing shall be impossible to you.

—MATTHEW 17:20

Soldiers in the Vietnam War scrawled slogans on their helmet covers, these according to the temperament and sentiments of the individual. Catchphrases such as "Kill! Kill! Kill!" and "Kill 'Em All, Let God Sort 'Em Out" were popular for those soldiers who were new in-country and had not yet confronted the reality of combat. Helmet graffiti changed dramatically as newbies became veterans. Crude inked-in Christian crosses appeared, along with "You and Me, God" and "Yea I Walk Through the Valley of the Shadow of Death."

It should not be surprising that soldiers turn to God to bring reason to chaos and sanity to madness when they live with death all around them. One reporter embedded with American troops in Iraq in 2004 asserted that not a single soldier he'd talked to was not seeking a stronger connection to God. Scorched by the fires of war, many warriors discover faith that has been missing from their lives. Others gain a greater sense of God. Few are not in some way touched by the supernatural as they struggle for understanding, comfort, and protection.

"In my . . . experience," noted Arthur Kammerer, 102nd Infantry Division, World War II, "I've seen [combat] make killers out of some, cowards of some, Christians of most."

Army Private Paul Curtis may have said it best. After being pinned down at Anzio, Italy, in May 1944, he tried to explain combat in a letter to his brother.

"It's beyond words," he wrote. "Take a combination of fear, anger, hunger, thirst, exhaustion, disgust, loneliness, homesickness, and wrap that all up in one reaction. . . . It's a comfort to know there's One Who is present at all times and . . . ready to help you through. . . . Without faith [in God], I don't see how anyone could stand this."

MARINE LANCE CORPORAL NATHAN JONES,
Vietnam, 1968

Just another day in 'Nam. "Death Defying Delta" Company, redubbed by "Chargin' Charlie" Company as "Dyin' Delta," moved out of Camp Evans in the late afternoon and slogged at a forced pace down the dusty road toward the village of Cam Lo some five klicks (kilometers) away. About three miles. An Army of the Republic of Vietnam (ARVN) company had stumbled onto a company of North Vietnamese Army (NVA) and got itself pinned down. Dyin' Delta expected to kick some serious ass, drag Marvin the ARVN's bacon out of the fire, and be back within Evans's wire-and-bunker perimeter by nightfall.

Marine Lance Corporal Nathan Jones, a wiry kid from Oklahoma, glanced back up the road at the black snouts of a 155mm howitzer battery silhouetted against the white-hot afternoon sky. He shifted the M-60 machine gun to a more comfortable position across his shoulder; he would trade out the gun later with his assistant gunner, a new in-country cherry called Bill. He wondered what they would be having for evening chow when they returned to Evans. NVA and Viet Cong (VC) rarely stood up to a Marine company on the prod.

Although only nineteen, Jones was one of the vets in the outfit, having just completed Operation Pecos to kick the enemy out of Khe San and back across the border into North Vietnam. He had been wounded there, a glancing head blow that earned him a certain respect in the Marines and, along with a quarter, a cup of coffee back in the States.

Cam Lo, a typical village of straw or tin huts, sat clustered between the road and rice paddy squares sectioned off by hedgerows of mangrove. Marines trudged into one side of the settlement and out the other, scattering pigs, geese, chickens, and bare-assed little kids. If ARVN was in contact out there, it was one *quiet* contact. Most likely, the NVA had already pulled up stakes and hauled out.

About a kilometer beyond the village, platoon leader Lieutenant Been ordered Jones and his A-gunner to set up their M-60 in rear security. Ordinarily, three Marines made up a machine gun crew, but Jones's section was short a man. That left him and Bill. While the rest of the company forged ahead to check on Marvin, the two Marines bipodded the M-60 in a hedgerow that overlooked a dry-season rice paddy. A 7.62mm M-60 machine gun, the infantry grunt's primary defensive weapon, was capable of chewing up terrain and flesh at five hundred rounds per minute out to a maximum effective range of 1,100 meters.

Dyin' Delta melded into the landscape, out of sight and sound. Shadows grew long. Jones watched the sun turn red as it sank into the horizon. Mosquitoes buzzed around his helmet.

Suddenly, all hell busted loose from the direction of Delta Company's advance. It started with the distant loose rattle of AK-47s in groups, the cyclic chop of enemy 51mm machine guns, the crash and bang of rocket-propelled grenades and mortars. Marines responded with M-16s, M-60s, and light mortars. It was immediately apparent that Delta was clashing with an enemy force far greater in size than its own—and that that force was standing up and determined to wipe out the Americans in full-scale battle.

Outside the perimeter of the fight, a klick away, Lance Corporal Jones and his A-gunner could do nothing but listen to the discordant thunder of the engagement and keep a nervous eye peeled into the gathering darkness to make sure no additional enemy moved in from the rear. As the fighting raged back and forth, Jones listened with alarm and dread as one M-60 after another ceased its chugging. Soon, all of Delta's M-60s were quiet, either killed, knocked out, or jammed. By comparison, the tinny cacophony of M-16 rifles sounded ineffectual and last-stand desperate.

What in hell had Delta walked into out there?

Darkness clasped the land firmly in its fist. Artillery from Camp Evans poured high explosives (HE) into the fray, trembling the earth and choking the air with smoke and dust. Illumination flares filled the sky like fierce miniature suns, skittering fearsome shadows like shape-shifters. From out of these shadows and light appeared a runner crawling, ducking, and dodging, shouting the password repeatedly to prevent being shot by rear security. He collapsed next to Lance Corporal Jones, panting, his eyes wide with terror.

"We walked into a battalion, a U-shaped ambush," he gasped. "Jones, the captain says you got to get your gun up there. It's the only one left. Jones, they're killing us! They're killing us all!"

Like good Marines whose buddies were in trouble, the two machine gunners grabbed their vital weapon and ammo and took off with the runner guiding them. They eluded NVA fighters several times in the darkness as the enemy began closing the trap around Delta. Breaking through the defensive perimeter, Jones was stunned by the numbers of dead and wounded dragged to a casualty collection point near a thicket of mangrove. Their moans and cries pulsed the night air. Dyin' Delta was living up to its name. It departed Camp Evans with 180 men; only eighty would return.

Lieutenant Been met the gun crew. He was a big man with courage to match. But tonight, like everyone else, he was scared. He directed Jones to the front of the ambush where the M-60 could do the most damage against concentrated attackers. Parachute flares blazed overhead. Howitzer shells banged around the outside perimeter, but to little effect since the enemy was close in and hugging Marine lines.

"Tanks are on the way, but they're not going to get here in time," Lieutenant Been explained. "We're surrounded, but the company is going to break out and leapfrog by platoons back toward Cam Lo. Our platoon will set up a base of fire to cover the rest of the company while it busts out. Then the company will set up and cover our asses while we pull back. Jones, we gotta hold the bastards. Understand?"

Muzzle fire twinkled from all sides as the ruthless NVA closed in. From the protection of a dike, Jones lay down a cyclic rate of fire while Bill fed belts to the gun, raking the machine gun back and forth, spraying steel and lead and death into the thickest concentrations of muzzle flicker, weaving red tracers like streaks of lasers. Lieutenant Been and Sergeant Jackson, the platoon gunny, fought desperately on either side of the M-60, emptying magazines of 5.56 through their M-16s. Jones was so absorbed in the brutal business of killing that Lieutenant Been's sudden exclamation failed to sink in for a moment or two.

"My God, they've left us!"

Jones's head snapped around. The eerie ghost light of parachute flares hanging against the black sky revealed their plight to be even more grave than they could ever have imagined. Orders had apparently been misunderstood in all the confusion and chaos. The stay-behind platoon had withdrawn with the rest of the company, leaving only four Marines behind to hold off an entire battalion of hard-core, pissed-off NVA: Lance Corporal Jones, his A-gunner Bill, Lieutenant Been, and Sergeant Jackson.

Terror jolted Jones's body like lightning. Violent death could be the only outcome of this screw-up.

"Let's get out of here!" Been hissed.

Jones leapt to his feet with the M-60 and its last belt of ammunition. Firing from the hip, he backed away from the dike, wheeled around, then bolted with the other three Marines across a rice paddy in a reckless bid to catch up with the retreating Delta. Maybe they had a chance if they could reach the hedgerow on the other side. Bullets lashed out at them from all angles, snapping. Green tracers threatened to entangle them in spider webs.

Run! Run! Run!

In their haste to decamp, they raced headlong into a squad of enemy soldiers left in the hedgerow to snare stragglers. The NVA opened fire with a startling crash of point-blank AK-47 fire. The four Marines hit the dirt. By some miracle, none of them was hit, although they found themselves in one awkward position—marines on one side of the hedgerow, gooks on the other. They had to go through the Viets in order to catch up with the company.

Muttering and sounds of movement came from the other side.

Jones had never felt such fear in his entire life, not even at Khe San. He was afraid his trembling hands would rattle his machine gun and give them away.

Overhead illumination faded as the last parachute flare sputtered out and fluttered into the rice paddies, returning full night to the battlefield. Dyin' Delta required cover of darkness in order to withdraw successfully. Uneasy quiet accompanied the return of darkness. Furtive movement all around signaled the gathering of enemy fighters to finish off the four cornered Marines.

A Chicom grenade sailed over the mangrove thicket and struck the ground nearby with a plop and the hiss of a burning fuse. Jones buried his face between his arms. The explosion shook dust out of the ground and almost kicked him off the earth. A tiny shard of red-hot shrapnel nicked his chin with enough force to almost tear off his head. It left his ears ringing. Lieutenant Been uttered a sharp sigh as an even larger piece of the grenade ripped into his arm.

They lay on their bellies waiting for the inevitable attack.

Jones had maybe a half belt of M-60 ammo left. The lieutenant was out of M-16 cartridges. Sergeant Jackson and Bill were on their last magazines. Jones removed his remaining grenade from his belt harness and tucked it against his ribs where he could reach the arming spoon. Determined not to be taken alive and tortured, he would fight as long as he was able. Then, at the end, he would pull the grenade pin and take as many of the bad guys with him as he could.

He began to pray, hard and earnestly, but silently. "Lord God, just get me out of this if it be Your will . . ."

His life seemed to flash before his eyes from the time he was a little boy in Oklahoma. He saw the faces of his mother and father, as though they were actually standing right in front of him.

Then, even more astonishing, even more unbelievable, a tiny light appeared. Like a dim lightbulb rising out of the earth. To his amazement, it grew and grew until it completely enveloped him in a cocoon of warm luminescence.

Suddenly, he no longer found himself in a scary place. Everything in the whole world turned silent. All was peace. Even the air he breathed was pure and sweet-smelling. A great and wonderful calm overcame him. He was no longer afraid.

A voice issued from somewhere, as from the light itself. It was so full of compassion and caring that the unseen speaker seemed to wrap the Marine in loving arms. The voice said, "Don't worry, my son. You are going to be just fine."

The light faded. An artillery round exploded somewhere off the left flank. Jones returned the grenade to his cartridge belt and whispered to Bill, "We're going to be all right."

Yeah? Bill was dead quiet, but his silence spoke. *Where have you been? We're surrounded.*

"Open up and give 'em what you got left," Lieutenant Been whispered. "We'll try to break through and catch up with the company. That's all we can do."

On his signal, the four Marines sprang to their feet and opened fire. Jones burned off the last of his M-60 ammo as they crashed through the hedgerow, stampeding directly over and through the assembling enemy soldiers. Incredibly, not a shot, *not a single shot,* was even fired at them. It was as if they were invisible.

Or *protected.*

Tanks that had joined Delta Company to establish a hasty defense outside Cam Lo village were the most welcome sight the lost Marines had ever seen. Later, Lance Corporal Jones asked his companions what they thought about the remarkable light at the hedgerow.

"What are you talking about, Jones?"

He told them about his experience. Lieutenant Been mulled it over.

"There was definitely *something* that got us out of there," he said.

Nathan Jones has devoted the rest of his life to serving God.

ARMY SERGEANT KEVIN CRAWFORD,
Iraq, 2003

The rising red sun hung two fingers above the flats. Temperatures were already approaching the 100-degree mark. Heat shimmers obscured the two-lane macadam highway that stretched like a single black ribbon from the outskirts of Baghdad to Tikrit. Here and there mud-colored cottages crouched next to the road. Little children scurried out laughing and shouting and waving at the convoy of eight lumbering U.S. Army tractor-trailers, each coated with a patina of desert dust.

Kids or not, Sergeant Kevin Crawford, thirty-three, constantly swept watchful eyes back and forth between the road and the children along its sides. Improvised explosive devices (IEDs) and the occasional ambush were common hazards. Intervals between vehicles allowed over-watch while at the same time keeping each clear should the truck ahead trigger something. As noncommissioned officer-in-charge of the convoy, Crawford drove the command truck second back from the lead.

Next to him in the cab, nineteen-year-old Private Rhoden rode shotgun. He seemed to absorb his sergeant's unease. He leaned forward, tense and sweating, peering ahead, hand resting on the stock of his mounted M-240 7.62mm machine gun. Dust swirling in through open windows caked his face and made his eyes shine round and oddly white.

The 24th Transportation Company out of Fort Riley, Kansas, put boots on ground in Kuwait in April 2003, some seven months before. As U.S. troops ripped across Iraq to take Baghdad, the 24th's "Bastard Children" had operational control to four or five different divisions, supporting the 3rd Infantry Division at jump-off, then transferring in order to the 101st and 82nd Airborne Divisions before finally ending up with the 1st Armored. After the capture of Baghdad, the 24th's trucks ran logistical support and major ammunition pushes to outlying units. Beans and bullets. Two convoys had departed base camp this

morning on different mission routes. Something, a little voice, a nagging feeling, *something*, had told Sergeant Crawford to say an extra prayer
with his soldiers.

Prayer was nothing unusual in the company. Crawford prayed every
day, morning and evening and before each mission. *Lord, keep us out of
harm's way and please help me protect my people.* He would clasp his Bible,
lower his head, and close his eyes. Other members of the 24th joined
him. Virtually the entire company came to expect prayer, to depend on
it. Even those who were unsure of their beliefs or who preferred not to
believe in God joined the sessions.

Each time the enemy mortared base camp near Baghdad Interna-
tional Airport, soldiers rushed to their assigned concrete-and-sand bag
bunkers to wait it out. Sometimes the lights flickered and went out.
Everyone huddled in pitch blackness and sweated through the stifling
heat while listening to muffled explosions outside.

Crawford led prayers at such times, then cracked jokes and made
light of the situation to alleviate tension and worry. "I sure hope this
is over soon so we can get back out where it's cool."

The temperature inside the bunkers was about 110 degrees, while
the "cool" outside reached only 100. People tittered here and there.

Often some truck driver, such as the single mom whose two kids
were living with her sister while she was in Iraq, approached the sergeant
after the "all clear." "Sergeant Crawford, will you pray with me?"

While other units suffered casualties, the 24th had not yet lost a
single soldier, even though the company and its vehicles were exposed
to hostile intent nearly every day. Commanders wondered what the
company was doing that made it different and seemingly safer than
many other outfits. At some point during the deployment, soldiers of
the 24th began to feel that *something* must be watching over them.

"You know, I don't quite know what I believe in," one soldier said.
"But I believe this, Sergeant Crawford: every day you pray encourages
others to do the same. I wonder if it is a direct reflection of your
prayers that we've never lost anyone."

Crawford thought it was due to a *lot* of people praying.

Private Rhoden, Crawford's gunner and almost-constant companion, frequently questioned his sergeant about his faith during their road trips together. The kid had been new to the company when it first rolled out from Kuwait into Iraq. Crawford, as usual, began the day with prayer.

"You really believe in God?" the kid asked the sergeant as they convoyed at the rear of an infantry unit in contact a few miles ahead.

"Don't you?" Crawford responded, glancing at the kid.

Rhoden was thin-faced with haunted, cautious eyes. He came from a broken home and had bounced around in foster care until he was old enough to enlist in the Army. He sometimes commented how the Army was the only real home he had ever known.

"I don't know what I believe," he said. "What's God ever done that I can see?"

Now, on the way to Tikrit, Private Rhoden was edgy and silent, disturbed only by squelch and magnified voices over the radio as drivers checked on one another and passed along road information. As usual, he had stood aloof during pre-mission prayer, with a perplexed look on his face, eyes open, head unbowed.

"Keep alert," Sergeant Crawford advised the convoy. He had a nagging feeling that refused to go away.

Halfway to Tikrit, the point truck suddenly braked, causing the entire procession to stop. "Sergeant Crawford, something's wrong," the point driver radioed. "There's something up ahead in the road."

The sergeant maneuvered his vehicle into the oncoming lane, stopped again, and squinted into the heat haze. Rhoden's finger curled around the trigger of his machine gun.

Ordinarily, the buckle in the road ahead, a mere interruption in the lane, would have gone unnoticed, dismissed as nothing other than what it appeared to be—a natural road hazard. However, Crawford decided that if God was looking after the 24th, the least he could do was his part. He ordered the convoy to turn around and return to Baghdad.

An Explosive Ordnance Disposal (EOD) team and a Ready Reaction Force, subsequently dispatched to the site, discovered a booby trap containing enough explosives to blow a Bradley fighting vehicle all the way to the Euphrates River. It would have demolished the first truck that ran over it while ambushers in hiding opened fire on the others. Sharp eyes—and perhaps *someone*—had again protected the 24th.

"The outfit that prays together stays together," a driver later commented.

That wasn't the only incident involving the transportation company that remarkable day. The other 24th convoy encountered a rocket-propelled grenade (RPG) attack near Fallujah. Although a rocket struck a vehicle and disabled it, the only casualty was minor. The driver sustained negligible burns to his arm. He sought out Sergeant Crawford once all trucks and personnel were safely behind the wire at base camp.

"What about it?" he asked. "You were praying for us, Sarge. It must have worked."

It went that way for the rest of the year while the company ran its trucks all over Iraq. Drivers gathered around their big dusty trucks and bowed their heads each morning, each evening, and before every mission. The 24th Transportation Company from Fort Riley, Kansas, suffered not a single serious casualty during its tour.

Private Rhoden looked thoughtful and introspective on the plane ride that took the intact unit back to the United States.

"Sergeant," he said at last, "you made me think about a lot of things the whole time we were in Iraq." He closed his eyes, then opened them again. "I'm led to believe there are greater things than any of us can ever know."

MARINE SERGEANT TOM COTTICK,
World War II, 1945

Word went out among Marines before they clambered aboard Higgins boats, tracks, and other landing craft to make everything "right" before they met the threat of eternity. Announcements boomed out over the PA systems of LSTs (landing ship, tank) and transports: *"Make out your wills. Write your letters home. Church services on deck for men of all faiths. Make peace with your Maker."*

Acting Platoon Sergeant Tom Cottick, Foxtrot Company 2/24 (2nd Battalion, 24th Regiment), 4th Marine Division, attended services, although he figured he didn't need it since the 24th would sit out Iwo Jima in reserve. It was about time. The regiment had been in and out of hell on earth since February 1944, a year ago, making landings at Kwajalein, Saipan, and Tinian. Cottick had already earned one Purple Heart and two Silver Stars for valor.

He got his Purple Heart and his first Star on Kwajalein for single-handedly knocking out an enemy machine gun nest that had bottled up the Marine advance. His second Silver Star, from Saipan, was not what he would remember most about that ungodly little piece of real estate. What he would always remember, what would sear his nightmares in the middle of sleep for the rest of his life, were Marine loudspeakers pleading with the civilian population and surviving Japanese soldiers as they rushed en masse to the tops of cliffs.

"Please surrender. You will not be harmed. We are taking prisoners."

Japanese soldiers considered surrender the ultimate dishonor. They bailed off the cliffs to smash themselves on the rocks below, followed by a disturbing number of civilian men, women, and children. Sometimes when Cottick closed his eyes he could still hear kids screaming like dying gulls as they sailed off the cliffs in the arms of their parents.

That he had survived all this while many of his buddies were killed along the way seemed nothing short of a miracle. Over 80 percent of the Marines who landed with him on Kwajalein were not there that day.

Sergeant Cottick, his men said, was "one tough bastard."

Iwo Jima, a pork-chop-shaped island one-third the size of Manhattan, was supposed to be a cakewalk. Three days at most. B-29 bombers had softened up the island for the past thirty days. Cottick and the other men of the 2/24 lined the railings of their transport several miles out to sea and watched in the predawn as fire and smoke roiled over the tiny island, which was being pounded by even more aircraft and battleships in advance of landings by the U.S. 4th and 5th Marine Divisions.

The first indication that things weren't going as planned came from loudspeakers aboard ship: *"Now hear this! Now hear this! All 24th Marines in reserve, on your feet and get ready to board your landing craft. You are going to hit the beach. The first wave has been wiped out."*

For the next thirty-six days beginning on D-Day, February 19, 1945, Iwo Jima was one of the most heavily populated 7.5 square miles on the face of the earth: 100,000 men on both sides fighting with everything from mortars and machine guns to clubs, knives, and fists. The enemy had dug deep into bunkers and caves and had to be burnt out with flamethrowers. The air itself was so lethal that Marines felt that if they inhaled too deeply they would suck in a fatal lungful of blazing lead and steel.

Mount Suribachi, the 550-foot volcanic cone at the island's southern tip, dominated the landing beach. Japanese gunners in defensive blockhouses and pillboxes on the high ground zeroed in on every inch of the island. Machine guns crisscrossed the beaches with blistering interlocking fire. Rockets and antitank guns scythed through American invaders. Every Marine, anywhere on the island, was always within range of enemy guns.

Unable to dig foxholes in the loose volcanic ash, Marines became sitting ducks. They had to fight from above ground; defending Japanese fought from below ground. The advance was measured in yards, a yard or two *a day*, real estate bought dearly in lost lives. The cloying stench of death and rot, of cordite and smoke, of fear and horror hung in the tropical air like a toxic cloud. Before the battle ended, 6,821 Marines would die, along with 21,000 Japanese.

Sergeant Cottick caught his foot in wire mesh and severely wrenched it on the first day while clearing an enemy pillbox with hand grenades. It swelled up to twice its normal size, but he had no time for medics. He cinched tight his bootlaces and soldiered on.

One evening at dusk, he glimpsed a Japanese soldier creeping up on a Marine machine gun position. The Jap sprang to his feet and charged, two-handed with a Samurai sword. Cottick yelled a warning. At the same time, he wheeled around and cut the attacker nearly in half with a burst from his tommy gun.

It wasn't the first man he killed. It wouldn't be the last.

By D-plus-eleven days, Easy Company 2/24 ceased to exist because of casualties. Those who remained merged into Captain Walter Redlon's decimated Foxtrot Company, which found itself pinned down at the base of Hill 382, known to Marines as "the Meat Grinder." For the past three days, that hellish little knob and its defenders had ground into hamburger every Marine unit that attempted to scale it, including what had formerly been Easy Company. Sergeant Cottick received orders that Foxtrot Company would make the next assault. There was nobody else.

Exhausted in body and soul, filthy, ragged, unshaved, stained with the blood of both friend and foe, the sergeant crawled into a deep shell hole for a moment of respite before he rallied his platoon. He lit a cigarette and lay on his back in the crater, looking up at the clear blue sky. For that moment he shut out the din of battle that surrounded him.

Sergeant Cottick had never been a particularly religious man. God was God and man was man, and God seldom interfered with the petty affairs of pitiful humans. But now, lying on his back in the shell crater below the Meat Grinder and gazing in the direction of where he assumed Heaven to be, he began examining his faith.

Every man he knew embraced the old truism that there were no atheists in foxholes. At least he did *after* his baptism of fire. Combat, especially sustained combat, was enough to cleanse the soul of any man. In a few more minutes he must lead his platoon up the brutal side of the Meat Grinder. Many of those who went up would not come back down alive. What would happen to their souls? What would happen to *his* soul if he were one of those carried back down wrapped inside his poncho? For the first time since he began making beach landings in the Pacific, he closed his eyes and prayed.

"Lord, if You can hear me . . . Lord, I would go through the first three invasions all over again if You will just get me out of this one alive . . . Lord, if we die today, please forgive one and all of our mortal sins and have mercy on our souls . . . We done our best."

He opened his eyes, smoked his cigarette, and looked into the sky. Foxtrot's CO, Captain Redlon, slid down the side of the crater and sat at the bottom next to Cottick. A filthy bandage wrapped tightly around his leg oozed blood from a previous wound.

"Sergeant Cottick, the time has arrived to do what we must do," he said.

Cottick's moment with God was over. The crash and rattle and shrill of battle returned with all its immediacy.

"What's left of the company will be committed to a frontal assault, a joint effort with other units on our left and right flanks," Redlon said. "It should break the enemy's resistance."

Cottick looked numbly about. A mortar shell exploded nearby, showering them both with dirt. In a weary voice, Cottick said, "Sir, I have had it. I would like to quit and just walk away."

Captain Redlon understood. He nodded and gently wrapped an arm around his sergeant's shoulders. "Sarge, I didn't hear that. This job must be done. We move out and take the hill on my signal, right after the artillery barrage."

Cottick sighed. That was how life was: hills and more caves and challenges to overcome. He glanced up at the sky one more time. By all accounts, he should have been dead by now. Maybe God and he already had a bargain. What was that old verse from the Bible? His mother quoted it. Oh, yes . . .

Why are ye so fearful? How is it that ye have no faith?

He flipped his cigarette away. He met Captain Redlon's gaze. "I'm ready, sir."

Foxtrot Company took the hill. A few days later, a mortar round exploded next to Sergeant Cottick, peppering him with shrapnel. The cigarette case in his breast pocket caught a piece of steel that likely would have penetrated his heart.

For valorous action on Iwo Jima, he received a third Silver Star and his second Purple Heart. He survived the war and lived into his old age in Michigan.

MARINE SERGEANT RICHARD "DICK" WILSON,
Korea, 1952

Diplomats fought a war of words in ongoing truce talks in Korea while the *real* war, the shooting war, settled into a Battle for the Hills, a vicious and primitive seesawing back and forth for the advantage of high ground. It was not unusual for a hill to change ownership two or three times. Fox Company 2/5 of the 1st Marine Division occupied a hill called "Warsaw" about four hundred yards forward of the main line of resistance (MLR). After seizing the hill from the communists, Marines moved into old trenches and bunkers formerly occupied by Chicoms, set up housekeeping, and prepared to fend off enemy probes and day and night mortar fire.

It was early spring, which meant drizzle during the day and ice at night, altogether miserable conditions. The only man who seemed unaffected by the weather and living arrangements was a lanky older Marine known to everyone simply as "Preacher." He was about thirty or so and had a wife and several kids back home. In combat, most men picked up appropriate nicknames like "Mad Dog," "Rag Bag," or "Boot." Preacher got his because he carried a Bible wherever he went and always appeared as cheerful as a meadowlark singing on a wire fence. He constantly found time to stop and read scripture to fellow Marines.

Sometimes Sergeant Dick Wilson envied Preacher his faith. At eighteen, Wilson was the youngest buck sergeant in the 1st Marines, possibly even in the entire U.S. Marine Corps. As a Latter-Day Saint, he had always derived comfort back home from attending sacrament, Sunday School, and priesthood meetings. Preacher helped fill the void in Korea. Together, they often huddled in the trenches, hunched in their ponchos against rain and sleet while they debated God's plan for mankind in general and for themselves as soldiers in particular.

It wasn't the same as peacetime back home surrounded by the Loving Spirit. Nonetheless, Wilson doubted he could have maintained his beliefs and his sanity without these sessions and Preacher's personal prayer and scripture readings. Preacher had an answer for any spiritual or moral question. Everything that man ever needed to know, he said, was in the Bible.

North Koreans and Chicoms commonly attacked or probed lines in the predawn hours when men were the sleepiest and most wretched. First bugles blew and whistles shrilled from the darkness at the bottom of Warsaw Hill. Next came the pounding of massed feet, the horrendous din of rifle and machine gun fire, and rolling sparkles of muzzle flashes. Finally, artillery flares burst like suns in the blackness to illuminate the field of battle.

Young Wilson marveled at the transformation in his friend whenever he put down his Bible to fight. He calmly tucked it into his pack or pocket, hefted his M-1 Garand, and, methodically, with unerring marksmanship, began picking off targets while ignoring bullets chewing the earth around him.

As soon as the probe broke, Preacher would retrieve his Bible and read out loud in the lingering light of flares. *"Though an host should encamp against me, my heart shall not fear: though war should rise against me, in this will I be confident."*

"Aren't you ever afraid?" a fellow Marine once asked him.

"Everyone is afraid," he said. "I'm afraid I will never see my wife and children again in this life. But the Lord has promised that He is with me, even until the end of time, and that should I die I will see my loved ones again."

On a surprisingly pleasant morning without rain, Preacher left the chow bunker on his way back to his own fighting position, striding cheerfully along with his rifle slung over one shoulder, the Bible as usual in his hand. He tarried along the way to clap a comforting hand upon the shoulder of a young Marine, to utter encouragement to another friend. Preacher being Preacher.

Unexpectedly, a mortar shell whistled low over the trenches. Chicoms were always lobbing in random rounds to keep Marines on the edges of their nerves. The shell exploded a geyser of dirt, water, ice, and shrapnel almost directly on top of Preacher. When the smoke cleared, he lay on his back in the churned-up mud of that forlorn Korean hilltop, an expression of superb tranquility on his face, the Bible still clutched in his mangled hand.

Wilson had seen dead Marines before, but Preacher was the first personal friend he had lost. It left him numb. One moment Preacher was merrily alive and vital. The next, he was gone—in a twinkling of an eye, as the scriptures said. It made Sergeant Wilson aware of how suddenly one could meet his Maker. It was a harsh awakening for youth who tended to view themselves as immortal.

Later, Preacher's comrades gathered his personal belongings to ship back with his body. Someone murmured the question on everyone's mind: "How can someone so good, so spiritual, and so religious lose his life while others live who are not so good or who have never even attended church or read the Bible?"

Dick Wilson, rolled up in his poncho, thought about it a long time that night. Preacher, he knew, would have had an answer.

2

PRISONERS OF WAR

*The Spirit of the Lord God is upon me: because the Lord hath . . .
sent me . . . to proclaim liberty to the captives, and the opening of
the prison to them that are bound.*"

—ISAIAH 61:1

One of the greatest tragedies of war has been the suffering of military servicemen seized and held captive by the enemy, not only in recent times but all the way back to the Revolutionary War. From the beginning of the nation, American prisoners of war have undergone hardships and atrocities ranging from sadistic torture and deliberate starvation to brainwashing and murder.

"Death camps" like the Confederate's Andersonville during the Civil War, Japan's hellholes of Cabanatuan and Camp O'Donnell during World War II, and the "Hanoi Hilton" in North Vietnam became infamous for their maltreatment of prisoners. In them, American POWs daily confronted abuse, starvation, disease, despair, and death.

During the Revolutionary War, the British used obsolete, captured,

or damaged ships as prisons. At least sixteen hulks, including the notorious HMS *Jersey*, were used to incarcerate thousands of Continental
soldiers and sailors from about 1776 to 1783. Over 10,000 died from
intentional neglect, more Americans than died in all the combined battles of the Revolution. Corpses were often simply tossed overboard to
wash up on shore where local women recovered them.

During the Civil War, approximately 45,000 prisoners entered the
gates of Andersonville Prison, the South's largest POW camp, located
in southwest Georgia. Nearly 13,000 of them died there.

"Five hundred men moved silently toward the gates that would shut
out life and hope for most of them forever," John McElroy wrote in
1864 of his stay in Andersonville.

Military historian William B. Breuer described conditions at Camp
O'Donnell, one of the internment camps operated by the Japanese for
the survivors of the Bataan Death March: "Death soon became the
norm. Most POWs were skin and bone, had pipe stem legs and arms,
and there was no flesh on their buttocks. . . . Lungs loaded with tissue
fluid fell easy prey to pneumonia. Hearts weakened by prolonged starvation suddenly dilated and stopped beating. Men standing shakily in
chow lines toppled over dead. Some straddling latrines slithered down
into fecal graves, too weak to extricate themselves. Others hobbled
back from long work details, lay down on their filth-covered pallets
and died."

U.S. Air Force Captain Howard Rutledge was shot down in his F-8
Crusader over North Vietnam on November 28, 1965, and caged for
seven years behind the cold stone walls of the Hanoi Hilton. What he
experienced was representative of conditions endured by modern-day
American POWs.

"[The guard] shackled me to my slab in rear cuffs and irons," he
wrote in his memoirs. "For five days I couldn't move. It was summer
and very hot. The humidity must have been in the 90s, the temperature
in the 100s. I developed one of those severe heat rashes where the red
welts turned to blisters and ultimately to boils. . . . They wouldn't come

to a head, so I had to pick them to stop the swelling. . . . In a few days I counted at least sixty boils about one inch in diameter over my entire body—under my arms, in my nose, in my hair, on my ears, legs, arms, hands, and fingers."

Prisoners of war who have miraculously survived internment or who have escaped or are rescued bring back stunning tales of the means they utilized to cope with captivity. The vast majority credit faith in a Higher Power for their survival.

ARMY AIR CORPS SERGEANT JAMES GAUTIER, JR.,
World War II, 1942

An aircraft mechanic with the 27th Bombardment Group, U.S. Army Air Corps, Sergeant James Gautier, Jr., arrived at Manila Harbor in the Philippines on November 20, 1941. The Japanese attacked Pearl Harbor six weeks later. Air raids against the Philippines began the next day, followed by the Japanese invasion on December 12. The 27th was bivouacked in tents on the parade grounds at a Filipino Scout base camp near Manila when General Douglas MacArthur declared "open city" on the capitol. This declaration meant he would not defend the city since his troops were greatly outnumbered by the advancing Japanese, and defense meant unnecessary sacrifice of American lives.

With the stroke of a pen, MacArthur transformed Gautier's support unit into the 17th Provisional *Infantry* Battalion. Gautier and the other aircraft mechanics were each issued a 1918 Springfield rifle, three bandoleers of ammunition, a box of Nabisco hardtack crackers, and a can of corned beef. Their orders: Withdraw onto the Bataan Peninsula and hold off the Japanese until help arrived.

Japanese forces closed in and trapped beleaguered American and Filipino defense remnants on the Bataan Peninsula. Cornered and starving, the soldiers fought on without resupply or reinforcement until, by March, it became clear that MacArthur wasn't coming back, at least not yet.

Strapping lean to begin with, Gautier lost thirty pounds he could little afford to spare. Malaria and lice ravaged the ranks, with the misery compounded by artillery shelling and constant attacks from enemy infantry. Weak and always hungry, GIs spent time away from the line scavenging for food like a troop of primates. Once all the horses and mules were devoured, they turned to edible roots, lizards, snakes, and monkeys. The jungle was soon picked so clean of edible plant and animal life that it appeared a plague of locusts had swept through.

During a shelling, one of Gautier's buddies, Corporal Jesse Knowles, took off running ahead of a stick of bombs. A piece of shrapnel slammed him to the ground. Afterward he discovered only a huge blister on the back of his neck.

"Better sign up with us Baptists right now, Cajun," Knowles teased Gautier, who hailed from Louisiana. "If I was a Methodist like you, I'd be dead."

Even hard-core atheists and skeptics turned into believers at the random, almost haphazard manner in which death continued to claim its victims. How else to explain why some died and others lived, except through the divine plan of Providence?

One afternoon, Gautier and two other sergeants were sitting on the ground in a small circle munching on peanuts and sugarcane purloined from nearby fields. Suddenly a 240mm Jap shell homed in with the sound of a flying boxcar. It struck a grove of guava trees about a hundred yards away, close enough to make the sergeants nervous but not near enough to pose a threat.

The sergeant directly across from Gautier, only an arm's length away, slowly toppled over, a single small, fatal fragment from the exploding shell having punctured the back of his skull.

The Japanese began their final push in April. Shooting erupted from every direction as the enemy closed in. A grim-faced platoon sergeant stared at Gautier and about fifty other survivors.

"Destroy your machine guns," he ordered. "Break up into small groups and head south. Try to avoid the Japs. You're on your own."

Gautier rounded up Knowles and another friend named Inzer. "I'm heading south. Ya'all coming?"

"Aw, Gautier," Knowles cracked, "you just want me with you 'cause you know God takes care of us Baptists."

"We'll make a good team then, because this Methodist is going to work as hard as he can to help the Lord save his skin."

Except for a few fortunates, however, escape from the encirclement proved impossible. General Edward King, commander of the remaining forces on Bataan, met with the Japanese on April 9th to surrender his troops so they wouldn't be annihilated. Gautier silently prayed as he trudged to the surrender assembly point with Knowles and Inzer.

In the Japanese culture, the Bushido Code governed the conduct of its military. Fighting to the last man, even committing hara-kiri at the end, was more honorable, and preferable, to surrender. Japanese soldiers treated the capitulating Americans and Filipinos with contempt. They went through the prisoner ranks taking money, watches, pens, rings, food, medicine, and everything else of value. Gautier stared in horror and disbelief as men who protested were kicked, slugged, and hammered with rifle butts. Some were jerked out of ranks and bayoneted on the spot, especially those who possessed anything that might have been taken as souvenirs from Japanese soldiers.

Guards divided prisoners into groups of one hundred and started them marching north on the National Highway. They were bedraggled, filthy, unshaved, and infested with lice and fungi. All wore rotted, torn clothing. Many had no hats to protect their heads from the merciless sun. The feet of those without shoes were soon cut and blistered. Gautier was fortunate because he had managed to replace his worn-out combat boots with a pair of white nurse's low-quarters, scrounged from the hospital.

Since the Japs appeared to pick on those guys nearest the edge of the processions, Sergeant Gautier positioned himself in the middle of a group. Good plan. Japanese troops passing by in trucks made sport of trying to whack prisoners on their heads with rifles or with long bamboo poles. Once a man was knocked down and couldn't get up, guards bayoneted him and left him on the road, wallowing in his own blood.

Men weak from wounds, sickness, or starvation received the same treatment. Soon the roadside was littered with corpses bloating in the burning tropical sun, emitting a hellish stench and crawling with maggots. Of the 75,000 captured American and Filipino soldiers who began the so-called Bataan Death March, more than 10,000 would die of hunger, disease, brutality, and murder before they reached Japanese POW camps—first the infamous Camp O'Donnell, then later force-marched the additional eight miles to the equally infamous Cabanatuan prison.

Temperatures reached triple digits. No one was allowed to stop for water or to relieve himself. Gautier saw a GI crazed by thirst attempt to sneak away and steal a drink from an artesian well. Guards shot him before he reached the water.

Stronger prisoners attempted to help the weak. All were in such bad shape, however, that they hardly had strength to help themselves. Weeping in frustration and fear, they went on automatic pilot, lurching along like wasted zombies. They were delirious, hallucinating, trudging through heat and dust in a trancelike state, obsessed with their own thirst and misery.

Those who collapsed were either shot, clubbed to death, or left to die.

Guards finally permitted Gautier's group to drink where a bridge spanned a small creek. Sergeant Gautier broke into a stumbling run. He dropped on all fours and thrust his entire head underneath the brackish water. He felt a little stronger after he drank. He looked around and saw fly-swarmed corpses floating in the creek. Dead for days, they were bloated up like balloons. Pieces of rotted flesh sloughed off into the water.

He forced himself to drink again, all he could hold. He had to survive.

"Lord, keep me from getting sick," he prayed.

At nightfall, marchers were packed two thousand or more into barbed wire compounds large enough for only five hundred. On the third evening, they reached the town of *Balangao*. At the entrance to the compound on the edge of town was stacked a grisly pile of men freshly killed.

Guards entered the compound that night with the severed heads of

GIs impaled on the ends of their bayonets, parading about to terror-
ize and taunt the American POWs. The heads were gruesome objects,
dusty and soiled, with glazed, bulging eyes and slack-open mouths,
jagged skin flaps hanging from the necks. Gautier dropped his head
and closed his eyes; he didn't want to give the guards any satisfaction in
seeing the horror on his face.

After five more days on the road, those still alive were corralled
inside a school yard at San Fernando, about 25 miles northwest of
Manila. They had walked in the searing sun for almost seventy miles,
each with only a single spoonful of uncooked rice and enough water to
keep him barely alive. They were so ravaged and spent that they hardly
recognized one another.

At that point, they received their first real food since capture, such
as it was. Gautier, who had become separated from his friends Knowles
and Inzer, staggered into line to get his share of boiled rice from one
of the large black kettles. Other prisoners served, scooping rice into a
man's cupped hands or whatever other "plate" he might have salvaged.
Gautier had found a slab of board. He held it out.

"Aw, Cajun. You're a pitiful sight. What have they done to you?"

Gautier looked up to find Jesse Knowles grinning at him while
ladling out rice.

"Have you seen Inzer?" Gautier wanted to know.

"Not since we left. Tough as he is, I think he'll make it."

Camp O'Donnell, only nine miles more up the road, proved to be
the destination for Gautier and his batch of POWs. As he and Knowles
tramped along together in a near stupor, he happened to notice a familiar figure in the road ahead. Inzer! The three friends reunited for their
arrival at what could only be termed hell on earth.

The prison compound loomed ahead by the side of the road. Japanese troops corralled the ragged hordes of prisoners through the gates.
Gautier prayed for his friends, for himself and other survivors, and
for the souls of the thousands who perished along the way. That he
had come through the long siege of Bataan and the march following

surrender could only mean that God wasn't through with him yet, and that he would make it the rest of the way, whether he be Methodist or Baptist.

Sergeant James Gautier, Jr., survived the nightmare and was rescued by American Rangers and Alamo Scouts in 1945. "Different things gave different men the will to live," he said. "For some it was their faith. They accepted their circumstances with the belief that God was still in control. . . . Other men survived on hate alone. They lived for the day when they might repay the Japs for all they had done to them and their friends. . . . For me, it was a combination of the two. Prayer was something the Japs couldn't take away, and although I was suffering I believed God was still in control. The Lord had His hand on my shoulder all the time I was a prisoner."

ARMY SERGEANT DAN PITZER,
Vietnam, 1964

On October 29, 1963, Captain Rocky Versace, Lieutenant Nick Rowe, and Sergeant First Class Dan Pitzer from the Tan Phu U.S. Army Special Forces camp accompanied a 129-man Civilian Irregular Defense Group (CIDG) of Vietnamese against a Viet Cong command post located on the Ca Mau Peninsula near the small hamlet of Le Coeur. Never before had American and Allied troops ventured so deep into the enemy's well-established sanctuary in the legendary Forest of Darkness.

It turned out to be an ill-advised venture. An estimated one thousand seasoned guerrilla fighters of the Main Force 306th VC Battalion trapped the much smaller band of CIDG in a farm village next to a stream. The battle raged for three hours. Finally, nearly out of ammunition and still facing large numbers of attacking VC, the surviving South Vietnamese and their American advisers attempted to withdraw and slip away through fields of cane and reeds. Machine gun fire nearly tore off Versace's leg, and grenade fragments struck Rowe in the chest and face before the VC captured all three Green Berets. They were stripped of their boots and led to a remote prison camp deep in the U Minh Forest, a dark labyrinth of canals and mangrove swamps.

Daily life was brutally difficult for American soldiers captured in South Vietnam. Rarely were more than seven or eight held in a camp at any one time. They were kept isolated from one another in small bamboo crates called "tiger cages," deprived of food, and exposed to insects, heat, and disease. Moved regularly to avoid rescue by U.S. troops, they were unable to grow vegetables or tend small livestock such as rabbits or chickens. Their diets consisted of rice and whatever they could catch or gather in the surrounding jungle, and this led to dysentery, edema, beriberi, malaria, eczema, and depression.

For propaganda purposes, guards and political cadres attempted to break the POWs down by deceit, force, and brainwashing, and indoctrinate them into the "enlightened" practice of communism.

"Do not think that merely because the war ends that you will go home," VC political officers cautioned prisoners. "If you unrepentant Americans ever wish to go home, you must denounce your Wall Street capitalists and declare the United States imperialistic, unjust, and illegal."

Pitzer and Rowe adopted a "sit and listen" posture to mandatory classes, preferring to keep a "low profile" and wait it out. Versace, on the other hand, attended only at the point of a bayonet.

"You can make me come to class," he conceded, "but I am an officer in the United States Army. You can make me listen, you can force me to sit here, but I don't believe a word of what you're saying."

Recalcitrant and defiant to the end, Captain Versace was finally taken away. He was singing "God Bless America" at the top of his lungs when guards marched him out of camp. Pitzer later learned that he had been escorted into the forest and executed.

Sergeant Pitzer spent his first year of captivity in virtual isolation. Although he attempted to escape a number of times, he was quickly recaptured on each occasion. A feeling of hopelessness and despair overcame him. Having had a fairly religious upbringing, he now began to blame God for putting him through this ordeal. He questioned God's motives. It was fist-shaking time in his bamboo cage.

"Why are You doing this to me?" he raged. "Why am I being put through this kind of torture?"

Jesus Himself had asked such questions during His sojourn alone in the desert.

On Christmas Eve at the beginning of Pitzer's second year in captivity, he was working outside the camp in the jungle attempting to gather something to eat when he heard the high drone of an approaching airplane. Overcome with excitement and hope, he watched as a light OV-10 FAC (forward air controller) aircraft used by the U.S. Air Force to "spot" targets appeared through a break in the forest canopy. Its pilot must have seen the enemy camp, for it dived and dropped red smoke to mark it. Almost immediately, a Huey helicopter gunship soared in at treetop level and opened up on the VC camp with its machine guns.

Pitzer's excitement turned to fear and disappointment. He hid in the trees, afraid to show himself since he might easily be mistaken for a VC in his issued "black pajamas" and be gunned down before he made his identity known. Profoundly exasperated, almost in tears, he cowered in the forest like a hunted animal until the chopper departed.

The camp had been all shot up. After nightfall, VC guards gave prisoners a handful of cold rice and ordered them to gather their meager possessions. They marched for several hours through the night along a river on their way to a new prison camp.

Just before midnight and the start of Christmas Day, the procession rounded a bend in the river. Pitzer gasped in astonishment. One of the guards exclaimed, "Choi-hoi!" That roughly meant, "My heavens!"

Directly ahead loomed a magnificent evergreen tree thirty or forty feet tall, standing alone next to the water. Something about the tree had attracted thousands and thousands of fireflies. The "Christmas tree" twinkled merrily, as though decorated by strands of lights, reflecting and displaying itself in the black river. Above its top branches hovered a brilliant light in the sky, like a Star of David. A very bright star.

A sense of peace and well-being engulfed Pitzer. He couldn't explain it, but somehow he suddenly knew that everything was going to be all right. The feeling persisted, even after he arrived at the new prison camp and had ample time to consider the spectacle. He decided God didn't have to use lightning bolts or burning bushes to communicate with men. In this instance, He had chosen something recognizable to all Americans every Christmas in order to let Sergeant Pitzer know He was with him.

From then on, whenever Pitzer spoke to God all alone in his little tiger cage, and communist guards asked him who he was talking to, the American replied simply, "Someone you will never know."

In November 1967, the VC National Liberation Front released two GIs in a propaganda move to demonstrate its "humane and lenient" treatment of captives. One of them suffered so badly from malaria, beriberi, hepatitis, and amebic dysentery that the VC also released Medic Pitzer to take care of him.

Because of his "unrepentant" and "reactionary" stubbornness, Lieutenant Rowe was sentenced to be put to death in December 1968. However, before the death penalty could be administered, he took advantage of the appearance of a flight of American helicopters and escaped.

CONFEDERATE PRIVATE JAMES PAXTON,
U.S. Civil War, 1863–64

Confederate General Joe Shelby raided into Missouri from Arkansas in the fall of 1863, one of his purposes being to recruit men to join the insurrection. Yanks surprised and captured several of his soldiers, including Private James Paxton, who had grown up in the Ozarks of Arkansas.

Prisoners were herded through Springfield and St. Louis on foot, in wagons and on horseback to Camp Morton, Indiana, where they arrived in November 1863. Located a mile or so north of Indianapolis, the camp was named in honor of the state's war governor, Oliver P. Morton. Nearly four hundred Confederate prisoners of war were confined on flat, hard soil inside box walls constructed of planks solidly nailed to timbers. Some fourteen feet tall, the walls blocked out the sun until midmorning. Guards oversaw the prison yard and its inmates from a walkway that ran around the outside of the stockade about four feet from the top. Old livestock sheds near the north and west walls served as barracks. Through the center of the compound ran a sewer drain. Prisoners called it the Potomac.

Paxton assumed his confinement was temporary, that the warring sides would soon hold a prisoner exchange. Weeks stretched into months. Word came that there would be no exchanges. Immediately after this, rations were reduced to the point of starvation—about six ounces of stringy beef and a half loaf of "duffer" bread per man per day. No coffee and no vegetables.

Men who died of disease, starvation, and deprivation were lugged outside the walls and buried in unmarked graves in the Indiana soil. Guards said the harsh treatment was retaliation for the starving of Union prisoners held in Andersonville and other southern prisons.

"You starve us down there, we starve you Rebel boys up here. That's how it works."

Lieutenant James A. Corry from Georgia, Paxton's friend, preferred to pass as a common private to avoid being singled out by vengeful guards. He was a strong Christian who joined several preachers among the inmates to hold Bible study and church services. Congregations met underneath shade trees in the summer and inside the shed-barracks in the winter. Old southern gospel singing and down-home fire-and-brimstone preaching by the self-ordained ministers rocked prison walls every Sunday. The more desperate conditions became, the more readily men turned away from gambling and other pursuits to join the "church." Private Paxton noted that a great many sinners came to a knowledge of their Savior underneath the shade trees at Camp Morton.

Lieutenant Corry died of pneumonia in the early winter of 1864. After his body was hauled away to be buried, the entire prison population turned out to hold a memorial service in his memory. Even some of the Union guards attended. Paxton wondered if the lieutenant's relatives in faraway Georgia would ever find out where and how he died.

"There won't be no more war up there where Lieutenant Corry has gone," the presiding preacher promised the silent and bowed-head assemblage. "That there is something we all can look forward to."

Private James Paxton survived Camp Morton and was released after the war ended in 1865.

AIR FORCE LIEUTENANT JACK M. BUTCHER,
Vietnam, 1971

Jack Butcher slowly circled his Cessna OV-10 above a river ford on the Ho Chi Minh Trail near the Laotian border with South Vietnam. A thousand feet above the jungle, he scanned the ford with a pair of binoculars, looking for movement or other indications of enemy activity. The trail was the primary route used by the North Vietnamese to bring in troops and supplies to pursue their war of subjugating the South to communism. FACs like Butcher and his partner Captain Tom Yarborough, who worked a second grid nearby, scratched and sniffed around enemy supply lines and other congested areas. If they spotted anything, they called in "fast movers" to dump rockets and napalm on-target.

The only movement Butcher detected through his binoculars were ripples reflecting sunlight where the primitive twin ruts of the trail crossed the shallow river. He thought he had caught sight of something else down there in the Big Green, but he must have been mistaken. He banked once more to make sure.

Flying FACs was one of the most, if not *the* most, hazardous aviation job in Vietnam. The low-flying, slow-flying aircraft literally invited anyone and everyone to take a pot shot, from the VC farmer-by-day with his antique .50-caliber single-action rifle to the surface-to-air missile (SAM) gunner. It didn't surprise Lieutenant Butcher that he would be shot at. What surprised him on that morning of March 24, 1971, was the suddenness of it, the unexpectedness.

Seemingly out of nowhere, originating from somewhere down in the jungle's vast expanse, a single antiaircraft shell streaked up at him trailing smoke. It slammed into the nose of his little airplane before he had time to react and exploded with a deafening bang below his left rudder pedal.

Of all the dumb luck! Every combat pilot lived with the nightmare of possibly being shot down over enemy territory and risking capture. Butcher's nightmare-turned-real was just beginning.

The OV-10 burst into a ball of flames. It shuddered violently and rolled forward. Although dazed from the concussion, barely conscious, Butcher reacted instinctively to training and managed to open the door and bail out. He blacked out as his parachute opened with a positive jerk.

Captain Yarborough, patrolling nearby, saw what happened. But by the time he reached the site, Butcher's airplane and Butcher himself had vanished into the green canopy below. However, the high-pitched shrill of the downed pilot's emergency beeper filled his headphones. That meant his friend had ejected and was possibly still alive down there. Yarborough radio-alerted search and rescue (SAR) helicopters.

Lieutenant Butcher awoke lying next to a tree. Still groggy, hardly aware of what he was doing, he crawled into some bushes to hide. *They* would be coming for him. Only a few weeks in-country and here he was already shot down. Shock and the aftereffects of the explosion in his cockpit made him pass out again.

The next time he opened his eyes, he was lying flat on his back in a dim place. At first he thought it was nightfall. He blinked rapidly, trying to orient himself. How much time had passed? Hours? Gradually, his senses returned. He discovered himself stretched out, still in his flight suit, on a reed sleeping mat inside what he assumed to be a Vietnamese hooch. He was looking up at the underside of a thatched-grass roof.

Other unsettling features about his environment came into focus. An IV needle protruded from his wrist. In the open doorway, staring in at him, stood a sentry dressed in peasant "black pajamas" and a cone hat. He pointed his AK-47 at Butcher when the American stirred.

Butcher studied the VC with a mixture of fear and curiosity. It was the first enemy soldier he had ever seen close up. All he could figure was that this guy and his comrades must have found him and whisked him away to their base camp. By the look on the guard's face, this was not going to be a pleasant experience.

"If I had my druthers," Captain Yarborough once drawled, "I'd druther die right away rather than end up in gook hands. Chances are they'll kill you anyhow—only it'll be so much slower and more painful."

Butcher wondered why they hadn't already finished him off. Probably because they intended to torture and interrogate him. *Then* they'd kill him.

The guard lowered his rifle and walked off a few steps, where he resumed his sentry duties. As Butcher lay helplessly gazing up at the thatched roof of his prison, he began to prepare himself mentally for what he felt to be certain and eventual execution.

He began to pray. He prayed for over an hour. He prayed the Sinner's Prayer: "Lord, I know I have sinned. In Jesus' name, forgive me of my sins and come into my heart." He accepted Jesus as his Savior and afterward felt much better. He believed God was listening and would guide him through his ordeal.

Except for the omnipresent guard, he was left alone in the hut for the next several days with nothing but his increasing apprehension. He soon recovered from being shot down, but he seemed to be getting weaker rather than stronger. The cause was his meager diet—a handful or so of boiled rice once a day. Maybe starvation was how they intended to accomplish his execution.

Butcher and his guard soon formed a symbiotic routine. After lunch, the guard sat down against the trunk of a tree and took a nap. Butcher used the opportunity to explore, peeping cautiously out the open door to discover his hooch was only one of several in some kind of small village camp. Guerrillas and gray-green uniformed NVA regulars were always about. There was no way he could simply walk away without being noticed.

On hands and knees, he patted down every inch of his hut's dirt floor before he found what he was looking for—an escape tunnel concealed underneath a reed mat. His in-country indoctrination course had been right on the money. The enemy *was* ingenious in burrowing a way to flee in case he was surprised and had to get out without being seen. His hopes soared.

The next day, during his guard's after-lunch siesta, Butcher said a prayer, grabbed his boots and a canteen that had been left in the hut, and wriggled into the tunnel. It was almost too small for the average American's body. He feared he might get stuck in it and starve to death. With great relief, he popped up in the jungle a short distance away.

He was free! *God had been listening!*

Running, stopping frequently to listen for pursuit, he made his way toward the western sun, away from the Laotian border and deeper into Vietnam, where his chances of being found were greater. He climbed a wooded ridge and worked his way along it until he came to a wide meadow. He heard voices drawing rapidly nearer on his back trail. Trackers.

He followed a trail that meandered along the base of the ridge between it and the meadow. He dared not try to make a run for it across the open; he would be spotted and promptly shot. At the same time, he knew by the sound of voices that his trackers were catching up to him. There was no way he could outdistance them in his weakened condition. Instead, he crawled into dense underbrush, covered himself with foliage, and prayed.

Armed and enraged searchers combed the ridge for him for the next several hours. Butcher lay motionless in his hide, hardly daring to breath. His heart pounded so hard when soldiers passed nearby that he feared they must surely hear it.

Finally, they seemed to give up. The forest grew silent. Butcher waited for another hour to be sure before he crept from cover. Sundown was only an hour or so away, and he needed to put as much distance between himself and the base camp as he could before nightfall forced him to hole up somewhere.

He pushed downhill to the edge of the meadow, where he could make better time and the growing dusk was not quite so thick. Suddenly, more than a dozen NVA stood up in the grass, bayoneted AK-47 muzzles pointed at him. They had been waiting patiently like deer hunters on a stand for him to show himself—and he had fallen into their trap. His few hours of freedom were over.

An English-speaking officer interrogated him for the next few days. Butcher refused to cooperate, playing dumb and pretending not to understand the officer's accented English. Soldiers congregated in the door of the hut to watch and cheer on their communist hero. The discouraged officer finally gave up.

"I am sorry you have chosen not to answer," he said. "We have decided to execute you."

Soldiers and villagers in the door scattered at that announcement. One guard remained standing behind the American. Butcher heard him chamber a round into his pistol. As the interrogator walked out, he turned back and sadly repeated how sorry he was that the American pilot refused to talk.

The muzzle of a handgun pressed against the back of Butcher's head. He felt his life about to stop. He sat on his little stool, eyes closed in a final prayer, hands clasped in his lap, the muzzle of the pistol jammed against his skull, and waited for his life to end.

To hell with them, he thought. *I'm not breaking the code. God's will be done.*

The guard did not shoot. It was a bluff. After a few minutes, the interrogator returned, looked at Butcher, and shook his head.

"We did not realize how much your President Nixon has brainwashed American soldiers," he said.

On May 4, six weeks after Lieutenant Butcher's initial capture, he and two guards started the long walk up the Ho Chi Minh Trail to Hanoi. On May 9, during a rest break in the jungle, he said he had to go to the bathroom. The guards moved to the other side of the trail to smoke while he nonchalantly walked into the forest. Once out of sight, he took off running.

Within a few hours, the top-secret Allied Joint Personnel Recovery Center (JPRC) intercepted an enemy radio message stating that an OV-10 pilot had escaped along the trail in southern Laos. JPRC was established by the United States earlier in the war to keep track of American and Allied POWs, and attempt to recover them. Immediately, the great hunt was on to find Butcher. JPRC monitored communications and filled the skies with SAR aircraft.

For ten desperate days, Lieutenant Butcher evaded the heaviest concentrations of NVA and VC troops in Southeast Asia while suffering from malaria, headaches, fever, and overwhelming hunger. Several times he spotted friendly aircraft flying overhead, but failed at contacting them because of heavy jungle.

On May 19, driven by hunger, he sneaked into a village to steal pineapples. An elderly woman spotted him. He fled the village and stumbled down a trail. He crossed a dry streambed and was hurrying through the woods when he heard shouts. Armed NVA soldiers promptly ran him down.

He resumed the long walk to Hanoi—with four guards this time. He knew God was by his side to see him through whatever came.

Lieutenant Jack Butcher survived incarceration at the notorious Hanoi Hilton until "Homecoming" at the end of the war, when the North Vietnamese released him.

NAVY LIEUTENANT COMMANDER JOHN MCCAIN,
Vietnam, 1970

During a bombing run over Hanoi in October 1967, Lieutenant Commander John McCain's A-4 Skyhawk was hit by a SAM missile, knocking off its right wing. Reacting automatically, McCain radioed "I'm hit!" and pulled the ejection seat handle as the aircraft spiraled toward earth.

Somehow, he struck the plane as he ejected and broke both arms and his right knee as he hurtled through the air. Knocked unconscious by the force, he revived only after his parachute dropped him into the center of shallow Truc Bach Lake in the middle of Hanoi in the middle of the day. Unable to use his arms, he inflated his life vest by pulling the toggle with his teeth.

Angry Vietnamese civilians hauled him ashore, shouting, spitting, kicking, and striking. Someone smashed his shoulder with a rifle butt. Someone else stabbed a bayonet into his ankle and groin. A female nurse and the arriving Viet military rescued him before the civilians could finish him off. They transported him to nearby Hoa Lo, the former French prison notorious among American POWs as "Hanoi Hilton." He was confined there and at "the Plantation" for the next five and a half years and endured unspeakable deprivation, hardship, and torture.

Denied initial medical care, he suffered further injuries and abuse at the hands of brutal military guards and interrogators. The camp officer of the Plantation, a short, fat Viet called "Bug" because of a cloudy right eye, finally decided the American pilot was going to die, no matter what.

"Are you going to take me to the hospital?" McCain asked.

"No. It's too late."

Just as McCain accepted his fate, Bug returned, excited. "Your father is a big admiral," he exclaimed. "Now we take you to the hospital."

Delivered because of his propaganda value, McCain was treated and placed in a cell with two U.S. Air Force majors, George "Bud" Day and Norris Overly. Day suffered from the aftermath of his own injuries and from incessant torture. Overly was in better shape. Together, the two men saved McCain's life. They cleaned him, fed him, helped him on and off the toilet bucket, and massaged his leg. Gradually, he began to recover.

Prisoners of war knew well the meaning of the term "steady strain." It meant to buckle down and endure, to take life in captivity and everything that came with it in a stoic, patient manner. They would go home when the time came. Nothing they did could hasten it.

North Vietnamese guards and interrogators were "mean sons of bitches," as McCain put it in describing Bug. Raised and indoctrinated through communism, which acknowledged no moral principle of a god or a higher being, they seemed to possess none of the restraining influences that might have tempered their harsh treatment of captives. Many of the guards and even some of the interrogators had never even heard the word "god" in any language. They beat and sometimes murdered prisoners without compassion or conscience.

"Interrogation," which meant torture, continued long after a prisoner no longer possessed useful military information. It became an effort to brainwash him into accepting communism and making statements against his own country. McCain, like other POWs, settled into the "steady strain" of a prisoner of communism.

The daily routine of life was both simple and excruciatingly dull. Each morning began at six with the ringing of a gong. POWs rose and folded their bedding. They sat while loudspeakers broadcast Hanoi Hannah and the "Voice of Vietnam" into their cells. "News from home" consisted of updates on antiwar activities, incidents of civil strife in the United States, and recordings of speeches delivered by prominent American opponents of the war.

POWs emptied their waste buckets and were fed two meals a day, each usually consisting of weak tea, a small slab of bread and a bowl of pumpkin soup with, sometimes, a piece of pig fat in it. The rest of the day, they simply waited in solitary with nothing to occupy their minds, boredom broken only by irregular interrogations.

Sometimes three or four weeks might pass between events in the interrogation room, a Spartan cell furnished only with a wooden table, a chair behind the table, and a low stool. At other times, a prisoner might be jerked out of sleep two or three times in a single night and hauled down for a session. McCain would shoot bolt upright in terror every time he heard the sound of jangling keys at his cell door.

The "Soft Soap Fairy" was an interrogator with delicate manners and a solicitous good-cop routine. He spoke fine English.

"How are you, Mac Kane? This terrible war. I hope it's soon over."

Bug, on the other hand, was a sadist filled with irrational hate. On occasion, he had McCain trussed in ropes with his hands and feet cinched behind his back so tightly that it cut off circulation and caused him to lose consciousness.

But whether the interrogator was a Fairy or a Bug, the POW could only accept it and endure. Only once during McCain's captivity did he encounter a Vietnamese who seemed to possess some true compassion toward his subjects. In 1970, a young interrogator practicing his English on the pilot appeared interested in American religious customs, especially the significance of Easter.

"It's that time of year when we celebrate the death and resurrection of the Son of God," McCain explained.

The Viet frowned in disbelief as McCain recounted the events of Christ's Passion: His crucifixion, death on the cross, resurrection, and ascent into Heaven.

"You say He *died*?" the interrogator demanded suspiciously.

"Yes. He died."

"Three days He was dead?"

"Then He came alive again. People saw Him. Then He went back to Heaven."

The Vietnamese stared at the American, and pondered, clearly puzzled. He got up without another word and left the room.

Shortly, he returned, his friendly manner gone. He glowered at McCain.

"Mac Kane," he barked, "the officer say you tell nothing but lies. Go back to your room."

Lieutenant Commander John McCain was released in 1972 and later became a U.S. senator and presidential candidate.

3

PRAYER

Then hear Thou in heaven their prayer and their supplication, and maintain their cause.

—I Kings 8:45

The very first motion on the floor of the Second Continental Congress after its members received news about the outbreak of war with Britain in 1775, "the shot heard 'round the world," was for a prayer to seek the guidance of Almighty God.

The significance of religion in making American society what it is, the importance of its religious roots, cannot be downplayed. Nearly half the men who signed the Declaration of Independence had at least some seminary training. George Washington drew on his religious convictions for both practical and philosophical help as he fulfilled his duties as general and as president. During the darkest days of the Revolutionary War, he urged citizens to ask for God's protection in prayer.

Benjamin Franklin rose to speak when the Constitutional Convention was mired in deadlock in June 1787. "I . . . believe that without

His concurring aid we shall succeed in this political building no better than the builders of Babel," he said. He then moved that the Constitutional Convention begin each morning with prayer.

Americans throughout the history of the union, from common soldiers in battle to generals and presidents, have looked to a Higher Power in times of chaos and war. Abraham Lincoln called for a National Day of Prayer while in the throes of the Civil War.

"Likewise, we need to pray earnestly for the power of the Holy Spirit to give us a precious revival in our hearts and among the unconverted," declared General Robert E. Lee.

President Franklin Roosevelt issued a "D-Day Prayer" prior to the invasion of Normandy in 1944: "Almighty God: Our sons, pride of our nation, this day have set upon a mighty endeavor, a struggle to preserve our republic, our religion, and our civilization, and to set free a suffering humanity. . . .

"They will be sore tried by night and by day, without rest until the victory is won. The darkness will be rent by noise and flame. Men's souls will be shaken with the violence of war. For these men are drawn from the ways of peace. They fight not for the lust of conquest, they fight to end conquest. They fight to liberate. They fight to let justice arise among all Thy people. They yearn but for the end of battle, for their return to the haven of home. Some will never return. Embrace these, Father, and receive them, Thy heroic servants into Thy Kingdom."

Harry Truman signed a joint resolution for such a national prayer day during the Korean War in 1952. In 1988, President Ronald Reagan approved an amendment to officially make the National Day of Prayer the first Thursday of each May.

In 2006, in a new and equally brutal "War on Terror" in Iraq, President George W. Bush honored the National Day of Prayer in his annual commemoration speech.

"America is a nation of prayer," he said. "It's impossible to tell the story of our nation without telling the story of people who pray. . . . At decisive moments in our history and in quiet times around family tables, we are a people humbled and strengthened and blessed by prayer."

CHIEF CHAPLAIN JAMES O'NEILL,
World War II, 1944

At about eleven o'clock on the morning of December 8, 1944, General George S. Patton telephoned Third Army's Chief Chaplain James H. O'Neill with an unusual request. Rain drummed steadily against the windows of Patton's temporary headquarters in an old French military barracks at the Caserne Molifor in Nancy. It showed no signs of letting up. Once Patton's army had been unleashed after D-Day, he had gone through the Germans, as he put it in his salty language, "like crap through a goose." Now weather and stretched supply lines prevented him from being the first Allied commander to reach and cross the Rhine River.

"Do you have a good prayer for weather?" Patton asked the chaplain. "We must do something about these rains if we are to win the war."

Although Patton's reputation had him crusty and often profane, Chaplain O'Neill also knew him as a man who possessed a genuine trust in God. The general was a regular in church on Sunday unless duty made it impossible. He was serious about the prayer. The chaplain immediately typed up a prayer on a three-by-five card and presented it to his commander.

> *Almighty and most merciful Father, we humbly beseech Thee, of Thy great goodness, to restrain these immoderate rains with which we have had to contend. Grant us fair weather for battle. Graciously hearken to us as soldiers who call upon Thee that, armed with Thy power, we may advance from victory to victory, and crush the oppression and wickedness of our enemies and establish Thy justice among men and nations.*

"Chaplain, sit down for a moment," Patton invited. "I want to talk to you about this business of prayer." He rubbed his face in his hands, then rose to his full six-two and stood at the high window behind his desk, looking out at the gray rainfall.

"Chaplain, how much praying is being done in the Third Army?" he asked.

"Does the General mean by chaplains, or by the men?"

"By everybody."

"I am afraid to admit it, but I do not believe that much praying is going on. When there is fighting, everyone prays. But now with the constant rain, when things are quiet, dangerously quiet, men just sit and wait for things to happen. . . . I do not believe that much praying is being done."

General Patton returned to his desk and leaned back in his swivel chair.

"Chaplain O'Neill, I am a strong believer in prayer," he said. "There are three ways that men get what they want: by planning, by working, and by praying. Any great military operation takes careful planning, or thinking. Then you must have well-trained troops to carry it out. That's working. But between the plan and the operation there is always an unknown. That unknown spells defeat or victory, success or failure. It is the reaction of the actors to the ordeal when it actually comes. Some people call it 'getting the breaks,' I call it God.

"God has His part, His margin, in everything. That's where prayer comes in. Up to now, in the Third Army, God has been very good to us. We have never retreated. We have suffered no defeats, no famine, no epidemics. This is because a lot of people back home are praying for us. We were lucky in Africa, in Sicily, and in Italy, simply because people prayed. But we have to pray for ourselves, too. A good soldier isn't made merely by making him think and work. There is something in every soldier that goes deeper than thinking or working. It's called guts. It is something that he has built in there. It is a world of truth and power that is higher than himself. Great living is not all output of thought and work. A man has to have intake as well. I don't know what you call it, but I call it Religion, Prayer, or God."

He paused, let his pencil drop to his desk.

"Chaplain, men should pray no matter where they are, in church or out of it. Sooner or later if they do not pray, they will crack up. I wish you would put out a Training Letter on the subject of prayer to all the chaplains. Write about nothing else, just the importance of prayer. Let me see it before you send it. We've got to get not only the chaplains but every man in the Third Army to pray. We must ask God to stop these rains. These rains are that margin that hold defeat or victory. If we all pray, it will be like what Dr. Carrel said [Patton's reference was to a press quote by a foremost scientist, Dr. Alexis Carrel, who described prayer as 'one of the most powerful forms of energy man can generate']. It will be like plugging in on a current whose source is in Heaven. I believe that prayer completes that circuit. It is power."

Chaplain O'Neill then wrote Training Letter No. 5:

At this stage of the operations I would call upon the chaplains and the men of the Third United States Army to focus their attention on the importance of prayer.

Our glorious march from the Normandy Beach across France to where we stand, before and beyond the Siegfried Line, with the wreckage of the German Army behind us, should convince the most skeptical soldier that God has ridden with our banner. Pestilence and famine have not touched us. We have continued in unity of purpose. We have had no quitters; and our leadership has been masterful. The Third Army has no roster of retreats. None of defeats. We have no memory of a lost battle to hand on to our children from this great campaign.

But we are not stopping at the Siegfried Line. Tough days may be ahead of us before we eat our rations in the Chancellery of the Deutsches Reich.

As chaplains, it is our business to pray. We preach its importance. We urge its practice. But the time is now to intensify our faith in prayer, not alone with ourselves, but with every believing man, Protestant, Catholic, Jew, or Christian in the ranks of the Third United States Army.

Those who pray do more for the world than those who fight; and if the world goes from bad to worse, it is because there are more battles than prayers. "Hands lifted up," said Bossuet, "smash more battalions than hands that strike."

Gideon of Bible fame was least in his father's house. He came from Israel's smallest tribe. But he was a mighty man of valor. His strength lay not in his military might, but in his recognition of God's proper claims upon his life. He reduced his army from thirty-two thousand to three hundred men lest the people of Israel would think that their valor had saved them. We have no intention to reduce our vast striking force. But we must urge, instruct, and indoctrinate every fighting man to pray as well as fight. In Gideon's day, and in our own, spiritually alert minorities carry the burden and bring the victories.

Urge all of your men to pray, not alone in church, but everywhere. Pray when driving. Pray when fighting. Pray alone. Pray with others. Pray by night and pray by day. Pray for the cessation of immoderate rains, for good weather for battle. Pray for the defeat of our wicked enemy whose banner is injustice and whose goal is oppression. Pray for victory. Pray for our army, and pray for peace.

We must march together, all are for God. The soldier who cracks up does not need sympathy or comfort as much as he needs strength. We are not trying to make the best of these days. It is our job to make the most of them. Now is not the time to follow God from "afar off." This army needs the assurance and the faith that God is with us. With prayer, we cannot fail.

Be assured that this message on prayer has the approval, the encouragement, and the enthusiastic support of the Third United States Army Commander.

The "Weather Prayer" and Training Letter No. 5 were distributed to every man in the Third Army and to all 486 chaplains by December 14.

Two days later, on December 16th, Germans crept out of rain, mist, and thick fog in Belgium's Ardennes Forest to catch the Americans by complete surprise. General Patton rushed his divisions north from the Saar Valley on December 19th to relieve beleaguered Bastogne. He was heard praying in a Luxembourg chapel.

"Sir, this is Patton talking. The past fourteen days have been straight hell. Rain, snow, more rain, more snow. I am beginning to wonder what's going on in Your headquarters. Whose side are You on anyway? In exchange for four days of fighting weather, I will deliver You enough Krauts to keep Your bookkeepers months behind in their work. Amen."

It appeared the Nazis' last-ditch gamble to defeat the Allies and win a truce might succeed. Had bad weather continued, the war may well have stalemated at the Battle of the Bulge with Hitler still in power. However, both German and American forecasters were astonished when the rains and snow ceased and the fog dissipated on December 20th. The next week brought clear skies and perfect flying weather.

Allied bombers knocked out hundreds of enemy tanks and killed thousands of German soldiers. Hitler's generals called a full retreat after suffering more than 100,000 casualties.

In late January 1945, Chaplain O'Neill ran across Patton in Luxembourg. The general cracked the chaplain lightly on the side of his steel helmet with his riding crop.

"Well, Padre," he said. "Our prayers worked. I knew they would."

MARINE LANCE CORPORAL PAUL DRINKALL,
Vietnam, 1968

U.S. Marine Lance Corporal Paul Drinkall was no praying Christian when he got shipped to Vietnam in 1968—but his mother was. She got down on her knees every night before she went to bed and prayed that her son would come home safely.

Thanks, Mom.

Marine Battalion Landing Team (BLT) 3/1 dug out a small fire support base (FSB) at the mouth of the Cua Viet River in late January 1968, just before VC violated the Vietnamese New Year's cease-fire and launched the Tet Offensive by attacking government buildings and military bases all over South Vietnam. The 3/1 FSB came under regular deadly artillery and mortar fire.

Drinkall was a section A-gunner—assistant gunner—for a six-gun 105mm howitzer battery. Although three men could fire a howitzer, a single 105 section normally consisted of seven crewmen: gunner, A-gunner, loader, two ammunition bearers, a radioman, and a section chief. Drinkall controlled the up-and-down movement of his gun, operated the breech, and pulled the lanyard to fire it.

Individual gun crews scraped out two-man fighting holes in the ground behind their guns. Tet and daily pounding by enemy artillery forced them to renovate their holes into bunkers, lined and roofed with sandbags, capable of withstanding anything short of a direct hit. Drinkall vacated the one he shared with Norman Cowell and set up housekeeping with James Kearney. Joe Dallea moved in with Cowell.

All they had to do now was hunker down when they were shelled, deliver fire missions when ordered, and stave off boredom while they crossed days off their "short timer's" calendars.

During a lull in the shelling one afternoon, Cowell and Dallea crawled from their bunker to take a look around at the damage. A respite could last anywhere from a half hour to as long as two or three hours; it generally meant Charlie had temporarily run out of ammo and was waiting for more to be brought up. The two Marines slipped into the bunker with Drinkall and Kearney to scuttlebutt for a few minutes.

The breather turned out to be a short one. A 130mm round from the resumed barrage scored a roof hit on the bunker Drinkall previously shared with Cowell, demolishing it in a geyser of mud, dirt, and sandbags. The four Marines, safe in Drinkall's new home, were stunned.

If Cowell and Dallea had remained in place, as they usually did, BLT could have shipped their remains stateside in their ditty bags. In another equally catastrophic scenario, all four Marines would have gone up in blood, guts, and mud had Drinkall kept his original hole and Cowell and Dallea ventured over to visit in it.

Thanks, Mom.

. . .

An artillery battery followed a set pattern in delivering a typical fire mission. A rifle company out in the field encountered stiff resistance and decided to call in artillery to see if the dinks could hang in there.

"I want a battery three rounds on that tree line," the company commander informed his accompanying forward observer (FO).

The FO calculated grid coordinates and relayed the request via radio to the FSB. "Fire mission! Troops in contact. From BC 218, add 500. Enemy in tree line. HE fuse, superquick and delay. Will adjust."

Rounds with superquick fuses exploded immediately upon hitting tree branches. Delayed or variable time (VHT) fuses allowed the shells to penetrate trees without exploding, then burst on the ground after a timed delay. VHT was not popular with gun crews because of is unreliability. Radio signals, rain, even low clouds or birds could sometimes inadvertently set them off.

Once the FO's mission request reached the FSB, radio loudspeakers mounted high on twelve-by-twelve timbers crackled and crews dozing in their bunkers sprang into action. Howitzers shimmered in the hot afternoon sun behind sandbag parapets. Number six fired. Smoke belched from its muzzle. The round soared through the sky toward its target like a crash of thunder.

Lance Corporal Drinkall threw open the breech of his gun to receive a VHT. The loader, Tim Miller, slammed the nose of the heavy shell at the breech—and *missed*. It struck the breech ring instead on its way in, shattering the fuse.

"*Aw, shit!*" he said.

Definitely an *Aw, shit!* moment. Little pieces of the fuse dribbled to the ground. Reacting, Drinkall slammed the breech on the round and locked it, his thought being to get rid of the damned thing before the delay ran out and it went off.

"Cease fire!" came the command.

"*Aw, shit!*" A round about to cook off in the tube and the CO wanted to hold it up! The section chief jumped at his radio mike to explain the situation. Crewmembers stampeded to their bunkers in case the gun detonated.

"Drinkall! The CO says fire it."

Drinkall quickly looped a long lanyard on the trigger. He expected the gun to blow up in his face at any moment. Running, he played out the lanyard, ducked behind sandbags, and yanked it. The round exploded with a great deafening air burst less than a hundred yards downrange.

Thanks, Mom.

During a scary night fire mission in which the FSB launched a mix of HE (high explosives) and Willie Pete (WP, white phosphorus) to support a Marine company in contact, the dinks dueled back with their own 130mm big guns. Exploding shells stomped all over the firebase with amazing accuracy, opening quick bright holes in the darkness. They were on target tonight.

Battery sections hunkered down behind their gun shields and waited out the more nerve-wracking moments. A near miss, sounding like a VW, hurtled through the air, whirred over Drinkall's gun, and exploded close behind with a blinding lightning flash and the crash of doom.

After the all-clear, Drinkall and his crew discovered how close they had come to meeting their Maker. The enemy shell that cruised close over their heads struck the Willie Pete ammo bunker blast wall, destroying it. Some idiot had left two WP rounds lying ready to fire on top of the bunker. The explosion flipped one of them back inside with the other stores of WP and hurled the second across the parapet where it landed in the entryway of the HE storage.

Had either one exploded and cooked off the stored artillery ammo, which by all rights they should have, nothing would have been left of that corner of the FSB except a smoldering crater filled with blood and scraps of human flesh.

Thanks, Mom.

. . .

"In 1973 I finally accepted Jesus as my Lord and Savior," Paul Drinkall wrote in a letter dated March 21, 2006. "I should have done it sooner, but I guess I wasn't ready. At least I was still able to receive Him. Thanks, Mom."

"THE ANGEL OF HADLEY,"
King Philip's War, 1676

In 1659, about fifty Puritan families led by Reverend John Russell carved out the settlement of Hadley, Massachusetts, in a bend of the Connecticut River on the edge of the western wilderness. Isolated and surrounded by Mohawk, Wampanoag and Abenaki Indians, who sometimes proved hostile, the colonists constructed a defensive palisade that enclosed most of the town's houses, the main street, and the commons.

A bloody war broke out in 1675 between English settlers and the Wampanoag tribe led by Chief Metacom, known to settlers as Philip or "King Philip." The war spread as far north as New Hampshire and as far southwest as Connecticut. By the spring of 1676, Indians were attacking outlying towns of Massachusetts, also known as the Bay Colony. Hadley was right on the frontier. Anticipating trouble and feeling especially vulnerable, the town voted to fortify the meetinghouse. Reverend Russell penned a letter to the Bay Colony council expressing his concern: "We must look to feel their utmost rage. My desire is we may be willing to do or suffer, to live or die, remain in or be driven out, as the Lord our God would have us."

In May 1676 he wrote another letter describing events unfolding around Hadley:

This morning about sunrise came into Hatfield one Thomas Reede, a soldier who was taken captive when Deacon Goodman was slain. He relates that they are now planting at Deerfield and have been so these three or four days or more, saith further that they dwell at the Falls on both sides the river, are a considerable number, yet most of them old men and women.

He cannot judge that there are on both sides of the river above 60 or 70 fighting-men [Indians]. They are secure and scornful, boasting of great things they have done and will do. There is Thomas Eames, his daughter and child hardly used [captives]; one or two belonging to Medfield and I think two children belonging to Lancaster. The night before last they came down to Hatfield upper meadow, and have driven away many horses and cattle to the number of fourscore and upwards as they judge. Many of these this man saw in Deerfield Meadow, and found the bars put up to keep them in.

This being the state of things, we think the Lord calls us to make some trial what may be done against them suddenly without further delay; and therefore the concurring resolution of men here seems to be to go out against them tomorrow night, so as to be with them, the Lord assisting, before break of day. We need guidance and help from heaven. We humbly beg your prayers, advice and help if it may be. And therewith committing you to the guidance and blessing of the Most High.

After two days of prayer, men from Hadley attacked the Indians in retaliation and in an attempt to rescue white captives. The Falls Fight resulted in considerable bloodshed on both sides, but the colonists soon took the upper hand and drove the Indians back.

That was not the end of it, however. On June 12, residents of Hadley were observing a Fast Day service at the meetinghouse when a large band of Wampanoag launched a surprise raid against the settlement. Villagers rushed out of the meetinghouse, guns in hand, to defend their homes. However, they were disorganized and ineffective, their resistance confined to individuals and small groups. Arrows or bullets dropped a number of them all up and down the commons.

Just when it appeared that Indians would prevail and destroy the town and all its inhabitants, an elderly stranger with flowing white hair and beard appeared as though out of thin air. Wielding an old sword in his fist, he threw himself into the melee with the bearing of a general who had seen battle previously.

He seemed to be everywhere at once, marshaling the townspeople, organizing and leading counterattacks, establishing effective pockets of defense and resistance. Inspired by his leadership, the townspeople of Hadley rallied and drove off the attackers, saving the village.

After the fighting ended, Reverend Russell and the others looked around to thank their mysterious savior—only to find he had vanished as suddenly as he appeared. Unable to explain logically what happened, the settlers proclaimed the white-bearded transient to be an angel sent by God in answer to their prayers. The Angel of Hadley.

Some historians speculate that the "angel" could have been one William Goffe, who fled to the colonies to hide out from King Charles II following England's Civil War and Restoration. Goffe made his way to the frontier of New England where he may have been granted asylum in Reverend Russell's basement. The residents of Hadley, however, always believed they were saved by an angel.

MARINE LIEUTENANT COLONEL NEIL LEVIN, *Vietnam, 1966*

Flight leader Lieutenant Colonel Neil Levin* delivered a little pep talk to his fellow Marine fighter pilots before they took off from the Chu Lai airfield. He wasn't sure how much good it did. The three younger flyers still looked grim as they hoisted their flight bags and helmets and followed him to their silver raptors waiting on the ready line. None of the usual grab-assing and joking around. Their target was a bridge that routed two major highways and a railroad track across a river south of Hanoi, North Vietnam. The bridge was a major enemy supply line into South Vietnam.

Six aircraft from the U.S. Air Force and Navy had been shot down during the past three days trying to destroy the bridge. Three pilots

---

* See also chapter 14.

were missing and presumed killed. Previous Marine air attacks that morning reported such extreme concentrations of flak over the target that the pilots had missed it and been driven off.

"Keep alert and follow my lead," Colonel Levin said before climbing into the high, narrow cockpit of his A-4 Skyhawk jet. "Are we ready? Let's go!"

The formation of four Skyhawks climbed out of Chu Lai airfield to 20,000 feet in a clear Asian sky, then skirted to seaward to avoid antiaircraft (AA) along the DMZ. In addition to 20mm cannon, each warbird carried six five-hundred-pound bombs. These were sufficient to do the job if the pilots were skillful enough—and lucky enough—to successfully run the enemy shooting gallery to reach the bridge.

The jets dived for the deck at full throttle over the South China Sea before slashing into North Vietnamese airspace at more than 600 miles per hour, so treetop low that a kid could have knocked them out of the air by tossing up his sandal. Their best chance of getting through enemy defenses depended on complete surprise, which meant flying the deck to pop up at the last instant to give the bad guys hell before they knew what hit them.

Terrain zipped past below like an unreeling mapscape. Levin recognized his last checkpoint, a bend in the river southeast of the bridge. He opened his flight into combat formation.

"Spread out and pop up to seven thousand feet on my signal . . . Arm bombs . . . Pop up now!"

The target lay dead ahead—a brown river twisting like a dying snake, traversed by a broad and modern bridge of concrete and steel. Several military vehicles were crossing it.

Colonel Levin gave the order: "Attack! Attack!"

At such speeds, air combat took on a quickened, unreal quality, like a film on fast-forward. Levin led the strike, diving from 7,000 to 3,500 feet, the bridge bracketed in his bombsite. Exploding AA shells, black and red blossoms of flak, charged the air with electricity and death, so thick it seemed they could be used like stepping stones across a running brook. Green tracer rounds webbed the sky with startling impact.

Diving! Diving! Into it hard, his jet engine winding up and shrieking. Target dead center. *Bombs away!*

Seconds in the attack, seconds over target, other seconds climbing out through flak and tracers. He jinked the Skyhawk from side to side in the climb, pulling up hard and right. A glimpse back through his canopy revealed a huge gap in the midsection of the bridge, twisted steel on either side like the jagged teeth of a dragon's mouth belching smoke and flames. He radioed his wingmen to abort. No sense risking them on a target already destroyed.

Ka-pow! A powerful thud jolted Levin's plane. Pain stabbed into his right side. He was hit—and hit hard. Winged like a chukkar in flight by a shotgun blast.

The Skyhawk continued to climb, although the cockpit filled with smoke. Once clear of AA, he did a quick assessment. His wound wasn't bad, a small piece of steel lodged above his right hip. He could live with it.

The blow to the jet, however, looked fatal. Nothing but twisted metal remained of the right jet intake. He opened an air vent to blow smoke out of the cockpit. He kept climbing as long as the plane would generate power, and was intent on getting as far away from the area as he could. His instruments weren't reassuring. Tailpipe temperatures redlined at over 2,000 degrees centigrade, well above the maximum tolerance level of 650 degrees.

"You are on fire! Eject! Eject!" a wingman screamed through the radio.

All manuals recommended ejection when confronted by a crisis like this one—bail out before the plane explodes. The colonel looked down and all he could think about was dropping into that wasps nest and, if he survived ejection and capture, ending up in a POW camp. Better to take his chances on dying in the air than being slowly tortured to death by the North Vietnamese.

The Gulf of Tonkin lay about twenty-five miles away. U.S. Navy and Coast Guard ships constantly patrolled the coasts to pick up downed airmen. He might have a chance if he could reach the gulf before abandoning his ship. What did he have to lose by trying?

He radioed *Mayday*, his voice sounding calmer than he felt, then ordered his three wingmen to return to base before they ran out of fuel and found themselves in a bad situation with him.

Miraculously, the crippled jet continued to respond to its controls. Levin climbed to 16,000 feet before heat and smoke inside the cockpit grew intolerable. He leveled off in the direction of the gulf. He saw its blue waters ahead.

Just a few more minutes . . . Please, a few more minutes . . .

The mottled green and tan of solid ground below turned to rimmed beach and the vast expanse of the sea. The Skyhawk shuddered and jerked across the sky, streaming a long tail of smoke. Within seconds now, it was likely to take over its own fate and detonate its fuel and ammunition. Levin was still too near land and the enemy for comfort, but he had better take his best shot now before it was too late.

He braced his back, locked his legs and feet, and pulled the ejection curtain over his face. What a kick in the pants! He whipped through the air, tumbling over and over, free-falling, plunging toward earth at 100 miles per hour.

The parachute opened automatically at 10,000 feet, almost two miles above the sea, the only sounds now the soughing and whining of a stiff breeze through his shroud lines. Farther out in the gulf, his Skyhawk smoked toward the sea, burning like a comet. It exploded before it hit the water.

Between his flight boots, he saw to his horror that he was tracking back toward the beach, blown there by the wind. Two enemy patrol boats inscribing white wakes sped out from the shore in anticipation of his landing. Bow-mounted machine guns sparked tracers curving up toward him. He took out his radio pack and called for help. His only hope lay in rescue reaching him before the NVA patrol boats either got his range or picked him up out of the drink.

He floated lower. The patrol boats kept coming, their fire intensifying.

Just when he thought his fate was sealed, two pairs of Air Force and Navy fighter jets rocketed out of nowhere and spotted the enemy gunboats. The jets dived and with one pass blasted them out of the water. Colonel Levin could have cheered had he not been so busy preparing to splash down in the sea.

Standard personal equipment for a pilot flying a combat mission included a sheath knife, a pistol, survival and first aid kits, shark repellent, and a single-man rubber life raft neatly compressed and attached to his parachute seat pack. At 500 feet above the water, Levin secured the raft lanyard to his harness and made sure his knife was accessible. He assumed those shadowy sinister shapes in the water were sharks. Injured, he was about to splash right in among them.

He struck the water hard, skittering across the surface because the 35-knot winds refused to let go of his canopy. Even when he sank into the sea, the canopy remained inflated and dragged him through the swells like a floundering skier. Sputtering and coughing, eyes burning and blinded from salt, entangled in his shroud lines, he thought it the greatest irony that he might drown after all he had gone through.

Struggling desperately, he finally recovered his knife and hacked himself free of his parachute. He immediately popped to the surface and yanked the handle of the rubber raft to inflate it before the neighborhood sharks signaled mealtime to one another. Panting and scared, he clambered into the raft and collapsed in exhaustion.

Any deserved relief he experienced proved short-lived. Now, the single-minded enemy began lobbing artillery shells at him from the shore. Waterspouts erupted a football field's distance away from him to his right; they approached him slowly like giant Neptune's splashing footfalls. He and his raft were a small and elusive target in the wave action, but it would take only one round to ruin the rest of his day.

Fate seemed determined to squash him like a bug. First, his plane was shot out of the sky. That didn't get him, so enemy gunners pecked at him with machine guns as his parachute descended. The 'chute almost drowned him once he landed. Sharks were everywhere in the water. And now commies were throwing artillery at him . . .

One damned thing after another . . .

Jewish, Colonel Levin had not practiced his religion in years. Still, he couldn't help feeling that God had sent an angel to Vietnam with him to ride his wing for protection. Maybe the angel was trying to tell him something with today's mishaps—that there would never be a better time to get right with God. He began to pray.

"God, You know I haven't been good about praying. I've only prayed for others and not for myself. Well, I felt Your presence in the plane. You or Someone told me to go for it to reach the Gulf. You also told me when to eject. They have been shooting at me and either they are bad shots or You haven't let them get lucky. Now, I need a little more help to get out of this mess. I sure would appreciate any help You would care to give. Well, that's all I have to say. Amen."

Praying appeared to be the turning point. Two Marine rescue helicopters arrived. Colonel Levin outsmarted his tormentors by dropping a smoke flare into the water next to his raft to give them something to shoot at while he dived overboard and swam away to be horse-collared out of the sea. He was airborne in a helicopter and gone before enemy artillery could rebracket.

Thank You, God.

4

CASUALTIES

O death, where is thy sting? O grave, where is thy victory?

—I CORINTHIANS 15:55

The origin of taps, a haunting refrain traditionally played at funerals, memorial services, and each evening on military installations to signal "bedtime," has been shrouded in controversy because of an oft-repeated myth that it was written by a Confederate soldier whose body was recovered by the soldier's father, a Union officer. The melody remains haunting and eloquent even though the story is entirely false. The true story is almost as interesting.

The British Army has used a similar call known as "Last Post" over its soldiers' graves since 1885. In the fledgling United States, the infantry used a call to "Extinguish Lights" borrowed from the French. The music for taps was adopted during the Civil War by Union General Daniel Butterfield, a brigade commander of the Army of the Potomac, with the help of his brigade bugler, Oliver Wilcox Norton. The two men wrote it to honor General Butterfield's men who died during the battles of the Peninsular Campaign. The bugle call quickly spread within the Union Army and was reportedly even used by the Confederates.

Day is done,
gone the sun
from the lakes,
from the hills,
from the sky.
All is well.
Safely rest,
God is nigh.

Fading light
dims the night.
And a star
gems the sky,
gleaming bright
from afar.
Drawing nigh
falls the night.

Thanks and praise
for our days
neath the sun,
neath the stars,
neath the sky.
As we go
this we know:
God is nigh.

MARINE LANCE CORPORAL
JESUS SUAREZ DEL SOLAR,
Iraq, 2003

*D*eath, as playwright Philip Massinger noted in the seventeenth century, *has a thousand doors to let out life.* The number of doors increases during wartime. Every Marine of Delta Company, 1st Light Armored Reconnaissance Battalion (1st LAR), was to become well aware of it when the division stepped off from Kuwait in March 2003 at the start of the Iraq War to depose Saddam Hussein. As the outfit driving LAV-25s (light armored vehicles) spearheaded along Highway 1 on the way to Baghdad, a number of men prayed for the first time.

"God, allow me to do my job and not let down my buddies."

On March 23, Delta, under the command of Captain Seth Folsom, pulled into a defensive posture on the highway and sent out a foot patrol to scout to the east. The land was barren, dry, and hot, not a building in sight. Lance Corporal Jesus Suarez del Solar hot-capped his weapon to accompany the patrol. Suarez was twenty years old. From Tijuana, Mexico, he had emigrated to the United States with his family in his early teens. He was still a teenager when he volunteered for the Marine Corps.

He also became Delta Company's first KIA (killed in action), victim of an unexploded duel-purpose, improved conventional munition (DPICM), an antipersonnel artillery round that releases tiny bomblets. Ironically, the weapon had been dumped early on enemy forces by the U.S. invasion. The little bomblets, the color of sand and stone and all but invisible when covered with blown sand and soil, were lying about on the ground waiting for someone to come along. Suarez stepped on one of them as the patrol set out.

For the battlefield memorial service, his fellow Marines erected in the sand the traditional monument to mark a fallen comrade: a bayoneted rifle stuck in the sand topped by a helmet. Suarez's dog tags and a small crucifix hung from the rifle's pistol grip. Inside a ring of company LAVs, Marines with dusty faces and stony expressions formed a circle around the tribute. The battalion chaplain, Lieutenant Mike Moreno, spoke first, stepping up to the battle cairn and slowly walking around inside the assembly.

"Marines and sailors, we are gathered here today to honor the memory of Lance Corporal Jesus Suarez del Solar. He will not be forgotten by his family. He will not be forgotten by you, and he will not be forgotten by God."

He sang the first verse of "Eternal Father" in a high clear voice that left few dry eyes.

"Marines die with honor," added the battalion sergeant major when it came his turn to speak. "Lance Corporal Suarez died with honor. Here on enemy soil."

He scooped up a fistful of sand and thrust it toward the sky. Grains of it sifted down onto his bare head. Tears wet the crusty veteran's cheeks.

"He died a long way from home, but he will be remembered," the sergeant major resumed after swallowing the lump in his throat. "We got to let his honor live on. We got to hold our heads up high. We got to continue to march, continue to fight . . ."

Chaplain Moreno called Captain Folsom's name. The company commander had to compose himself before he spoke.

"When I was commissioned as a second lieutenant about nine years ago, I understood the risks I was about to take." He paused and swallowed. "I knew the risks that my men might one day face. But back then I never would have guessed that I would spend my thirty-first birthday mourning the loss of one of my Marines. . . .

"Lance Corporal Suarez del Solar . . . was a motivator. He was always willing to do whatever he had to do to get the job done. He loved his fellow Marines and sailors and they loved him. During the past two years, I've spent more time with you men than I have my own family. As such, losing Lance Corporal Suarez is like losing someone in my family. . . .

"Sometimes I question my faith, but I know one thing. Suarez is in a better place than we are now. I know he's up there looking down at us and he's thinking, 'Don't worry about me; get off your asses and go kick the enemy's ass.'"

The service ended. Before the company scattered, Marines approached the upthrusted rifle and helmet, knelt or stood by it, and bowed their heads. First Lieutenant Doug Cullins, Suarez's platoon leader, came and stood next to Captain Folsom. Folsom laid a hand on the young lieutenant's shoulder.

"Are you going to be all right?" he asked.

"Man," Cullins said. "This really burns."

The CO looked out across the vast expanse of desert. Delta Company still had a long way to go.

"Yeah," he agreed. "Yeah, it does."

ARMY SERGEANT DAVID GRANT,
Vietnam, 1970

Medic David Grant worked at the U.S. Army hospital at Camp Zama, Japan, where wounded soldiers were transferred from Vietnam for treatment. He also operated the Army Military Affiliate Radio Station (MARS) maintained for the purpose of allowing patients to "patch through" calls to family back in the States.

There was no such thing as a private call through MARS; any conversation reached radio stations all over the net, from Vietnam to the United States. That was the way it worked.

One morning on Grant's call request log appeared the name "Clarence." Grant knew nothing about Clarence other than that he was a patient in the hospital and wanted to get a patch through to his family in Hawaii. Sergeant Grant attempted to put the call through on two separate days, without success. MARS stations did not always work the way they should.

The station NCO-in-charge (NCOIC) was on his way to Hawaii for R & R leave. He promised to contact the MARS operator in Honolulu and work on bringing in a call from that end.

Sure enough, the NCOIC came through the next morning loud and clear on the MARS Hawaii call sign. "We're getting the family now," he said. "Put Clarence on."

Sergeant Grant discovered Clarence was a nonambulatory patient who could not leave his bed. He sent a runner with a phone to Clarence's ward. Within a few minutes, the wounded and recovering victim was hooked up with his father, mother, and numerous siblings, all of whom wanted to talk to him. MARS calls were normally limited to three minutes, but Grant stretched the time. He and countless other operators netwide monitored the conversation.

"We understand you were wounded," Clarence's father said. "We don't have any details. What happened?"

"Dad, I've lost both my legs at the knees."

"I understand, son. How are you doing?"

The father was inquiring about his son's spiritual well-being as well as about his physical health.

"I'll be okay, Dad. The doctors say I have a good chance of getting artificial legs."

Clarence's father offered a prayer at the end of the family conversation. He prayed for his son, for those at the hospital caring for him, and for all the soldiers still fighting in Vietnam. Sergeant Grant could barely see the controls and meters on his radio because of tears flooding his eyes.

"Amen," Clarence's father concluded.

Immediately, a MARS on the net somewhere broke in with its call sign and offered, "Amen."

Other MARS followed in line, over thirty of them, one by one closing on the same note.

"Amen."

"Amen."

"Amen . . ."

MARINE LIEUTENANT COLONEL MIKE STROBL,
Iraq War, 2004

Marine Private First Class Chance Phelps died on Good Friday, 2004, when his convoy came under intense fire outside Baghdad. The military provides a uniformed officer or senior NCO to escort home men and women killed in combat. The escort makes sure the fallen comrade's body is delivered safely to the family and that it is treated with dignity and respect along the way. Phelps's funeral was to be in Dubois, Wyoming, population less than one thousand. Marine Lieutenant Colonel Mike Strobl volunteered to accompany the remains.

Colonel Strobl met the casket shipping container at Dover Air Force Base in Delaware and accompanied it by hearse to Philadelphia, where it was loaded into the cargo bay of a Northwest Airlines carrier for the flight to Wyoming. Tears welled in the eyes of the woman behind the Northwest counter when she learned the nature of the colonel's mission; she upgraded his government travel voucher to first class. One of the pilots personally saw to Strobl's carry-on, while flight attendants appeared choked up and went out of their way to make him comfortable.

Shortly after the plane climbed off the landing strip, a flight attendant bent over the Marine and clasped his hand in hers.

"I want you to have this," she said, depositing into his palm a small gold cross with a relief of Jesus on it, a lapel pin that appeared well used.

In Dubois, flyers distributed all over town announced the funeral service: *Dubois High School Gym, two o'clock.* Mourners began arriving hours ahead of time to fill neatly lined rows of chairs on the gym floor. Everyone in town, it seemed, as well as from the surrounding area, drove in to pay respects: Ranchers in boots and hats, children with scrubbed faces, wearing their Sunday best. Colonel Strobl doubted this many people would have attended a military funeral in a large city like Detroit or San Francisco. Antiwar activists would probably have turned out to chant and shout in protest.

When he met with Private Phelps's mother and stepfather, father and stepmother in a school computer lab, they all tearfully shook his hand, embraced him, and repeatedly thanked him for his military service and for bringing Chance home. People were still patriotic and grateful in America's heartland.

He opened the pouch containing the dead Marine's personal effects, taking the items out one at a time and placing them on a table around which the parents sat: Chance's watch still set on Baghdad time; a large wooden cross on a lanyard; a Saint Christopher's medal; his dog tags. Parents and stepparents touched them with reverence. Colonel Strobl felt their pain resounding in his own heart. The catch in his throat made speaking difficult.

"I have one other thing to give you," he said. He took the flight attendant's crucifix pin from his pocket, told the story of how he acquired it, then laid it on the table with Chance's other things.

Later, after he checked the dead private's uniform to make sure it was correct, even though the service would be closed casket, he noticed Chance's mother was wearing the crucifix on her lapel. After services, military pallbearers transferred the casket to the traditional horse-drawn carriage for the mile-long journey to the cemetery. The main street, posted with American flags at half-staff, was lined with people waving other small American flags.

The carriage climbed a steep hill to the graveyard. Local Boy Scouts stood on the hill road with still other large flags. It took more than a half hour for all the mourners to pour into the cemetery. School buses brought many of them along the procession route.

VFW and the Marine Corps League formed up at the carriage on the high ground overlooking the town. Pallbearers removed the casket from its caisson and carried it the last fifteen yards to the open grave. A chaplain said final words. Two Marines removed the flag from the casket and slowly folded it before presenting it to Private Phelps's mother.

Chance's father placed on the casket a ribbon from his service during the Vietnam War. His mother then approached the grave. She unpinned something from her blouse and reverently laid it on the casket.

The afternoon sun glinted off the flight attendant's little gold crucifix as it accompanied Private Phelps into the open earth.

ARMY SERGEANT TERRY M. JORGENSEN,
Vietnam, 1969

Lanky and good-looking and only a couple of years out of high school, Buck Sergeant Terry Jorgensen pulled his share of duty in the bush as a boonie rat with the 9th Infantry Division, then got a "pud" job in the "rear" with the Army Supply Section. On Sundays, after he delivered fuel to the 82nd Airborne, operating outside Saigon, he often parked his tanker truck at the end of the Tan Son Nhut runway. There he watched F-4 Phantoms take off and listened to the Mormon Tabernacle Choir and the "Spoken Word" of the Church of Jesus Christ of Latter-Day Saints over Armed Forces Radio.

On other days, the Mormon sergeant flew crew on helicopter support missions to outlying firebases, kicking out beans and bullets for guys in the field. One afternoon he learned that his best friend from the "old days," Jay, had departed his fire support base three days previously on a platoon-sized patrol deep into Indian Country. The platoon made hard contact and lost a number of soldiers. Survivors were forced to withdraw, leaving their dead behind. Jorgensen's buddy was presumed either KIA or missing in action.

Jorgensen appealed to Captain Holloway, his Huey pilot. "When Jay and I were in the bush together," he implored, "we made a pact that we would never leave the other behind. Sir, is there any way we can help search for him and still complete our mission?"

Captain Holloway looked at the earnest young sergeant, whose eyes were filled with concern. "We'll do what we can," he promised.

On a supply run to the next firebase, Captain Holloway detoured over the area where the ill-fated platoon had been ambushed. Patchy swamp and jungle checkered with occasional rice paddies stretched south toward the Forest of Darkness, legendary refuge of thieves, scoundrels, murderers, and Viet Cong. Jorgensen lay on his belly in the bay of the chopper with his head stuck out the open cargo door, scanning the terrain for signs of the massacre. Suddenly, he pointed.

"I see them!" he shouted through the intercom.

The pilot banked the UH-I and circled above a small clearing surrounded by forest giants. Several bodies lay strewn in tall grass. They were twisted and distorted like disjointed dolls dropped from the sky. They had to be the MIAs from Jay's platoon, corpses not yet recovered by the 9th Infantry.

"They're all dead by now," Captain Holloway said.

"Sir, we don't know that for sure. Can't we go down?"

Landing a chopper in enemy country was risky, even with a secured landing zone (LZ). Putting it down blind could be suicide. Charlie sometimes set up ambushes over dead GIs, knowing that Americans always came back to retrieve their casualties. Nonetheless, Captain Holloway buzzed the clearing while the keen eyes of his crew looked for signs of danger. The door gunner tethered to his safety cord leaned far out over his mounted M-60 machine gun, which was loaded and cocked for action.

Nothing stirred down there.

"We're going in," Captain Holloway decided. "You got three minutes on the ground, Jorgensen. Make 'em count."

"Yes, sir."

The helicopter and crew may well have ended up contributing to the carnage except for the presence of an excitable Viet Cong hiding in the surrounding forest. He got nervous as the American chopper flared toward the opening and opened up prematurely with his machine gun. Green tracers lashed at the bird. Bullets penetrated the chopper's aluminum skin with a resounding *tick-tick-tick!* Holloway threw in power and snatched the Huey back into the air, zipping back over treetops to get out of the fire zone.

"We can't just leave him," Jorgensen pleaded. "You don't understand, sir. Jay might be alive. He needs me. I promised him, sir. I *promised*."

"It's suicide," Captain Holloway argued.

"Drop me off somewhere near, sir. Please? I'll go myself and try to bring him back—and anybody else who might still be alive."

"Sergeant, gooks are all over that place, like maggots." Besides, it violated army regulations. More than that, it was against common sense.

Nonetheless, friendship in combat was a thing of loyalty and trust. Captain Holloway knew he would do the same thing in Jorgensen's boots. The enemy, having given his presence away, would probably *di di mau*, get the hell out of Dodge, anyhow, before American gunships returned to work *them* over. It was a chance Jorgensen seemed willing to take.

The pilot finally relented. Out of sight of the enemy, he hovered over another jungle opening a mile away while Jorgensen shouldered a small pack containing water, food, a first aid kit, and prepared to leap out into the rotor-whipped elephant grass.

"I still don't think it's worth it," Holloway said. "Your buddy and everybody else are probably already dead. You're throwing your life away. I'll pick you up here at 0600 in the morning—if you make it."

Jorgensen stood in the field as the helicopter flew away, watching it diminish against the Vietnam sky, feeling so alone and afraid that he began to sob quietly. Wiping away tears, he prayed to God to see him through. Then he turned and worked his way cautiously toward the scene of death. Frigate birds and circling vultures helped guide the way.

It had been late afternoon when Holloway let him out. Purple night spilled like ink across the land before he was halfway to his destination. The darkness was vicious because of the horrors it concealed. Armed with his faith in God, drawn through the jungle blackness by the stench of death and decay, and by loyalty to his friend, Jorgensen reached the site several hours before moonrise. He realized he couldn't simply walk out in the clearing and start checking the dead. Chances were the enemy machine gunner had departed, but he couldn't depend on that.

With a deep sigh of determination, he dropped to his belly and wriggled out into the grass. The bodies were mangled and stiff and blood-crusted. It was ghoulish business, crawling among the rotting corpses of fellow American soldiers, feeling his way from one to the other, quelling the gorge that welled in his throat. He had to inspect each one individually, thrusting his face close to lifeless faces in order to determine in the darkness if one of them might be his friend Jay.

He dragged himself around in the grass for hours. He wept. He prayed silently for the souls of the departed. Sometimes, heart pounding at some jungle sound, he stopped to listen, resisting the all-too-human impulse to flee that hellish necropolis. But he kept at it.

At last he came to his friend. The corpse stirred. Miracle of miracles! He was alive!

"Jay!" Jorgensen whispered, sobbing with relief. "It's me. Terry."

Jay mumbled something, words so weak Jorgensen had to place his ear next to Jay's lips to hear them.

"You don't have to talk if you don't want to, buddy. I've come to see you home."

It took the sergeant the rest of the night to drag his gravely wounded comrade off the field and then carry him through the jungle to the pickup point. Staggering from exhaustion, often tripping and falling over rocks and roots, fording leech-filled streams and swamps, he somehow reached the forest opening where Captain Holloway promised to collect him shortly after daybreak.

He collapsed against the trunk of a banyan tree where he could watch for the returning chopper. Captain Holloway found them there—Sergeant Jorgensen, fatigued and used up, cradling his friend's body tenderly in his arms. The pilot knelt next to them, placed a hand on the sergeant's shoulder. Jorgensen's lips were cracked from the effort, his face haggard and coated in filth.

"I told you it wouldn't be worth it," the pilot said softly. "Your buddy is dead."

Jorgensen managed a wan smile. "It was worth it, sir."

"Listen to me, Terry. I'm telling you, your friend is dead."

"Yes, sir. I understand. But it was still worth it."

"How do you mean, worth it?"

"Because, sir, when I got to him, he looked at me and he said, 'I knew you would come.'"

5

CULTURES

*His hand will be against every man, and every man's hand
against him.*

—GENESIS 16:12

W hile religion often proves to be a source of contention between peoples, or a means of exploitation of one by the other, it can also provide at times a common meeting ground between enemies, a way to express universal humanity.

In World War I, American and German soldiers confronted one another in trenches on Christmas Eve in 1914, and spontaneously called a truce for the night. Sharing a common heritage, they exchanged gifts of food, candy, and tobacco while serenading one another with "Heilige Nacht" and "Silent Night."

A similar incident occurred during the Korean War. U.S. Army Chaplain Kermit D. Johnson visited a British unit whose soldiers seemed bent on making the war more civilized. They erected a Christmas tree in the shelled wastes of No Man's Land. Not only

did Chinese communists hold their fire, they sent men out to deco-
rate the tree.

The Japanese of World War II were especially cruel to prisoners
of war since their Bushido Code considered it a shameful dishonor
for a soldier to let himself be captured by the enemy. Now and then,
however, American POWs encountered a Japanese with whom religion
provided a common ground.

Survivors of the cruiser USS *Houston*, sunk in a duel with the Japanese shortly after Pearl Harbor, were imprisoned on Java at a former
Dutch military base called "Bicycle Camp." Guards deprived their captives of food and water, beat them with little provocation, and executed
a number of them.

One guard, nicknamed "Smiley" because of his mouthful of gold
teeth, professed to be a Christian and said he had lived in the United
States before the war. He still had a brother in California. His having
spent time in the United States seemed to bond him to some degree
with the prisoners. "At nighttime, you'd hear some noise around your
cell door," Marine Sergeant Charley Pryor remembered, "and there'd be
a little tin of water [Smiley] slid under the door or maybe a tin of rice
that he had taken from the natives' kitchen."

ARMY SERGEANT RICHARD KILEY,
World War II, 1944

During the late autumn of 1944, as the Allies pushed rapidly
toward Germany, Sergeant Richard Kiley's artillery battalion set
up temporary headquarters in an abandoned castle on the outskirts of a
Belgian village. German infantry were dug in only a short distance away
on the other side of the village. Each side seemed content to accept the
momentary stalemate and catch its breath before going at it again.

Young Kiley had landed in France shortly after D-Day, over four months before. He was curious about the locals. He wandered away from the castle early one morning and discovered townspeople walking toward the center of the village, drawn by the pealing of church bells. It was Sunday. People were on their way to attend Catholic Mass.

A former altar boy from Philadelphia, Kiley fell in with the locals and soon arrived at an ancient brownstone chapel with a thick steeple piercing the sunrise. Having been unable to attend church since his battalion struck French soil, he removed his helmet and ventured inside.

The priest appeared from the sacristy—a tall man in his thirties clad in sweeping black. Since the father had no altar boy, nineteen-year-old Kiley walked into the sanctuary in his combat woolens, knelt next to the priest, and rotely began performing the functions of an acolyte.

The priest accepted him without comment. The traditional service was performed entirely in Latin.

"Quia tu es Deus fortitudo mea . . ." For Thou, O God, art my strength . . .

"Confiteor Deo omnipotenti . . ." I confess to Almighty God . . .

The priest and the uniformed American sergeant conducted Mass as though they had done it many times together—water and wine; the ritual of washing hands; changing the book; the prayer of acceptance . . .

After the final blessing, the altar boy preceded the priest into the sacristy, as is the custom, and stood silently apart with his hands in the prayer position while the priest derobed. Off came the chasuble and the cincture, followed by the alb. Kiley's eyes bulged in astonishment. He thought his heart would stop beating.

There before him stood a uniformed enemy officer. The priest was a German chaplain. During the twenty minutes of the Mass, he had displayed no outward sign of discomfort with his GI altar boy.

Kiley spoke only a few words of German. Stammering, he finally managed, *"Guten Morgen, Vater."* Good morning, Father.

Apparently, the chaplain spoke even less English. Flustered at his inability to communicate, he merely smiled. Nazi priest and U.S. altar boy shook hands. The priest left to return to his lines. Kiley walked back to the castle.

Two strangers whose countries were at war with each other had met by chance and found common ground in an ages-old ritual of Christian worship.

ARMY CHIEF WARRANT OFFICER PAUL HOLTON,
Iraq, 2003–2004

Before "shock and awe" at the start of the Iraq War in 2003, U.S. psyops (psychological operations) airdropped leaflets behind enemy lines suggesting that Saddam Hussein's commanders lay down their arms, instruct their men to return to their homes, then drive out to meet oncoming forces to surrender their bases and equipment. The top-heavy Iraqi Army was weighted down with more than 11,000 officers of the rank of brigadier general or above, compared to only three hundred in the U.S. Army. While many Iraqi officers stripped off their uniforms, abandoned their posts, and went into hiding, only fourteen generals actually turned themselves in to Allies. They expected to be treated well, expedited through the enemy prisoners of war (EPW) process, and released as quickly as possible after the war ended.

To contain the anticipated influx of EPWs of whatever rank, the United States erected Camp Bucca on a large expanse of unused desert near the southern port city of Umm Qasr. A propaganda radio station and huge antenna were the only construction at the site prior to the erection of tents and barbed wire. At its peak, the detention camp held 10,000 prisoners. The fourteen generals and other high-ranking former officers were kept apart from the general population in a special section of the facility called Hoover 7, a takeoff on the infamous "Hoover camps" of America's Great Depression.

Chief Warrant Officer (CWO) Paul Holton, fifty-three, tall, lanky, a veteran of the 1991 Gulf War, had been an interrogator for the U.S. Army for more than three decades. When he arrived at Camp Bucca, he found his senses assailed by the stench of open slit trenches, and the buzz of flies scuttling back and forth from the waste pits to the chow tents. Keepers and kept shared Spartan living conditions and the unforgiving heat of the tents.

As a ranking experienced member of the 141st Military Intelligence section, Holton was assigned to interrogate the Iraqi generals and obtain from them everything they knew about the times and crimes of the Hussein rule. He had received extensive training in the advanced art of using the most effective psychological approaches to quickly obtain vital information from captured individuals. Most interrogation tactics used by the American military were very different from those "exposed" by the American mainstream media as brutal. As a professional and as a devout Christian, Holton believed the most effective interrogation was built on mutual respect and trust.

For six months Chief Holton questioned the fourteen generals one-on-one and in groups. He often lunched with them. When temperatures cooled in the evening, he frequently went to their large Bedouin-style tent to chat informally. Always as he entered the tent where a lamp glowed, he followed a greeting ritual by addressing each man by name and looking him straight in the eye. After shaking hands and exchanging a few Arabic pleasantries, they placed their hands over their hearts to imply that they were brothers and therefore understood each other's hearts.

Most of the generals spoke English. All were Muslim. Five times a day they got on their knees and bowed toward Mecca, chanting prayers. The generals were curious about Holton's Christianity, but he avoided all proselytizing. That was not a part of his mission.

Time passed. The generals proved cooperative, providing important information that led to the capture of terrorists and the dissolution of underground enemy bands. Of the fourteen, one in particular stood out from the others.

Former Iraqi Air Force general Hakim was a very accomplished fighter pilot who had won many decorations during the Iran-Iraq War in the 1980s. Stocky in build, in his late forties, several inches shorter than Holton, General Hakim had black hair and sincere eyes almost as dark. Holton considered him one of the most unselfish persons he had ever known, a man who viewed his detention as a time to prepare for the rebuilding of Iraq.

"I will be the last general to leave the camp," he confided in his interrogator. "I must make sure the other officers get out first."

Gradually, the two men from vastly different cultures became fast friends. In the evenings, they took walks together inside the wire perimeter of Hoover 7, holding hands as is the custom of Middle Eastern men, talking of their families, their hopes, and, sometimes, even their religions, as friends do anywhere in the world.

One discussion focused on the war itself and its cost in lives and resources. Chief Holton found himself troubled by heated political debate back in the United States, news of which was beginning to discourage and demoralize American soldiers in the field.

"Many people back home question why we came to this country to free it of Saddam," Holton said.

General Hakim turned and faced the American, his expression strong with conviction and passion.

"As America is the leader of the free world and the last superpower," he said, "it is your responsibility and duty to help the oppressed people of the world enjoy the freedom that you do. Not just because it is your duty, but because you can. You have the ability, the resources, the manpower, and the will. Your very nature as free people compels you to want to provide the opportunities of a free and independent society to others. You have always shown a genuine compassion for the oppressed of the world."

Hakim turned his head. A look of sadness came over him. Almost to himself, he added, "If you don't, who will? Who else is going to step forward to make this dream possible for us?"

As the bond grew between the two men of different worlds, so did the depth of their communication. One evening, as the sun was setting red against the desert and evening dusk was spreading over the stark landscape of Bucca, the friends began speaking of God as they walked hand in hand inside the perimeter of Hoover 7. Of God, of the purpose of life, of the importance of faith. Muslims were Old Testament people and related easily to the language of the Bible.

"I sometimes wonder," mused General Hakim, "if God is punishing Iraqis for the things we may have done in our past."

Chief Holton felt the Spirit working in his heart. It was one of those moments when, solicited about his Christian beliefs, he opened his feelings about the Holy Spirit and bore testimony to the love of Jesus Christ.

General Hakim paused. They stopped walking. The Iraqi caught his breath. His eyes widened. They glistened with tears. His free hand flew to his heart.

"I am feeling something different tonight," he gasped, startled. "Something warm inside."

Holton squeezed the hand he held. "That is the feeling of the Spirit bearing witness to the truthfulness of things we've been talking about," he explained.

Inside the bleak EPW camp where one man was a prisoner, the other his keeper, they continued their walk, holding hands and sharing their worlds.

General Hakim is not the general's true name. After his release, he and his family had to flee Iraq and seek asylum in another country since terrorist assassins from Iran are searching for him.

ARMY AIR CORPS LIEUTENANT CHARLIE BROWN,
World War II, 1943

Ye Old Pub, the B-17 Flying Fortress piloted by Lieutenant Charlie Brown of Oklahoma, left Kimbolton, England, near the front of a massive formation of more than four hundred B-17s and B-24s on their way to bomb the Folke-Wulf aircraft factory in Bremen, Germany. Luftwaffe ME-109 fighters attacked like swarms of wasps as soon as the 379th Bomber Group crossed the German border, darting and buzzing, ripping and slashing with their machine guns and cannon, desperately fighting to destroy or drive back the intruders. The clear morning sky of December 20, 1943, filled with tracer webs and black smoke as American machine gunners in their bombers fought back just as desperately to throw off the fighter packs and survive.

One by one, bombers picked from the flight staggered and streamed toward earth. German fighters in smaller streaks of flame showed them the way.

German cannon fire knocked out one of Lieutenant Brown's starboard engines. He increased RPMs in his remaining three in an attempt to maintain position and stay with the formation. There was safety in numbers. A ship that fell behind in hostile skies became a crippled gazelle abandoned by its fleeing herd and left to the mercy of lions.

Bombers and Messerschmitts clashed all the way from the border to the outskirts of Bremen. Pilots and gunners yelled warnings and advice to one another over the radio net. Eerie electronic screams accompanied dying aircraft on their last, long and fiery journeys to earth.

Sweating profusely from tension in his cold weather flight suit, Brown struggled to keep his B-17 with the airmada. Gradually, however, he slid out of place with only three engines turning and lagged behind the lead squadron. Krauts seemed to sense his plight and singled out *Ye Old Pub* for special attention, raking it with machine gun bullets time after time.

German fighters retired from the battle just short of Bremen airspace. Heavy 88mm antiaircraft guns took their place, filling the air with black and red bursts throwing off deadly ack-ack. Bombers tore apart in midair, slinging out their crews like broken puppets. Others, streaming oily black smoke, tipped into death dives. Lieutenant Brown lost his tail gunner to shrapnel. One of his waist gunners had a leg ripped off. His navigator cried out suddenly from a bad chest wound. A piece of flying steel gashed Brown's shoulder. Of the ten-man crew, only six remained unscathed so far.

Ye Old Pub was taking an even worse beating than its crew. From reports Brown received from his gunners and flight chief, he gathered that the plane's Plexiglas nose and its tail stabilizer were gone, blown off, while the wings and horizontal stabilizers were riddled with bullets. Rents in the slim fuselage exposed crew inside frantically treating their wounded while trying to keep themselves from being sucked out into space. It took the combined strength of both Brown and his copilot on the vibrating yokes to keep the crippled plane flying. Riding it was like being tossed into the back of an old pickup truck and driven full speed over a rubboard country road back in Oklahoma.

Through skill and sheer doggedness, Lieutenant Brown nursed the wreck over Bremen, dropped his load of bombs, and turned back for England. A second engine went, popping and throwing metal, hissing fuel and oil into the wind stream. *Ye Old Pub* rapidly lost altitude and fell even farther behind the formation. Now the wounded aircraft was on its own, easy prey as rearmed and refueled Messerschmitts resumed the attack to pick off as many bombers as they could before the armada reached safe skies.

German fighters nipped at the stricken B-17, damaging a third engine and destroying the plane's oxygen supply. Flying at 20,000 feet, air cut off, Brown found his vision blurred. He and the copilot passed out at the controls while throughout the rest of the plane the crew simply went to sleep.

The Flying Fortress, unrestrained, slid into a wing and, then, nose down, began its four-mile plummet to earth while everyone aboard remained unconscious. Satisfied of having killed it, attacking ME-109s peeled off and went after the main bomber formation to select other victims.

Air below 10,000 feet became breathable once again without artificial aids. When Lieutenant Brown regained his senses, he sat strapped in his seat looking straight down at the ground rushing up at him. Wounded and oxygen-deprived, horror-stricken at what he believed to be his last few minutes alive, he wrestled with the controls to pull the B-17 out of its slow spiral. Through his earphones he heard his crew coming back to life, shouting and praying and screaming hysterically through the intercom.

Gradually, *Ye Old Pub* began to respond. Whether in time or not remained the question.

Somehow—a miracle, perhaps—he pulled up the nose, and the damaged bird suddenly soared in level flight only a few hundred feet above the treetops of Germany.

"Thank You, God," someone muttered through the intercom.

Disoriented and unable to depend on his malfunctioning instruments, Brown banked the airplane in the direction of where he assumed England to be. Actually, he was flying deeper into Germany.

The erratically flying wreck soon attracted the attention of Luftwaffe pilot Lieutenant Franz Steigler. Steigler caught up to it, intending to deal it a final blow. As he drew near, approaching from the rear, he was amazed that the B-17 was still able to fly at all.

He saw that the tail gunner was slumped over dead in his bloodsplattered bubble and that the other guns were unmanned. Through holes in the fuselage, he glimpsed airmen desperately endeavoring to save their wounded comrades. Curious, but with his finger on the trigger just in case, Steigler held his fire and made a second pass. He pulled throttle to keep pace with the slow-flying B-17.

The American pilot stared back at him. Steigler signaled for Brown to lower his landing gear and surrender. Brown continued to stare, still too groggy to comprehend. Finally, the exasperated German gave up on capturing the bomber. Instead, he signaled that Brown was going the wrong way and should turn around and follow him. Lieutenant Brown had no other choice but to trust the enemy fighter pilot.

Implausible though it might have been, the ME-109 escorted the battered B-17 to the North Sea coast. On the other side of the sea lay

England and safety. Steigler eased alongside the bomber one final time, saluted, rolled his fighter into a hard right turn, and headed back to his own base.

Brown and six members of his bomber crew survived the war, thanks to the grace and honor of an enemy pilot. Fifty years later, Charlie Brown located Franz Steigler living in British Columbia, Canada. That was when he learned that his Good Samaritan above war-torn Germany that December morning so long ago had studied to become a monk before the war. Steigler had merely extended Christian charity to a fellow human being in need.

AIR FORCE STAFF SERGEANT EDWARD GYOKERES, IRAQ, 2003

Flying aircraft in a combat zone can be a harrowing, even life-changing, experience. This is especially true for those new in-theater. For Staff Sergeant Ed Gyokeres, a career Air Force NCO active in youth ministry prior to enlisting eleven years before, assignment as a flight escort crewman on giant four-engine C-130 Hercules aircraft in Iraq in 2003 was enough to bring him back to his Christian roots. Episodes of random horror took him on a long journey to a closer relationship with God.

Flight escorts transported cargo and personnel all over Iraq and back and forth from Kuwait. C-130s approaching an airfield jinked through the sky to avoid and evade possible enemy ground fire. Dodging and weaving on final approach, they flew high and threw in flaps at the last moment to literally drop out of the air. The first time Gyokeres flew into Balad, a treacherous locale known as "Anaconda," he couldn't keep from thinking he was going to make his wife a widow on his first day in Iraq.

Am I the best person I could have been? he asked himself. *Will I get a chance to do better?*

That was the beginning of his renewed spiritual exploration. Constantly flying in and out of Iraq, he witnessed unimaginable scenes of carnage and destruction. When terrorists attacked the Italian mission headquarters at An Nasiriyah, blowing it up, there were so many casualties that medics treated them in a hospital parking lot. Sometimes, a medical evacuation mission resulted in the cargo bay being splattered with blood and gore.

Sergeant Gyokeres's plane received orders to transport wounded friendly Iraqis out of Tallil to improved medical facilities in Kuwait. The Hercules landed, dropped its rear ramp, and waited as a local box-like ambulance squalled onto the hot midday tarmac and approached. It stopped. Attendants opened the back doors. Inside on a stretcher lay a patient moaning and mumbling in agony, an Iraqi cop so critically wounded by an IED that he had lost both arms below the elbows and suffered numerous other injuries. The stench of infection and encroaching gangrene seeped from the ambulance like noxious gas. It appeared the fellow had little or no chance of survival.

A female American medic attached to the C-130 climbed inside the ambulance to comfort the victim as he was unplugged and prepared for transfer from ground transport to airplane. She was a small young woman in desert camouflage, her brown hair knotted in a bun, her face like the girl next door back in Madison, Wisconsin. Tears flooded her eyes when she saw the patient's condition.

Bending over the unconscious cop, she bowed her head, closed her eyes, and silently prayed. Four of the wounded man's companions had accompanied him to the airstrip. They stared in astonishment.

"What is she doing?" they demanded of an interpreter.

"She's trying to help your brother by praying," the interpreter explained.

That elicited an outburst of mocking laughter.

"Where is your faith?" the interpreter asked.

The men ceased laughing. They looked at each other. They looked at their dying friend and at the young American woman praying for him in the ambulance. Then, in unison, they spontaneously dropped to their knees, facing the direction of Mecca, and commenced praying with her.

Standing nearby at the ramp of the C-130 waiting to receive the patient, Sergeant Gyokeres watched the scene unfold, unable to wrench his eyes away. The dynamics of it shook him to the core.

"A Power exists," he reflected later, "one that is getting me through time after time of man at his worst and helping me to contribute to acts that represent man at his best. As a younger man, I would have said faith has nothing to do with whom I am. Now, I'm no longer ashamed to say my strength comes directly from my faith in God."

6

CHURCH SERVICES

Upon this rock I will build my church; and the gates of hell shall not prevail against it.

—Matthew 16:18

For Army Chaplain Tim Sturgill, deployed to Baghdad in 2006 in support of the Iraq War, one of the saddest passages of scripture comes from Psalms:

By the rivers of Babylon, there we sat down, yea, we wept when we remembered Zion. We hanged our harps upon the willows in the midst thereof. For there they that carried us away captive asked of us a song, and they that wasted us required of us mirth, saying, Sing us one of the Songs of Zion: How shall we sing the Lord's song in a foreign land?

Prior to deployment, Chaplain Sturgill said, "The Lord spoke very plainly to me on Sunday during the praise and worship time in church. The message was, 'Tim, I'm sending you to do my work. Many chaplains have already gone before you, and now it is your turn to go sing the songs of Zion by the river of Babylon.'"

The passage carried particular relevance because American soldiers *were* in harm's way in a foreign land along the rivers of Babylon. An old quote attributed to various pundits states that good people sleep peacefully in their beds at night only because rough men stand ready to do violence on their behalf. It is a tradition in the American military that wherever "rough men" go, chaplains go with them—and with the chaplains go the church.

From the sands of Iwo Jima to the cold muds of Korea, from the jungles of Vietnam to the wastes of Iraq, American men and women under arms have gathered in foxholes, bunkers, tents, beneath blistering sun and in the rain and snow, to seek God's comfort in times of peril.

"Soldiers who regularly attend church, [and] profess their faith . . ." Army Chaplain Kevin Wainwright observed from Iraq in 2003, ". . . are handling their deployment better than the average GI. They have more hope and a more positive attitude."

AIR FORCE CHAPLAIN GEORGE R. BARBER,
World War II, 1944

At the end of May 1944, Britain was the greatest operating military base of all time. The American buildup in preparation for the invasion of occupied France had brought in 50,000 tanks and armored vehicles, 450,000 trucks, and a half-million tons of ammunition. An invasion fleet in excess of 7,000 ships waited offshore. All roads leading to the south coasts were choked with military traffic; some convoys were one hundred miles long. An air of expectation swept through nearly a half-million Allied troops. They knew a landing was imminent, but no one knew exactly when or where.

May in southern England was full of spring sunshine and pretty girls in summer dresses. But bad weather closed in on June 1, bringing rain and gusting gales. On June 4, two days before D-Day, although no one outside General Eisenhower's staff knew it, chaplains caught motor launches in order to conduct Sunday services aboard the troop transports and ships.

One of these chaplains was a thirty-year-old six-footer with blue eyes and black hair, buzzed short. Chaplain George Barber teamed up with a Catholic priest to conduct shipboard church for their respective flocks in Weymouth Harbor. They went from morning to dusk, from ship to ship, holding services in galleys or on open decks where men in full combat uniforms, minus helmets and weapons, gathered in numbers sufficient to reinforce the old saying that there are no atheists in foxholes. They sat cross-legged or sprawled out on deck, serious men, quiet, and contemplative, all knowing that within a short time—days, perhaps *hours*—they must face their own mortality. At such times men look beyond the known world to the unknown.

Gray seas churned into spray by errant winds matched the mood of the soldiers. Wind-, rain-, and spray-whipped, Chaplain Barber clutched his Bible in the open air.

"Remember your mothers, your fathers, your brothers, your sisters," he reminded his congregations. "They all love you. They are praying for you, too. . . . We're on His side, and we're going to win. Jesus gave His life for us and we may have to give our lives for Him and for our country."

He handed out hundreds of pocket Bibles. Everyone wanted one. A rather thin man who had already become famous for his war correspondence approached the chaplain and asked for a Bible.

"Chaplain," Ernie Pyle said, "I will see you on the beach."

Slightly more than twenty-four hours later, the invasion fleet set out to cross the thirty-five miles of English Channel to the coast of France. Battleships, torpedo boats, cruisers, destroyers, troop transports—*thousands* of them—dotted the ocean for as far as the eye could see, beneath a moon playing hide-and-seek with scattered wisps of cirrus cloud. It was the greatest invasion force ever assembled. It seemed a man could almost walk from ship to ship all the way across the channel without getting his feet wet.

Barber would be one of only four chaplains to make the landing on D-Day. He circulated among the silent, battle-garbed men on his transport, bringing with him comfort in prayer.

Troop transports anchored twelve miles offshore in a strong swell while warships and bomber aircraft barraged the Normandy coastline with preparatory fire. Volleys of rockets flashed across the sky. Shock waves from battle wagons' enormous fourteen-inch guns threatened to swamp smaller boats nearby. Continuous thunder-shocks of fire tossed great barriers of smoke and vapor all along the coastline.

As heavily laden invaders prepared to clamber down scaling nets into landing craft, Chaplain Barber stood on the bridge of his transport and called his ship to prayer through the PA system. Everyone paused for a brief moment, removed his helmet, and bowed his head while the chaplain prayed for God to be with them all during the terrible day ahead.

Later, he derived great comfort in discovering that General Eisenhower had prayed with his chaplain just before he gave the word to go.

Between ships and shore, waves of landing craft plowed toward the beach like a hatch of turtles, bucking in the swells, LCIs loaded with troops and LCTs carrying tanks and tracks. The seas kept rolling and rolling, the surf accelerating over tidal runnels as it bashed mindlessly against the sand. Waves crashed down and sunk ten Higgins boats, drowning most of the three hundred men aboard them.

Wide beaches ahead designated Omaha seemed to glow under the moonlight. Obstacles erected by the Germans cast shadows of harsh lines and stark patterns across the sand. Cliffs rising in back of the sea-wall bristled with pillboxes, bunkers, trenches arranged for interlocking fire, bulwarks, parapets, machine gun emplacements, strongholds . . . The entire coastline looked impenetrable, impervious to assault by the combined armies of all the world.

Prohibited from accompanying the first onslaught, Chaplain Barber paced the railed deck of his transport, fretful and impatient, and watched this great and terrible drama unfold. He paused frequently to pray for the soldiers he had come to know and love.

The rolling, earsplitting thunder of the naval barrage quit as the first waves of landing craft approached sand. Eerie quiet returned, except for the steady plopping of German mortars landing in the water. Germans on the bluffs above Omaha Beach held their fire and waited.

Landing craft touched bottom some forty yards offshore, bucking up and down in heavy swells as they lowered their steel landing ramps. Dogfaces burdened with weapons and combat kit poured out into the surf and waded toward the beach in long lines, rifles held above their heads. Here and there, men plunged out of sight into deep tidal runnels. Some struggled into the shallows and crawled up on the beach. Others drowned.

Germans finally opened up with machine guns and mortars as the first ranks of GIs reached the sand and advanced across open killing fields. The slaughter was fast and merciless. Men fell in every direction.

The air crackled with bullets. In very short order, corpses lay strewn on the beach and bumped against one another in the shallows. Mangled human parts were scattered everywhere. The sea turned red.

The seawall offered the only cover and hope of survival. Few invaders from the first waves would reach it. The invasion all along Omaha bogged down, its soldiers pinned in place. Some men tried to dig foxholes in the hard sand. Others slithered forward, using corpses for cover. The few Americans still alive provided target practice for the entrenched Germans. Aerial bombing and naval artillery seemed to have done remarkably little damage to German defenses.

Although first accounts of the battle to reach ships offshore proved disheartening, landing craft continued to shuttle soldiers into the roaring maelstrom. Chaplain Barber's ears throbbed with pain from the crackle and clatter and ear-shaking thunder.

Early in the afternoon, the chaplain received the word to go. He scrambled over the side and down a rope ladder into a Higgins boat filled with thirty enlisted men and their gear. Since chaplains never went armed, he carried only a backpack containing his Bible and a few personal items. While the wind blew sea spray, he crouched below the gunwales with the soldiers and assured them that with the help of God they would prevail, even though it didn't seem that way at the moment.

Corpses bobbed in the water. Pocket Bibles that had been handed out to troops on Sunday floated in the surf. Machine gun bullets spattering against steel ramps proved that defenders were still dug in and dangerous.

Clutching his Bible, Chaplain Barber rushed out of the boat with the other soldiers and waded toward sand. Gunfire thundered all around. A Nebelwerfer rocket sliced off a lieutenant's legs and left him writhing and howling in agony. Ammo cooked off inside a burning tank and blew off the hatch, shooting fire into the sky. A snarling machine gun chewed up a sergeant. GIs fought to reach the beach, some swimming, some wading, others crawling or slithering like salamanders, all praying and helping one another.

The furnace roar of the battle was like nothing Chaplain Barber had ever experienced. Bullets electrified the air, chewed up the hard sand at his feet. The Bible was his armor.

Eyes dry and burning from smoke, heedless of his own safety, the chaplain responded to wounded men who cried out for help and mercy, and ran to as many of them as he could. He knelt over the maimed and dying, and prayed aloud, promising, "I'm your chaplain and I'm here to help you. God will see us through. God loves you. He knows you. God will help you if you make the supreme sacrifice. God has prepared a place for you in his kingdom."

He assisted combat medics in patching up the wounded and dragging them to the cover of the seawall. He raced from place to place, always under fire, here ministering to a soldier as he died, there bandaging a mangled arm or leg, everywhere tarrying with little knots of terrified GIs to lead them in prayer before they again rose and took on the enemy blazing down at them from the cliffs. Truly, it was the longest day of his life. Never had he ministered under such horrendous and perilous conditions.

Not a bullet touched him.

Darkness in June arrived an hour or so before midnight. The Germans had managed to pin down an assault force of 35,000 men. Realizing he wasn't going to get off the beach for a while, Chaplain Barber dug a foxhole behind the seawall at the base of the bluffs while tracers weaved intricate patterns in the gathering nightfall. He dug as if everything depended on it, and prayed as though everything depended on God. At least he could get his head down and stay away from bullets when he wasn't needed.

By 0330, the tide of battle was shifting. Americans destroyed enough of the enemy that they could scale the cliffs and carry the fight directly into German trenches. The shooting was less intense than before. Chaplain Barber helped evacuate casualties.

Bloodstained and filthy, weary to the core, Barber collapsed in his foxhole at daybreak and opened a can of Spam. The sun rose and painted the surf foam pink. He wondered if the tint was sun or blood. Clumps of bodies still littered the relatively narrow beach like bags of old clothing.

Ernie Pyle dropped into the foxhole next to him. Like the chaplain, the correspondent carried no weapons, only his camera, a portable typewriter, and a canvas bag full of his papers.

"Padre, I figured I'd see you here," he greeted.

"Ernie."

They shared the tin of Spam, taking a few minutes' respite in the midst of turmoil. Afterward, Chaplain Barber sighed and turned to look up at the cliffs towering above his head. He picked up his Bible.

"Time to get back to work," he said.

Chaplain George Barber served a second combat tour as a chaplain in Korea. He retired to California and died in 2004.

ARMY CAPTAIN MOLTON A. SHULER, JR.,
Korea, 1952

Although no major offensives were launched against the North Koreans after the autumn of 1951, United Nations warplanes, primarily American, continued to pound enemy targets. While truce negotiations languished, the warring sides dug in, fought, and died in more or less static battles to maintain the status quo along the 38th Parallel. Army Captain Molton Shuler, a company commander with the 45th Infantry Division "Thunderbirds," tramped to the rear late one afternoon just before dark to attend "chapel." Getting to the "rear" was a simple matter of walking down one hill and into the valley below.

It was summertime but, as Shuler wryly noted, the living was not easy. The weather was warm, which meant staff meetings, memorial services, chapel, and other ceremonies were conducted in the open. Church tonight was to be on a grassy hillside protected by a rise of

mountains on all sides. The chaplain was from Division, which meant
he made his rounds like a Bible-toting circuit rider of the early American West to minister to his various subordinate units for whose col-
lective souls he was responsible. He carried with him everything he
needed. Everything, as one wag noted, except the collection plate.

By appearance, little separated the chaplain from his rough congregation, other than that he wore crosses pinned on his soiled fatigues,
and he and his assistant trudged unarmed among these dangerous hills.
He was certainly as rugged-looking as any hardened warrior, with
his crew cut, weathered features, toughened hands, and lean, hungry-
looking frame. His pulpit was a couple of machine gun ammo boxes
stacked on each other, on top of which he placed his government-
issued folding podium with its red velvet cover and brass candelabra.
The candles themselves had long ago been lost or used up.

The assistant, a young corporal, took his place to the chaplain's
right and slightly uphill, sitting on a five-gallon gasoline can at the keys
of a battered portable organ painted olive drab. Three self-conscious
South Korean boys in black peasant trousers and mix-and-match Yank
uniforms stood ready to serve as a choir. Their hands were pressed in
prayer while they waited for the organ to play.

About fifty men, each war-weary and battle seasoned, settled in
"pews" downhill of the pulpit, sprawling on the trampled grass. One
soldier wore a blood-crusted field dressing on his hand. The bare knee
of another stuck up through a rent in his fatigues. A third wiped at
tears running down his thorny cheeks. M-1 Garands, .45 Thompsons,
Browning automatic rifles (BARs), and other weapons, all fully loaded,
lay on the ground next to the fighters, within easy reach should an
enemy attack disrupt services.

The chaplain opened his Bible and closed his eyes in a moment of
silent prayer. Captain Shuler removed his helmet and sat on it between
a blond, baby-faced private and a rugged sergeant with a dark beard
and dirty fingernails.

Olive drab (OD) tents housed Shuler's company tactical operations center (TOC) clustered farther up the valley. Bunkers and sandbagged, concertina-wired trenches surrounded them. In the opposite direction were blasted-out Chicom bunkers and old gun emplacements. Up the side of the hill on the military crest, a battery of 105mm howitzers pointed their ugly snouts menacingly toward the north. They remained silent for the time being. Several gunners stood and looked down the green hill where services were about to begin in the open purpling air of approaching dusk.

The chaplain's assistant passed out pocket Bibles to those who did not already have them. He returned to his organ and began to play. His sweet, lingering notes filled the air, rising up out of the valley to the ears of friend and foe alike. The choir boys sang "Amazing Grace" and "Old Rugged Cross."

Captain Shuler had never heard anything like it. Only a few times in his entire life before this evening had he felt God's presence in such a powerful way. God must be in this open-air chapel, so near a man could almost reach out and touch Him.

The tough chaplain led his congregation in an opening prayer. Then he began his sermon. "Men, in the days to come," he preached, "you must remember the words of Christ when He was asked where He lived. 'Come and see,' He said. . . ."

Three weeks later, on August 16, 1952, Captain Molton Shuler was wounded by exploding shrapnel. He died at a hospital in Tokyo.

AIR FORCE CAPTAIN VIRGIL N. KOVALENKO,
Vietnam, 1971

Soldiers and airmen desiring to attend the Church of Latter-Day Saints (LDS) on Sunday mornings, afternoons, or evenings waited next to roads on either the sprawling American military base at Bien Hoa or its outlying camps. A large blue Air Force bus, dubbed the "Mormon

Battalion Bus Line," came by to pick them up. No smoking or swear-
ing was allowed, which struck those who merely wanted a lift from one
point to the next as peculiar. After all, this was Vietnam, a combat zone.
It was a soldier's God-given right to smoke, curse the weather, the dirtbag country, the enemy, and everything else within sight.

"Fellows, this is the chapel bus," Air Force Captain Virgil Kovalenko
reminded such blackguards. Kovalenko began each Sunday's routine by
checking out the bus from the motor pool and cheerfully driving his
rounds.

A light would come on. "Oh! This is the God Squad."

A native of Arizona and a retread from the Korean War, Captain Kovalenko was assigned to the Political Warfare Division,
Vietnamese Air Force Logistics Command. During his free time,
other than driving the church bus, he served as group leader for
the Bien Hoa LDS Servicemen's Group, where he participated in
Priesthood and Sunday school. Often, Sunday evening services
ended after nightfall, even though Americans were warned to stay
in their bunkers and not roam about in the dark. Viet Cong liked
to sneak up close to the outer perimeter at night and pop in mortar rounds and rockets.

Raid sirens began screaming one night at an evening service just
before Christmas. Explosions banged here and there around the base
as the VC had themselves a little practice and provided the Americans
a workout. South Vietnamese airmen standing outside the Quonset hut
windows of the church listening to the music scattered to find cover.
The LDS meeting quickly adjourned to the chapel bus.

Kovalenko jumped behind the wheel. "Hold on to your hats," he
advised passengers. "The Mormon Battalion Bus Line is on the move."

In all the excitement—sirens blaring, rockets bursting—Kovalenko
drove the blue bus fast and with lights extinguished to avoid appearing
even more of a great big target. Peter Bell and Merwin Ruesh, a pair of
Army Green Berets active in the Priesthood, assisted Kovalenko in the
process of delivering passengers to their bunkers. As soon as a soldier

stood up when the driver called out the name of his destination, Bell yelled out, "Stand in the door!" That was one of the five paratrooper jump commands.

The bus skidded to a halt. The door opened. Bell planted his size-eleven combat boot against the guy's rump and shoved, shouting, "Airborne!"

Weather conditions suddenly deteriorated as Kovalenko made his rounds of the outlying camps. Thundering rain in an electrical storm, a common tropical occurrence, scudded across the airbase, making it difficult to distinguish the crack of lightning from an exploding mortar round. Kovalenko got all the Saints back to their units and hooches in spite of driving in the pitch dark and blinding rain without lights. The Green Berets remained on the bus with him as he dashed back from the Army side of the base to the Air Force side.

A poncho-slickered corporal with his M-16 at port arms blocked the road at the boundary. Another sentry stepped out of the guard post and shone a red-lensed flashlight in Kovalenko's eyes. The blue bus skidded on the slippery macadam to avoid running him down. Kovalenko threw open his passenger doors.

"Get out of the way!" he roared into the driving rain.

The sentries were in no mood for a discussion. Vehicles were not allowed on the roads during an attack. In no uncertain terms, the corporal ordered Kovalenko to "get your *expletive, expletive, expletive* bus off my *expletive* road!" As further emphasis, he leveled his M-16 at the bus and its driver. He meant business.

There was nothing for the captain to do except whip the blue bus off the pavement and into a shallow open depression near the guard shack, a position that afforded no cover or concealment for so large a vehicle. He cut the engine. Rain drummed on the roof in deafening crescendos. There he sat in the dark with the two Green Beret soldiers, Bell and Ruesh, and himself anxiously gripping the steering wheel while artillery blasted, sirens screamed, and flares went off all around. He fully expected to be blown into eternity at any moment. The bus made a ripe target for the discerning enemy gunner.

Sentries at the guard shack began firing an 81mm mortar, the concussion effect of which proved quite interesting in the rain.

Ruesh sighed. "Well, what do we do now, Kemo Sabe?"

Kovalenko shrugged and watched a VC rocket explode strobelike inside one of the revetments that sheltered aircraft next to the runway. This side of the base was taking a pounding. But there seemed to be no other cover near the bus except the guard shack, which was an even juicier target, considering how the guards were firing their mortar tube.

Attempting to remain calm in the midst of chaos and threat, Kovalenko suggested, "We can't go anywhere now. Why worry about it? We may as well start compiling group reports for the district."

Using shaded red-lensed flashlights, the three Mormons clustered in the bus aisle to work on the day's church minutes, flinching whenever a rocket or mortar round landed too near for comfort. As they pored over paperwork, Kovalenko suddenly sensed something extraordinary about to happen. The Green Berets felt it as well. They snapped erect and looked at one another.

No words could adequately describe the phenomenon, or their reaction to it. Awed, mystified, thrilled, stunned . . . A giant transparent bubble, glowing faintly, appeared at the rear of the bus and slowly, ever so slowly, stretched itself over the entire vehicle, closing itself off at the front to cradle the bus inside a protective balloon.

The Air Force officer and the two Special Forces noncoms could still see and hear everything occurring around them, but even though they couldn't explain it they somehow knew instinctively that they were being shielded from all harm. An amazing tranquility replaced their initial astonishment. They relaxed and were no longer afraid.

All clear sounded in about twenty minutes. The bubble retracted and vanished when Captain Kovalenko fired up the bus engine to head for the motor pool. None of the three aboard spoke of the bubble again. It was too incredible to believe—even though it *had* happened. The only way Kovalenko could explain the "bus in the bubble" was that God must protect those who do His work.

NAVY LIEUTENANT SYD BRISKER,
World War 11, 1943

Lieutenant Syd Brisker and the cook were the only two Jews serving aboard the gunship USS *Beaumont.* They decided to attempt to celebrate Passover with a traditional seder, even though they were at sea, bound on a mission of war. Passover commemorates the exodus of the Israelites from ancient Egypt after four hundred years of slavery. The startling parallel of Jews celebrating their deliverance from the persecution of an ancient fascism and the current war against the rise of a new fascism called Nazism did not escape them.

"It can be said, without fear of contradiction, that there are no Jews in the ranks of the enemy," Lieutenant Brisker cracked.

Their Passover celebration on the *Beaumont* was unusual . . . to say the least.

Each course in the seder meal is a symbol, as is each type of food that's offered. In anticipation of the event, Lieutenant Brisker obtained two boxes of matzoh at the ship's last port of call. The protestant chaplain donated a copy of the Haggadah, the text that goes along with the Passover seder service. Prune juice would have to do for wine since alcohol was prohibited aboard U.S. warships, and no grape juice was available. With the captain's cooperation, the cook took two chickens from the commissary. Chinese cabbage served as the "bitter herb," while celery tops substituted for parsley. The officers' steward baked a sponge cake. Salt water and hard-boiled eggs completed the preparations. There would be no knaidels due to the lack of matzoh meal.

Using two blankets, the lieutenant and the cook partitioned off a bay in the chief petty officers' quarters and set up a table. In addition to Lieutenant Brisker and the cook, the gathering included a Protestant pharmacist's mate, a Catholic cook, the ship's chaplain, and the officers' steward, who was black. Brisker related the story of Passover in English. It required little stretch of the imagination to substitute Hitler for the Assyrian Laban, who threatened to kill all the Jews.

He concluded with, "And it is this same promise which has been the support of our ancestors and us, too. For at every time enemies rise against us to annihilate us, the most Holy, blessed be He, hath delivered us out of their hands."

They prayed for peace. "May He Who maketh peace in His heavens grant peace on us all in Israel, and say ye Amen."

It was an ancient prayer repeated year after year. Lieutenant Brisker added a silent prayer of his own—asking God for a victory over modern fascism and for everlasting peace in a world where Jew and Gentile, white and black, of all religions, creeds, and colors could live in peace, harmony, and security. Even as those of different faiths and races had sat down at Seder that night aboard the USS *Beaumont*.

ARMY CHAPLAIN GEORGE WHITEFIELD RIDOUT,
World War I, 1918

Army Chaplain George Ridout, one of the oldest men in his 38th Infantry Regiment at nearly fifty years old, advised soldiers to wear the New Testament in their left breast pockets over their hearts. He believed the little book to be as capable of saving lives as redeeming souls. He moved into France's Argonne Forest with his regiment, trudging through terrible country plowed raw with shell holes. The forest was a ruins of shattered and splintered trees. Scarcely a green leaf or a green blade of grass remained. Nothing but barbed wire, trenches, dugouts, and the awful, sour stench of rotting corpses.

Medics set up a dressing station behind lines near Montfaucon in dugouts recently abandoned by retreating Germans. Chaplain Ridout served with the frontline first aid stations whenever he was not lecturing and preaching. He had barely got his pup tent erected when someone shouted a warning.

A swoop of three German airplanes appeared against the summer sky. The pilots dropped hand grenades from their open cockpits and raked the first aid station with machine guns, even though it was clearly marked with red crosses. Doughboys returned fire with rifles and machine guns. The engine of one flimsy biplane coughed and went dead, wobbling back toward its own lines, struggling to stay in the air. It crashed several hundred yards away and burst into flames and oily black smoke. American troops cheered and waved their arms.

As was his habit, Chaplain Ridout rose early each morning to brew hot chocolate and coffee and prepare bread, bacon, rice, or whatever else might be available to serve the hungry and wounded, sick and cold, or any stragglers who happened along. One morning he noticed a strongly built young corporal reading his Bible in an abandoned shack. That was his introduction to Fletcher "Happy" Benson, a former student of the ministry who had volunteered for the infantry when war broke out. He had been on the front lines since the Battle of the Marne.

"I was singing one of these hymns before you came along, Chaplain," Happy Benson said, indicating an Army hymnal open on his knee. "I'll sing you a verse if you don't mind."

He had a clear, fine voice.

> O Jesus, I have promised
> to serve Thee to the end;
> Be Thou forever near me,
> my Master and my Friend!

> I shall not fear the battle
> if Thou are by my side. . . .

He stopped singing and smiled. "In a peculiar way," he said, "I feel He is standing at my side when the shells are busting all around me. I feel He is sheltering me from the shrapnel and comforting me."

The chaplain and the infantry corporal became fast friends and got together to chat and worship whenever their separate duties permitted. Benson never seemed out of sorts, nor did he indulge in coarse behavior and language.

"I'd sure like to know what keeps Benson so happy in the miserable surroundings we have to put up with," another soldier mused.

Benson overheard and explained. "This is what makes me happy. I try to keep the fear of the Lord ever before me. I have my New Testament, which I read every day. And I say my prayers regularly."

"There you go again with your religious business, Benson."

Chaplain Ridout's division moved into the Saint-Mihiel sector to relieve an attacking division. Artillery, ammo, rations, infantry, engineers, signal corps—all seemed to be trying to get to the front at the same time. Congestion was so bad for the last ten miles that scarcely a wheel turned. A German mine went off in the road and overturned a truck, further blocking the road.

The 2nd Battalion Medical Corps established a first aid station as far forward as safety for the wounded permitted. Casualties from the front began arriving, carried on foot by their buddies and medics. Road congestion prevented ambulances from getting through. Dead and wounded littered the ground all around the aid station. Surgeons, nurses, aidmen, stretcher bearers, and Chaplain Ridout worked continuously for twenty-two hours.

On the second afternoon, four doughboys carrying an Army captain on a stretcher came trotting wearily across the battlefield. The captain was seriously wounded, shot in both legs and in the shoulder. One of the litter bearers was Happy Benson, now promoted to sergeant. He had volunteered to help carry out the captain after German snipers picked off the first four bearers.

Since it was almost dark, Benson decided to wait until morning before returning to his unit. He and Chaplain Ridout kindled a small fire in a trench at the opening of an old German dugout. They boiled coffee and chocolate in big pots for the wounded and for those hungry and thirsty soldiers who dropped by two or three at a time.

"I hope this will be the last war this old sin-cursed world will ever see," Sergeant Benson said. "One thing I'll never do is glorify war when I get home. Not after what I went through yesterday and today."

He stared into the flames of the fire for a long time. The chaplain waited.

"We were up against a nest of German machine guns, one-pounders and snipers," Benson went on presently. "I saw one of our lieutenants shot in the head and fall dead instantly. Ten of my own platoon went down one after the other. Our company got so shot to pieces that I believe there are no more than sixty or seventy left. The Germans were shelling everything in sight. One shell fell about fifty feet away from us and killed four of our boys and wounded eight others. A fellow riding a horse was shot to pieces and his horse torn in two.

"War is the most horrible monster the Devil ever invented. The marvel is that I'm still alive. Through it all, God has mercifully spared me and I am still alive to praise Him. These days I think about Psalms a lot, the ninety-first verse: 'A thousand shall fall at thy side and ten thousand at thy right hand, but it shall not come nigh thee.' I think of that hymn we used to sing at camp meeting—'God Will Take Care of You.'"

Chaplain Ridout produced his little Army hymnal. Together, he and Benson sang the first verse.

> Be not dismayed whate'er betide,
> God will take care of you;
> Beneath His wings of love abide,
> God will take care of you.

The singing in the night from the trench around the fire quickly attracted other soldiers and so quite a congregation gathered. Doughboys lifted their voices to join in the last verses and chorus. Fire glow illuminated faces gaunt, soiled, bewhiskered, and weathered.

Through days of toil when heart doth fail,
God will take care of you;
When dangers fierce your path assail,
God will take care of you.

Chaplain Ridout reflected, "We have all had close calls these past few days. Many of our friends have gone, never to come back. I propose that we have prayer before we separate to go to our dugouts. Sergeant Benson, will you lead us in prayer?"

Helmets were swept from shaggy bowed heads. Sergeant Happy Benson closed his eyes. The fire reflected against his face.

"Heavenly Father, we give Thee thanks that our lives have been spared during the awful fighting of these past two days. We have seen many comrades go down, many others wounded and carried off to the hospital. We thank Thee for Thy loving care over us. Bless my comrades here, O God. Forgive us of our sins, and don't let any of us go down to death without saving our souls. Protect us this night from the shells and from gas. Grant that soon this war might be over and peace shall come on the earth again. Bless our dear loved ones in America. Protect them and grant we may all meet again. For Christ's sake. Amen."

Chaplain George Ridout and Sergeant Fletcher Benson survived the war.

ARMY CHAPLAIN DELBERT KUEHL,
World War II, 1943

Boyish-looking and of slender build, newly commissioned Chaplain (First Lieutenant) Delbert Kuehl* prepared to conduct his first church services at Fort Benning, Georgia. His *potential* congregation

---

* See also chapter 13.

consisted of 1,800 paratroopers of the 504th Parachute Infantry Regiment, with which Kuehl had been undergoing training since early 1942. He held no illusions that he would pack the little white chapel on the training post, but he did expect a goodly number.

He arrived well beforehand to make sure hymnals were distributed to all the pews and that enough pocket Bibles were available to go around. Nervous about his first official sermon, he went over his notes a final time and opened his marked scriptures to today's message. Then he combed his hair, made sure his uniform was presentable, and waited for his flock to come.

Two men showed up. One of them was falling-down drunk.

The chaplain was devastated. Paratroopers were a hard lot, volunteers for the most hazardous duty of the war, rough men not prone to examine their inner feelings or to consider the fate of their souls. How was he to reach them?

Kuehl, twenty-four, was raised on a farm in Minnesota until he was sixteen and the Great Depression stripped his family of its land and left it poverty-stricken. Young Delbert wore his sister's hand-me-down shoes and had to borrow a sweater from the Red Cross to attend his high school graduation. He planned to work his way through the University of Minnesota, study hard, obtain his degree, and never be poor again. To the lean, hardscrabble kid, religion was nothing but superstition. It wasn't for people who were smart.

If he was right, he wondered, then how could his neighbor, a brilliant electrical engineer, also be a devout Christian? The question left him baffled.

"Delbert, you need to be a Christian," his neighbor told him.

"I'm too busy."

The more he considered it, however, the greater his curiosity grew about how such a bright man could embrace both science *and* religion. He secretly began reading the Bible, trying to find answers. He read through both the Old Testament and the New. One night, alone in his room, he climbed out of bed, dropped humbly to his knees, and began to pray.

"I believe you are there, God . . ."

The young man who rose to his feet afterward was different from the one who fell to his knees. The entire course of his life changed. Instead of attending the University of Minnesota to get rich, he earned a degree in theology from Northwestern Seminary to become a minister. He immediately enlisted in the army after Pearl Harbor, even though ministers were exempt from military service.

After attending chaplains school at Fort Benjamin Harrison, Indiana, he volunteered for the airborne. A tough kid himself, the little "sky pilot" in baggy pants with a big heart quickly won the respect of his fellow paratroopers. However, judging from the abject failure of his first Army church service, he wasn't winning *their* hearts and minds. He tried to console himself with the words of Jesus: *For where two or three are gathered in my name . . .*

But there were only *two*—and one was so drunk he probably didn't even realize he was in church!

"God, You have to do something," he prayed. "There are going to be a lot of casualties with these men, and they will need to hear Your Word."

The solution came as though God Himself spoke: *If they won't come to you, you'll have to go to them.*

From that point on, instead of attending to typical chaplain duties, the young chaplain stuck with the men. He engaged in full-pack twenty-five-mile hikes; qualified with every weapon in the regiment's arsenal; participated in "war games"; made countless parachute jumps to "get ready." His slim figure and boyish grin became a familiar and welcome sight to every man in the regiment, from the commander down to the greenest private. He was *their* chaplain, *their* "Battling Padre of the 504th."

The regiment shipped overseas in April 1943 en route to North Africa to link up with the 82nd Airborne Division, its parent organization. After porting in Casablanca, the 504th caught trains to Tunisia to prepare for its first combat jump into Sicily.

Chaplain Kuehl scheduled church services on the night before action. This time, there was barely standing room. Bible open at the pulpit, the chaplain looked fondly out over all those hardened, familiar faces. Tears brimmed in his eyes. After tomorrow, he realized, some of these men would never be able to attend church again.

"Let us pray," he said, bowing his head.

7

BROTHERHOOD

Am I my brother's keeper?

—GENESIS 4:9

The single greatest motivator for American troops in combat is the Brotherhood of Arms. Although faith and spirituality are factors in a warrior's makeup, men do not fight for abstract concepts as much as they do for one another and for a bond that is stronger than one between brothers. Those who have not personally experienced combat find it difficult to understand why men would willingly sacrifice, or offer to sacrifice, their lives for comrades. Of the 3,461 men and one woman awarded the Medal of Honor since the Civil War, most of them received it for risk in defense of fellow soldiers.

On November 13, 2004, Army Sergeant Benny Alicea had little time to think when terrorists ambushed his rifle company in Fallujah, Iraq. Struck by shrapnel from two grenades, Alicea led his squad through a courtyard and back into the street. When intense enemy fire seriously wounded three other GIs who were unable to seek cover or fight back, Sergeant Alicea stayed with them, shielding them with his own body.

Enemy rounds slashed all around him. He grabbed magazines of ammo from the wounded and held off attackers until a Bradley fighting vehicle came to the rescue.

"I just kept firing my weapon, just shooting, waiting to get hit," he said. "I'd pretty much figured at any given point, it was all over. I didn't think I was going to make it through it."

That same year, Marine Corporal Jason Dunham was killed near Husaybah, Iraq, when he dived for an enemy grenade and covered it with his Kevlar helmet in order to save the lives of his friends.

"When you are in a war situation," said the fallen Marine's father, "that guy beside you is your brother or sister. I think that most of us would give up our lives for our family."

The words from the Gospel of John seem to resonate through the lives of American combat heroes: *Greater love hath no man than this, that he lay down his life for his friends.*

NAVY CHAPLAIN GEORGE S. RENTZ,
World War II, 1942

The roar of big naval guns and the blast of Japanese torpedoes ceased at midnight of March 1st, 1942, letting the quiet and the night retake Sunda Strait off the coast of Java. The night was moonless, the only light coming from a crippled Japanese cruiser blazing against the black horizon. The oil-smeared seas also burned. Persistent threads of acrid smoke from the recent battle drifted like veils across the stars.

Only three months after Pearl Harbor, a Jap invasion force had all but wiped out the badly outnumbered and outgunned Allied naval presence in the southwest Pacific, sinking an Australian light cruiser, HMAS *Perth*, and the U.S. cruiser USS *Houston*, the flagship of the Asiatic fleet. Castaway sailors of the *Perth* and *Houston* floated in the drink, grasping whatever scraps of flotsam they could find in a desperate struggle for survival.

About twenty *Houston* seamen clung to the pontoon of a destroyed seaplane. Strong currents in the strait slowly dragged the pontoon and its passengers out to sea. Spilled oil from sunken ships, both Allied and Japanese, smoothed out the chop and kept sharks away. At least for the time being.

Among the castaways was *Houston's* chaplain, Commander George S. Rentz, fifty-nine. Nine years senior to the cruiser's captain, Rentz received his chaplain's commission during World War I and served with the U.S. 11th Marine Regiment in France. Decorated for valor in 1918, he again demonstrated courage when the Japanese fleet attacked *Houston*. He circulated among the ship's gun batteries as the sea battle raged, dropping words of encouragement, praying for and with the gunners. Men who saw this man of God walking fearlessly among them knew they were not alone.

He was still with them in the sea after the fighting was over, in the black

night with the current sucking at their feet and oil on the surface burning
their eyes. The chaplain appeared in better shape than many, even though
abandoning ship had taken a lot out of a man nearly sixty years old. Several of his pontoon mates endured dreadful wounds sustained from flying
shrapnel. Oil glued shut the eyes of one sailor, who kept crying out that he
was blind. Several others had skin roasted off their limbs, faces, or bodies.
They wept from the excruciating sting of salt water on torn flesh.

The overcrowded pontoon was slowly sinking, taking on water
through a rent in its top. It could not much longer remain afloat with
so many bodies clinging to it. Chaplain Rentz led the men in prayer
and a hymn. The haunting refrain of "Amazing Grace" was never ren-
dered with such raw and poignant emotion.

Grueling hours passed. Most of the men had life jackets, but Seaman Walter Beeson, hanging on to the float next to the chaplain, did
not. Weakened by his wounds, his hands stiffening, he kept losing his
grip and sinking into the sea. His neighbors kept pulling him back into
position.

Finally, Chaplain Rentz said, "You men are young, with your lives
ahead of you. I am old and have had my fun. I have lived the major part
of my life and am willing to go with God."

With that, he removed his life jacket and thrust it at Beeson. "Put
it on," he ordered.

Beeson refused. "No, Chaplain," he protested weakly.

"Beeson, lad, put it on."

Rentz let go of the pontoon and swam off. Marine Sergeant Jim Gee
retrieved him. Beeson insisted the chaplain take back his life jacket.

"Chaplain, sir, we need you. God will listen to you."

"He will listen to you as well," Rentz countered.

Waves washed over the surface of the pontoon, gradually filling it
with water. It wouldn't be much longer before it sank, leaving the men
with only their life jackets to keep them afloat. Beeson and one or two
others would surely drown.

With a catch in his throat, Chaplain Rentz led a last short prayer in which he asked God to forgive these shipwrecked sailors of their sins and protect them in their hour of need. He was gasping for breath when he finished. Clearly, he was about done for. Fatigue and exposure had taken their toll.

"My heart is failing me," he said to Beeson. "I'm old and can't last much longer."

No one tried to stop him this time when he removed his life jacket and gave it to Beeson. Beeson accepted it, although he declined to put it on for the moment. The castaways watched in horror, too exhausted themselves to do anything to stop him when the aging chaplain suddenly kicked free of the float and immediately vanished beneath the black chop of Sunda Strait. One moment he was among them, the next he was gone, sacrificing his life so that a younger man, a kid really, might have a chance to live.

Most of the "pontoon sailors" were captured by the Japanese and survived the war, Beeson among them. Chaplain George Rentz was posthumously awarded the Navy Cross for valor, the only Navy chaplain so honored during World War II. In 1984, a U.S. guided missile frigate was commissioned USS Rentz in his honor.

NURSE CLARA BARTON,
Civil War, 1862

Clara Barton, who became known as the "Angel of the Battle-field" because of her compassionate and fearless nature, was forty years old when the Civil War erupted. She was among more than three thousand women who volunteered to serve as nurses during the war. Although she stood only four-eleven in her bare feet, one Union soldier observed how she had to be the tallest human being spiritually he had ever known. Most of that frail body, he marveled, had to be made of nothing but pure heart.

Often working for days with little or no sleep, she tended wounds under fire, cooked meals, comforted frightened soldiers, and risked her own life repeatedly to help and heal. A prolific letter writer, she described to her cousin Vira the haunting calm that pervaded the soldiers' camp the night before the Union assault on Fredericksburg, Virginia. It was 2 A.M., December 12th, 1862. The depth of this remarkable woman's selflessness and devotion to *her* soldiers emerged in her letter.

My Dear Cousin Vira:

Five minutes time with you; and God only knows what those five minutes might be worth to the maybe-doomed thousands sleeping around me.

It is the night before a battle. The enemy, Fredericksburg, and its mighty entrenchments lie before us, the river between. At tomorrow's dawn our troops will essay to cross, and the guns of the enemy will sweep those frail bridges at every breath.

The moon is shining through the soft haze with brightness almost prophetic. For the last half hour I have stood alone in the awful stillness of its glimmering light gazing upon the strange sad scene around me striving to say, "Thy will O God be done."

The camp fires blaze with unwanted brightness, the sentry's tread is still but quick. The acres of little shelter tents are dark and still as death, no wonder for as I gazed sorrowfully upon them, I thought I could almost hear the slow flap of the grim messenger's wings, as one by one he sought and selected his victims for the morning sacrifice. Sleep weary one, sleep and rest for tomorrow's toil. Oh! Sleep and visit in dreams once more the loved ones nestling at home. They may yet live to dream of you, cold lifeless and bloody. But this dream, soldier, is thy last, paint it brightly, dream well. On northern mothers wives and sisters, all unconscious of the house, would to Heaven that I could bear for you the concentrated woe which is so soon to follow, would that Christ would teach my soul a prayer that would plead to the Father for grace sufficient for you. God pity and strengthen you every one.

Mine are not the only waking hours. The light yet burns so brightly in our

*kind hearted General's tent where he pens what may be a last farewell to his
wife and children and thinks sadly of his fated men.*

*Already the roll of the moving artillery is sounding in my ears. The battle
draws near and I must catch one hour's sleep for tomorrow's labor.*

*Good night, dear cousin, and Heaven grant you strength for your more
peaceful and less terrible but not weary days than mine.*

Yours in love, Clara.

*After the Civil War ended, Clara Barton formed a bureau to search for missing men
and later founded the American Red Cross. She died in 1912.*

ARMY PRIVATE FIRST CLASS DESMOND T. DOSS,
World War II, 1945

Army Private First Class Desmond Doss fought to clear his blurred
vision and force his brain to function. A small, lean man of twenty-
five with black hair and a thin mustache disappearing into unshaved
bristle, he blinked out the fog, only vaguely aware of being carried by
stretcher to emergency surgery aboard a hospital ship off the coast of
Okinawa.

He had suffered his first wound shortly after midnight at the
base of the Maeda Escarpment when Nips tossed a grenade into
his foxhole. He stomped on the little bomb to smother its effect
and protect the three dogfaces in the hole with him. The explosion
blew him out of the pit, inflicting massive wounds to the flesh of
his foot and leg.

Himself a medic with B Company, 1/37 of the 77th Division, he
didn't want other medics risking their lives for him. He treated his own
injuries and waited for stretcher bearers to pick him up after daylight.

As the litter bearers were carrying him downhill toward the beach
and the aid station, they came upon a soldier whose wounds were even

more severe than Doss's. The little Seventh-Day Adventist insisted he be replaced on the stretcher by the other casualty.

"You can come back for me," he said. "I'll make it until then. He might not."

Doss crawled among some rocks and waited in the morning sunshine for the litter bearers to return. Rifle fire and grenade and mortar explosions continued to boom and growl from the direction of the escarpment where the Japs had the 1st Battalion pinned down. Sadness seeped into the wounded medic's heart. Americans were falling up there. Men *depended* on him. He was letting them down.

A soldier with bloody field wrappings around his chest spotted Doss. Together, leaning on each other, they started the laborious journey to reach the beach and safety. Halfway there, an enemy sniper hiding somewhere in the bush fired two quick shots. One bullet missed. The other shattered Doss's wrist and elbow.

Undeterred, Doss splinted his arm with his new friend's rifle, perhaps the only time in his life the little conscientious objector had used a weapon in any manner. The two soldiers crawled another agonizing three hundred yards to the battalion aid station. From there, partly sedated, Doss found himself transferred to the hospital ship and an onboard operating room.

Lying on the operating table, groggy from morphine and exhaustion, he reached for his breast pocket and discovered his most precious possession missing. Somewhere back there on the Maeda Escarpment he had lost the little book his new bride gave him before he shipped out to the Pacific.

"Please?" he croaked.

A surgeon leaned close to hear his feeble appeal.

"Please get word back to my men. I've lost my Bible."

Doss could have readily avoided military service, and the war altogether, when he received his draft notice in April 1942. Not only was he a shipyard worker, a job critical to the war effort, he was also a conscientious objector who refused to carry a weapon, to kill, or to work on Saturday, the Sabbath for the Seventh-Day Adventist Church. He could have been deferred on any of these counts.

Nonetheless, extremely patriotic, he volunteered to serve God and country in the military, choosing to become a medic and save lives rather than take them. Fellow trainees reviled him for his refusal to handle weapons or to violate the tenants of his religion. They called the little Virginian a coward. One boot grabbed him by the shirt collar and slammed him against a wall.

"You yellow bastard," he snarled. "If the Japs don't kill you, I'll kill you myself."

In the coarse vernacular of the Army world, Doss became the "company shitbird." Nonplussed and passive through it all, the little man continued to kneel at his bunk each evening to pray and spend time with God. Ignoring taunts and thrown boots, he read from the Bible his young wife had given him.

His company commander, Captain Jack Glover, offered him a way out on a Section 8 as unfit for military service. Doss declined, boldly assuring the review board that "I would be a very poor Christian indeed if I accepted a discharge saying I was mentally off because of my religion. I'm sorry, gentlemen, but I can't accept that kind of discharge."

It seemed the Army was stuck with its "coward."

The 77th Infantry Division and Doss with it shipped to the Pacific to become part of the "island hopping" campaign on its way to the eventual invasion of Japan. Unarmed except for his bag with the red cross on it, medic Doss participated in landings on Guam and Leyte. On Leyte, he dashed onto the open battlefield to retrieve a wounded GI crying out for help. Enemy snipers on high ground had the field zeroed in and had already plugged several Americans.

Heedless of the danger, Doss ran to the wounded GI, knelt to stop his bleeding, then picked him up in his arms and started back toward friendly lines. A Japanese sniper concealed among bushes and boulders popped up with his rifle aimed directly at the medic and his patient.

Doss's fellow soldiers were unable to fire because of the angle and because they feared hitting other GIs.

For some reason, the sniper held his fire. Years later, a former Japanese soldier told an American missionary, "That sniper could very well be me. I remember having a soldier in my gun sights, but I couldn't pull the trigger."

Doss was awarded the Bronze Star for valor. Baker Company's initial assessment of the little Bible pounder, that he was yellow, began to change. Even the boot who threatened to kill him if the Japs didn't had second thoughts. Doss was obviously no coward. He was just *different*.

Okinawa was the largest island of the Ryukyus chain. Lying only seven hundred miles from Japan proper, it offered a staging site for bombing Japan and for the expected final invasion to end the war. The campaign to capture it began on March 26th when the U.S. Tenth Army captured islands near there and turned them into naval bases. The amphibious assault took place on April 1st, 1945. Since the Americans were invading what Japanese considered their home soil, the defense was bitter and frantic in the extreme.

The Maeda Escarpment bisected the island near its southern end. Riddled with caves and tunnels, the ridge provided the Japanese a near-unassailable stronghold at the top. Beginning on April 29th, American forces bashed themselves at the objective again and again and were hurled back each time with bloody losses.

On May 5, Doss's 1/37 was ordered into the fray. As Baker Company and its platoons staged in the predawn under cover at the base of the escarpment, Doss suggested that the men should be provided a few minutes of private prayer.

"I believe prayer is the best lifesaver there is," he said.

Platoon leader Lieutenant Goronto called out, "Fellows, come over here and gather around. Doss wants to pray for us."

The lieutenant's tone carried no derision. Attitudes about God and the hereafter have a way of changing when bullets start flying.

Bursting flares against gray morning mist initiated the attack. Men threw themselves against the ridge and began scaling it like so many insects. From a distance, it appeared anthills had been ripped open to send ants scurrying about in a mist of smoke, fire, blinding detonations, and unbelievable noise.

The tide turned against the Americans. Japanese swarmed from their foxholes and caves to repel another attempt by the hated Americans to take the high ground. GIs clinging to the sides of the rugged slopes were forced to withdraw to the Maeda base. Of the 155 men of Baker who started the assault, only fifty-five were able to retreat without assistance. The rest lay strewn across a rocky slope at the top of a cliff, some dead, many wounded, tossed about like old sacks of bloody rags. Those able to hold a weapon, no matter how serious their wounds, continued to fight back in a last desperate attempt to survive.

Singed by the defeat, the remnants of Baker Company clustered in disarray below the cliff and listened to the bedlam above as their wounded comrades fought on. Commanders of the decimated battalion were organizing an attempt to rescue Baker Company's wounded when a thin figure in helmet and fatigues suddenly appeared at the top of the cliff. To everyone's amazement, he began lowering a rope-supported litter down the sheer rock face. In it lay strapped a wounded GI.

"It's Doss up there!" someone shouted.

Smoke, fire, explosions, and tracer rounds painted a chaotic background for the little medic as, hand over hand, with his end of the rope wrapped around a tree stump, PFC Doss gently lowered his patient to waiting hands below. Then he pulled up the empty litter and disappeared to go for another casualty.

The desperate fight between Nipponese and wounded GIs raged around Doss as, one after the other, he dragged disabled and unconscious comrades to the edge of the cliff and eased them down into eager hands. He seemed to be protected by some greater power. He dodged through hails of bullets as through a summer rainstorm, dancing between raindrops to pull, drag, and carry men to the cliff edge. Yet nothing touched him.

A pair of Japs charged him with long rifles blazing and bayonets fixed. He was too busy dragging away a comatose GI to bother with them. They were only yards away when a less seriously wounded American mowed them down with a Thompson. Both dropped almost at Doss's feet. He cast one look, sidestepped the convulsing corpses, and proceeded with his self-appointed task of tending and rescuing as many of Baker Company's soldiers as he could.

Men below the cliff began cheering each time the skinny Virginian appeared at the top of the cliff with another man saved. Tears filled the eyes of tough GIs who had lived with the horrors of war for the past year.

It went on like that for five hours. Doss chanted a single prayer as he worked: "Lord, help me get one more. Just *one more.*"

Exactly how many he saved was anyone's guess. Those at the base of the rock receiving casualties lost count after thirty or forty. The Army later determined he must have lowered at least one hundred men down the rock face, among them Captain Jack Glover, the company commander who had tried to Section 8 Doss as unsuited for the military.

"He saved my life," Glover told everyone. "The man I tried to have kicked out of the Army ended up being the most courageous person I've ever known. How's that for irony?"

News of Doss's exploits immediately reached nearly every soldier on the island. The coward from boot camp, the skinny, unarmed CO from Virginia, became a living symbol of courage and service to those who once jeered him.

Doss was wounded later that same night when he stomped on a live grenade to save two fellow GIs. He recovered from both shrapnel and the sniper's bullet. On October 12th, 1945, President Harry Truman summoned him to the White House to present him the Medal of Honor, the nation's highest award for valor, for his exploits in saving Baker Company's wounded soldiers.

"All the glory should go to God," Doss said. "No telling how many times the Lord has spared my life."

The men of 1/37 had a surprise for him following the White House ceremony. They had not forgotten the request he made while lying in the OR aboard the hospital ship. Soldiers who once mocked him had returned to the Maeda Escarpment after the battle for Okinawa ended, fanned out across the rocky terrain, and searched until they found his Bible and mailed it to him.

Private First Class Desmond Doss died peacefully on March 23, 2006, at the age of eighty-seven.

ARMY CORPORAL DAMIEN LUTEN,
Iraq, 2003

Sandstorms—savage, blistering, *alive* entities—roared and hissed across northern Kuwait and southern Iraq the day before the ground phase of Operation Iraqi Freedom began on March 20, 2003. Sand abraded exposed skin, filled mouths and throats, and made blinking painful. It took its toll on machines as well as humans, gunking up oil and moving parts, and burying whatever it could.

Coalition combat forces crossed into Iraq in the early morning hours. Although still bruised-looking, the sky promised fair weather for the next few days. Thirty-three vehicles and sixty-four soldiers of the 507th Maintenance Company departed Camp Virginia in Kuwait as the rear element of a march column of six hundred vehicles, whose destination was Objective Ram, 350 kilometers away.

The 507th, out of Fort Bliss, Texas was a Patriot missile support outfit, its mission to transport supplies and maintain vehicles. Its thirty-three vehicles consisted of heavy five-ton tractor-trailers and trucks, wreckers, and smaller HMMWV command trucks dragging trailers.

"Don't worry," Sergeant Matthew Rose reassured his wife and six children before he deployed. "We're a supply company in the rear of the fighting."

The desert has a way of fouling up even the most optimistic plans. By late that first evening of the war, the 507th had bogged down several of its vehicles off-road and redlined others due to mechanical problems caused by sand. Company commander Captain Troy King left First Sergeant Robert Dowdy behind with enough people to repair the seventeen trucks and get them unstuck. Captain King and the rest of his vehicles continued with the main convoy. The fragmented element would catch up the next day at traffic control point (TCP) *Lizard*.

Corporal Damien Luten was one of those left behind. The husky black soldier stood in the day's accumulated swelter next to the high fender of his tractor-trailer and watched the main convoy surge away in billowing dust. The supply trains stretched from horizon to horizon across the barren flats of the Iraqi desert before they faded into haze and mirages. A desolate wind whined and nipped around the few vehicles left behind, keening directly into the soul to empty it of all hope.

Specialist Jamaal Addison shuddered. "Man, I'm not looking forward to spending a night out here. What if the ragheads find us?"

"We can see 'em coming a hundred miles away," First Sergeant Dowdy said. "Let's get to work."

Luten thought he better understood what it must have been like for Jesus and his forty days and nights alone in the wilderness. The Army supply clerk was an unabashed Christian. One young soldier to whom he ministered had been baptized before the unit took off for Iraq. A chaplain caught in a scheduling conflict during up-training asked for a replacement—and Captain King selected Luten for the job.

By morning, the vehicles of Sergeant Dowdy's left-behind column were back online and moving. They arrived at TCP *Lizard* at 1400 hours, on March 22. Captain King and his driver, Private Dale Nace, were waiting to guide the trucks around the city of An Nasiriyah to catch up with the main convoy.

The element consisted of thirty-three soldiers and eighteen vehicles, two of which were being towed. One of the towed vehicles, and the ten-ton wrecker pulling it, belonged to the 3rd Forward Support Battalion rather than the 507th. Sergeant George Buggs and Specialist Edward Anguiano of the 3rd had also had mechanical problems.

Captain King's hummer led the order of march. First Sergeant Dowdy's Humvee brought up the rear. Corporal Luten, his assistant driver, and his tractor-trailer were fifth in line behind another five-ton pulling a trailer and in front of a hummer occupied by Chief Warrant Officer Mark Nash and Sergeant Tarik Jackson. There was little communication between and among vehicles, only five of which were equipped with satellite SINCGARS radios. The batteries in all the handheld radios had died.

The truncated convoy departed Lizard at 1930 hours and traveled cross-country over rough terrain. Five hours later, it came out on Highway 8, designated Route Blue, and followed that straight ribbon of narrow, dark macadam through the night. Drivers switched off in order to provide everyone a chance to grab a few winks.

At some point in the predawn, the convoy missed its turnoff onto Highway 1. Corporal Luten stirred from his turn at fitful sleep and leaned forward over the .50-caliber machine gun mounted on the passenger's side of the cab. A bright canopy of stars lit up the flat desert, the only illumination anywhere. Convoy trucks ran tactical without lights.

"Where are we?" he asked his driver, Private First Class Marcus Dubois.

Dubois shrugged. Their handheld radio hadn't worked since before Lizard. In convoy, a driver simply followed the vehicle ahead of him.

At 0530 hours, just before daylight on March 23, Captain King stiffened and looked around. He assumed the twinkle of lights ahead on the horizon to be some sort of industrial complex, perhaps an oil refinery. He radioed Dowdy in the rear over SINCGARS. They talked it over and decided to continue straight ahead.

The convoy proceeded north on Route 7/8 where it and Route 8 intersected. It was Captain King's second missed turnoff. Route 8 led around An Nasiriyah; Route 7/8 took them toward the city still occupied by the undefeated Iraqi Army.

Daylight came swiftly in the desert. All in a single moment, it seemed, the stars faded and a hot rim of fire popped up beyond the eastern horizon.

The highway was narrow and potholed, sometimes deteriorating into sand. It ran between partially drained marshlands. The trucks at this point couldn't have turned around and gone back even if Captain King ordered it.

Wide awake, Corporal Luten nervously surveyed the terrain outside his windows as the trucks crossed a bridge spanning the Euphrates River and entered the eastern outskirts of An Nasiriyah. None of the buildings was taller than four or five stories, and the streets and alleys were narrow. The stench of raw sewage filled the air. The impoverishment, the squalor, were ungodly.

The convoy rumbled past sandbagged checkpoints manned by armed soldiers wearing the gray-green uniform of the Iraqi Army. Many of them merely waved, showing no hostile intent. "Technicals"—civilian pickups mounted with machine guns and other weapons—drove past the convoy on the narrow street, their drivers and occupants also waving. The anxious Americans waved back, not knowing what else to do.

Luten began to think SNAFU—"Situation Normal, All Fouled Up." He felt as though he had been transported into some kind of alternate universe. Were the guys in this city friendlies? Or were they so astonished by the bold appearance of Americans among them that they didn't know how to react?

"I don't think we're in Kansas anymore, Toto," Dubois commented drily.

Captain King led the convoy across another Euphrates River bridge and a canal. The road junctioned with Highway 16, then with Highway 7 about two kilometers on the outskirts of the city. King finally realized with a dreadful start that the convoy had gotten off Route Blue during the night and was now heading deeper and deeper into enemy-held territory.

He called a halt while he and First Sergeant Dowdy consulted maps and their GPS. They decided the main convoy route lay to the west of their current position. The only road back was the way they had just come. They would have to retrace their route through An Nasiriyah.

The drivers of the 507's "Lost Convoy" knew they were in a world of deep fecal matter. Could they brazen a path through the city once more and pick up Route Blue on the other side? Or would this morning's chain of unfortunate events finally catch up with them?

Word passed in tense monosyllables from truck to truck: "Lock and load. Be vigilant."

The convoy reentered the junkpile of drab mud buildings at 0700 hours. This time, there were no smiles and friendly hand waves. Corporal Luten checked his machine gun and murmured a brief prayer.

An Nasiriyah stirred and cleared its throat. Sporadic small arms fire broke out from the roofs of buildings and from alleyways. A driver with a working radio gabbled indignantly into his mike: "They're *shooting* at us!"

Captain King ordered the column to increase speed—and to hell with whoever or whatever got in the way. Frightened pale, his driver Nace slumped low behind the hummer's wheel and jammed the gas pedal to the floor. King unlimbered his M-16 and began pot shooting at armed figures darting furtively about. The streets turned into a gauntlet of terror. The Rangers' plight when they got lost in Mogadishu in 1993 came to mind.

Muzzles winked from shadows. RPGs with their wobbling, smoke-hissing flights streaked at the speeding Army trucks. Bullets striking vehicles sounded like hailstones on tin barn roofs. Some of the assailants were uniformed; many others wore traditional head wraps and long dirty robes.

Preoccupied with the fight, Captain King failed to notice when his driver barreled right past where the convoy should have hooked a right onto Highway 8 to get out of town. Sergeant Dowdy in the trail vehicle watched with dismay as his hummer flashed past the junction.

"You missed the turn!" he shouted into his mike.

They had to find a place in the narrow streets wide enough for the monstrous trucks and trailers to whip a U-turn. Spacing between the vehicles widened because of their different sizes and acceleration rates. The ferocity of hostile fire increased.

The tractor-trailer driven by Private Brandon Sloan and Sergeant Don Walters bit the dust with its engine popping and a loud flapping of its bullet-punctured tires. It careened crazily off the road and ended up teetering precariously at the lip of a half-dried-up canal. Bullets sputtered like firecrackers from buildings on the other side of the canal and from a line of storefronts on the street.

Sloan tumbled out on the ground behind one of the truck's huge tires and squeezed rounds back at ambushers with his M-16. Sergeant Walters combat-rolled into the canal. The last Sloan heard from him, he was across the canal and shooting furiously while running toward the enemy.

Three kilometers down the road, Captain King found a place wide enough for the convoy to turn around. Sergeant Bugg and Specialist Anguiano of the 3rd Forward Support Battalion abandoned their ten-ton wrecker and towed supply truck when they got stuck in soft sand. They scrambled into the Humvee occupied by First Sergeant Dowdy and his driver, Private First Class Lori Piestewa. They took the backseat, each next to a window from which he could shoot. Private First Class Jessica Lynch sat between them.

The convoy split into three separate elements during the turn and roared north again, back toward the city and that vital T-junction with Highway 8 that would lead it out of the miles-long death trap that threatened to enclose and destroy it.

PFC Patrick Miller and Sergeant James Riley in their wrecker were the first to reach Sloan and Walter's out-of-action tractor-trailer. Sloan was still putting up a fight. In what was to be one of many selfless acts of courage, Miller braked the wrecker under fire to make a combat pickup of the truck's stranded occupant. Sloan dived over Riley into the cab.

"Where's Walters?" Miller yelled.

"He's . . . he's dead."

Captain King's hummer whipped back into the lead. With him in Group One were two other vehicles, both five-ton tractor-trailers. Sergeant Joel Petrick and Specialist Nick Peterson crewed one. Specialist Timothy Johnson and Sergeant Tony Pierce were in the other. The three vehicles exploded through a roadblock of debris—old sofas, a pickup truck body, burning tires—and sent trash and would-be ambushers flying. Under heavy fire, Group One skidded a turn onto Highway 8 and poured on the gas, racing south out of town and out of the kill zone.

A quarter-mile behind roared Group Two with five vehicles: three five-ton tractor-trailers, a HMMWV pulling a trailer, and a fuel truck. Specialist Jun Zhang and Sergeant Curtis Campbell took the lead in their truck, followed by PFC Marcus Dubois and Corporal Luten in theirs. In third place came the five-ton crewed by Sergeant Matthew Rose and Corporal Francis Carista. CWO Nash and Sergeant Tarik Jackson had the hummer. The fuel truck with PFC Adam Elliot and Specialist James Grubb brought up the rear. Small arms fire and RPGs blistered them from all sides.

Corporal Luten pounded off a few rounds with his mounted .50-cal machine gun before it jammed. Desert sand was hard on weapons. Luten slapped the gun in frustration and, praying a little in the wildly swerving cab, reached for his M-16. Hostile lead drilled sparking holes and furrows in the truck's hood and doors.

He screamed in agony when a round shattered his knee cap, splattering the inside of the cab with blood and bone chips.

"Luten!" Dubois shouted.

"Drive this thing! Drive it!"

Directly ahead of them, a ball of RPG fire enveloped the lead fivetonner driven by Zhang and Campbell. The dying truck jackknifed off the road and swerved toward a drainage ditch. Dubois slammed on his brakes, stopping alongside the other truck for a combat pickup.

Critically wounded, Luten shouldn't have been able to walk. Nonetheless, dragging his bad leg, he jumped out and braved a rain of bullets to help the stunned Zhang into the blood-bathed cab with him. Nash and Jackson, who had moved into third place, pulled over to pick up Campbell. Campbell went down hard as he sprinted to the hummer, his legs shot out from underneath him. He got up and piled into the Humvee's backseat with Jackson, who had sustained multiple small arms and shrapnel wounds.

The four surviving vehicles sped toward Highway 8.

Smoke poured from the engine of the tractor-trailer driven by Sergeant Rose. His rearview mirror showed one tire flat, shot out. Rubber flapped and smoked. He began praying that he'd live, that he'd see his children again, that the truck would hold out long enough to get them out of this mess. Carista joined in the prayer as he blazed away with his M-16.

Luten, Dubois, and Zhang were now in the lead, followed by Chief Nash's hummer. Machine gun tracers streaming from an open alley hammered the Humvee, causing the engine to explode and leaving it stalled and smoking on the road. Luten and the men with him might have made it safely to Highway 8—except they couldn't leave their comrades to fight against such overwhelming odds.

Dubois pulled a hazardous U-turn, clipping the corner off a building, and gunned the truck back to where Nash, Campbell, and Jackson had gone prone behind their little truck and were putting up a valiant fight. Dubois jacked the tractor-trailer across the road against the direction of heaviest incoming. He and his two passengers jumped out and joined the fray.

Minutes later, the fuel truck and Sergeant Rose's tractor-trailer filled in the defensive perimeter. The wagons were circled. The addition of Rose, Carista, Elliott, and Grubb increased the stronghold's number to ten soldiers, five of whom were badly wounded. They prepared for a last-ditch stand, the Alamo.

In the meantime, Group Three had had difficulty with the U-turn due to the large size of its vehicles and because all were dragging trailers. That left this element a considerable distance behind Group Two and strung the six trucks out for more than a quarter-mile along the road. The Iraqis took advantage of its plight and heaped burning trash, cars, even a tank across the road in an effort to halt the trucks. Ambushers hammered the hapless lost convoy with small arms, and machine gun fire and rockets.

Specialist Edgar Hernandez and Specialist Shoshana Johnson took the lead with their five-ton tractor-trailer. First Sergeant Dowdy's HMMWV followed, driven by PFC Lori Piestewa with Anguiano, Buggs, and Lynch in the backseat. Next came a five-ton wrecker with PFC Patrick Miller, Private Brandon Sloan and Sergeant James Riley. Specialist Joe Hudson and Chief Warrant Officer Johnny Mata drove a heavy expanded mobility tactical truck (HEMTT) wrecker towing a five-ton tractor-trailer. Finally PFC Howard Johnson and Private Ruben Estrella-Soto came in another tractor-trailer; behind them were Specialist Jamaal Addison and Specialist James Kiehl, both in a five-ton truck pulling a trailer.

Strung out along the road as they were, each vehicle was essentially on its own. Fate and enemy action contrived to pick off these trucks one by one, as a pack of predators might bring down stragglers from a herd. Not one of them made it as far as where Group Two was fighting desperately for its survival.

Under heavy fire, the tractor-trailer crewed by Hernandez and Shoshana Johnson ended up in a ditch when it veered sharply to the right to avoid crashing into an Iraqi truck blocking the road. Approaching next at full speed under the same withering fire, PFC Piestewa also lost control and rammed her hummer into the rear of the stalled tractor-trailer. Hostile fire from both sides of the gauntlet blazed into the wreckage. Dowdy, Buggs, and Anguiano were killed either by the crash or enemy bullets. Piestewa and Lynch survived and were later captured; Piestewa died in captivity.

Miller, Riley, and Sloan's wrecker, disabled by fire, coasted to within several yards of the other smoldering vehicles before it went up in a screen of boiling smoke. Machine gun bullets raked out the windshield and killed Sloan.

Sergeant Riley's M-16 malfunctioned, probably because of sand. He dashed to the twisted hummer to secure a replacement weapon. The inside of the utility truck was a bloody mess, all five bodies twisted around one another, everyone apparently dead or unconscious.

While Riley was searching frantically for a weapon, Miller charged an enemy mortar pit, rifle chattering. He may have killed as many as nine Iraqis before he ran out of ammo and had to surrender.

Three soldiers were still on their feet among the ruins—Sergeant Riley, Shoshana Johnson, and Edgar Hernandez. Hernandez and Johnson were wounded, and Riley was still unarmed. Realizing that further resistance was tantamount to suicide, Riley surrendered himself and his two subordinates to the enemy.

Three vehicles remained of Group Three. But not for long. All met similar fates shortly after they executed U-turns to return to the Highway 8 junction.

Chief Warrant Officer Mata took rounds through his chest and was bunched in the gory corner of his HEMTT wrecker cab, dead, by the time ambushers stopped the truck and took driver Hudson prisoner. Addison and Kiehl died in a hail of rifle fire after their truck hit the gun barrel of an Iraqi tank blockading the road; rocket explosions killed Howard Johnson and Estrella-Sota.

These deaths brought the lost convoy to a standstill—with the exception of Captain King's Group One. After breaking out of An Nasiriyah, King and the soldiers in the two trucks with him ran into a U.S. Marine tank battalion, Task Force Tarawa, ten kilometers south of the city on Highway 8. After King hurriedly briefed the tank commander on the situation, the Marines headed north in a cloud of dust.

. . .

Back at the Alamo, the ten survivors of Group Two treated one another's wounds inside their ring of stalled trucks and held off Iraqi advances in a temporary stalemate. Corporal Luten, field dressing drawn around his knee to stop the bleeding, prayed intermittently and waited for the end to come while keeping his rifle ready and his eyes peeled for enemy tricks. He had no idea what had happened to the rest of the convoy. All he knew was that the standoff here could have only one outcome—the ten of them either dead or captured.

Time and again that day, the soldiers of the ill-fated 507th had risked their lives in attempts to save their brothers-and-sisters-in-arms. Now, there was only one place to turn.

Thy will be done . . .

Suddenly, to the astonishment of the small band of defenders, hostile fire slackened. Luten spotted enemy fighters running away across a field beyond the canal. He glanced up the road and hardly dared believe his own eyes. Rushing toward their makeshift truck fortress rumbled a long enfilade of tanks, *American* tanks, their turret guns blazing steel at enemy positions. The most wondrous sight he had ever seen! God had answered his prayers.

Corporal Luten's knee was seriously infected. Doctors at Walter Reed Army Medical Center in Washington, D.C., told him they thought they might have to amputate his leg. Even if they didn't, they warned, chances were he would never walk again.

Luten continued to pray and place his faith in God. Doctors were amazed at what could only be his miraculous recovery. The infection simply went away. He began to walk again without assistance.

Of the thirty-three soldiers of the 507th who made a wrong turn into An Nasiriyah that March morning, eleven were killed: Private Brandon Sloan; PFC Howard Johnson III; Specialist Jamaal Addison; Specialist James Kiehl; Sergeant Donald Walters; PFC Lori Piestewa; 1SG Robert Dowdy; CWO Johnny Mata; Private Ruben Estrella-Soto; Sergeant George Buggs; and PFC Edward Anguiano.

Captain King and the soldiers with him reached Task Force Tarawa in safety. Marines rescued Group Two's ten soldiers shortly thereafter. Special Operations soldiers recovered the five living members of the 507th who had been captured along the road in An Nasiriyah (Lynch, Miller, Riley, Shoshana Johnson, and Hernandez), and recovered Piestewa's body. Lynch was the first U.S. prisoner of war to be rescued from behind enemy lines since World War II, Shoshana Johnson the second.

MARINE PRIVATE FIRST CLASS EDGAR SHEPARD,
World War II, 1942

U.S. Marines on Guadalcanal were tasked with the mission of defending the island and its crucial airstrip, Henderson Field, against the Japanese.

Edgar Shepard and Russell Whittlesey, both PFCs, were best buddies. Shortly after dusk settled on a day in September 1942 following the Marine raid on Toranboca, their platoon was ordered to move into the jungle in front of Bloody Ridge and set up observation near a lagoon the Japanese had to ford in order to attack the airfield.

As scouts, Shepard and Whittlesey manned an observation post forward of the Marines' defensive line, in a patch of jungle next to the shallow lagoon. They crouched in a night as black as Tojo's heart. Everything was quiet until around 9 P.M.

Hearts pounding, the two young Marines listened intently to the swirl of stagnant water around stealthy legs as Japanese troops waded the lagoon on their way to Henderson Field. Before they could sneak back to report the movement, a leatherneck on the platoon's MLR opened up with a machine gun. The Japanese charged. Outnumbered five to one, the Marine platoon battled savagely hand to hand to repulse the assault.

The two scouts found themselves isolated in the midst of chaos—blaring bugles, rifle fire blossoming flames of death, bursting grenades, screaming men . . . Flitting, sinister shadows kept popping up everywhere.

Shepard discharged his carbine at a form splashing out of the bog. It vanished. At the same instant, from another quarter, a Nip drilled him through the arm. The bullet passed through his lungs and out the other arm. The force of the blow slung his weapon into the lagoon and slammed him onto his back.

He couldn't get up. His breath came in liquid-sounding gasps. Panic overtook him as he realized he had a sucking chest wound, usually fatal unless promptly treated. Whittlesey stood astraddle his fallen friend, carbine blazing as he fought off shadowy demons.

"I'm done for, Russ," Shepard gasped. "Leave me. Save yourself."

"Go to hell, Shep. I ain't leaving you here, buddy."

A Jap bullet knocked Whittlesey's carbine from his hands, rendering it useless other than as a club. That left the two Marines armed only with KA-BAR knives. Whittlesey dragged Shepard into thick bushes. There, he tore his own shirt into pressure bandages to stanch the flow of blood from his friend's wounds while the Japanese ran about shouting *"Banzai!"*

"Russ, you can still get away—"

"Hush! You want the Nips to hear us?"

After a while, things quieted into a stalemate. The Marine platoon had held out, but it was probably withdrawing back to Bloody Ridge by now. The skipper undoubtedly assumed his scouts at the observation/listening post (OP/LP) had been overrun and killed.

Night insects burred, tree frogs chirruped, and from somewhere off in the jungle a drowsy bird sounded an inquiry. Water in the lagoon nibbled at the edges of the jungle, disturbed by the passage of Japanese in two-toed boots.

"Shep, do you think you can walk if I help?" Whittlesey whispered.

The only hope they had was to exfiltrate the Japanese to reach their own lines. Shepard's arms were shattered, and he could hardly breathe. He started to protest that he would only hold up the escape. Alone,

Whittlesey had a chance. His chances diminished considerably if he was half-carrying, half-dragging a wounded man.

"I said I ain't leaving you, Shep. Are you ready?"

"The longest journey," Shepard managed, "begins with the first step . . ."

Whittlesey heaved Shepard to his feet. They listened for enemy noise nearby. Then, with the wounded Marine leaning on him, Whittlesey picked his way back through the jungle, hunkering in place whenever they saw a shadowy figure.

They came to a narrow trail that provided quieter and more rapid transit. Together as one, they followed it toward friendly lines. Refuge couldn't be far away.

Just when they thought they might make it after all, hostile forms suddenly blocked the way. Faint moonlight filtered through the open jungle canopy and glinted off Jap pith helmets.

Both sides, surprised, hesitated for a heartbeat. Then the three Japs yelled something and charged, bayoneted rifles stabbing. Whittlesey dropped Shepard to the ground and shouted back at them. He whipped out his KA-BAR and feinted to the right to draw the patrol away from Shepard.

Sprawled helplessly on the jungle trail, Shepard could do nothing other than watch in horror as grunting shadows parried and thrust at one another. He could barely discern his friend from foe in the strange desperate drama playing itself out almost within his reach. It may have all been over in seconds, but to Shepard it seemed hours.

Whittlesey eliminated the first two Japs by ripping out their guts with his big-bladed knife. As they fell to the ground, writhing and screaming in agony, the third Japanese plunged his bayonet into Whittlesey's back. Whittlesey grunted and staggered back a step before he wheeled to confront his remaining foe.

This Japanese soldier had witnessed his two comrades cut down by this tall devil and he had had enough. He turned and fled into the jungle.

Staggering from his wounds, the savage figure in the Marine helmet and bare chest sank to his knees next to his friend.

"Oh, Russ!" Shepard cried. "Why didn't you go when you had the chance?"

Whittlesey lay down on his back on the night trail. He smiled and gripped Shepard's hand. His face in the wan moonlight looked at peace as he began to hum his favorite old hymn, "I'm Getting Tired so I Can Sleep."

He breathed deeply once, and said, "Well, Shep. I guess this is where I came in."

He closed his eyes, this big, loyal man who refused to leave behind his best friend, even if it cost him his own life. Then he stopped breathing and drifted into eternal sleep.

PFC Edgar Shepard crawled on without the use of his arms until some miracle of God, he said, helped him reach Marine lines.

8

DOUBT

O thou of little faith, wherefore did'st thou doubt?

—MATTHEW 14:31

The principle that underlies the concept of God in the Christian world is that He has absolute power in the universe and therefore absolute control. Sometimes it seems God stands on the sidelines of human suffering and makes capricious judgments in deciding whom He will pull from which conflagration and whom He will leave to his fate. Nearly every soldier spared from the bomb or bullet credits God for his survival. But he also wonders why the buddy on the left was allowed to die, while the buddy on the right was spared. Does God really listen? Does God truly intercede?

A Vietnam veteran regularly visited the Vietnam War Memorial in Washington, D.C. "Sir," someone asked him, "how long have you been coming to the Wall to pray?"

"For about thirty years."

"That's amazing. What do you pray for?"

"I pray for peace between Christians, Jews, and Muslims. I pray for all the hatred to stop. I pray for all our children to grow up in safety and friendship."

"How do you feel after doing this for thirty years?"

"Like I'm talking to an [*expletive*] wall."

Although it is often pointed out that the battlefield allows few atheists, doubt invades combat as it does ordinary life. But doubts or not, rounds cracking over a soldier's head usually prompt him at least to consider the presence of God and his own human mortality.

Army Sergeant Jeremy Lussi served with the 10th Mountain Division in Afghanistan at the beginning of the War on Terror. During one action, several members of his outfit were wounded, and one was killed. In a letter home, he wrote, "I had a long talk with a buddy [about] how some guys don't and won't believe in God [even] after [all that has] happened."

ARMY PRIVATE JAMES WALSH,
Korea, 1953

Is it true you were going to be a priest?" a soldier asked Private James
Walsh.

Walsh looked at him. "Does it make any difference now?"

He crouched in his trench with a man he knew only as Clouse and
another guy, waiting for the command to attack. His hands trembled.
His mouth felt like someone had stuffed a raw boll of cotton in it. He
was scared. Damned right he was. Only a fool or a madman wouldn't
be. The chaplain was probably scared, too, and he wasn't even charging
the hill.

But when the time came to cross the line of departure (LD), Walsh
knew he would be ready, as always. Not like some guys who went up
a hill once or twice and then froze up. What was that one guy's name?
Smith? Jones? Something simple and American like that.

They had been waiting one morning. A morning just like this, clear
and crisp with the sun still behind the hills, purple shadows in the
valleys. Hiding in his hole, Smith or Jones, whatever, flew into about
a jillion pieces. He lost control of his nerves, then his bowels, finally
his senses. He curled up in the bottom of his hole as if in his mama's
womb, and whimpered and sobbed while he waited for the end of the
world. He wouldn't move out of it no matter how First Sergeant Shoemaker cursed him and threatened him and kicked him in the butt.

Afterward, after the hill, they found him still in his hole, curled up
like a fetus. Only he wasn't whimpering and sobbing anymore. He was
dead. A hunk of shrapnel from an exploding shell had found him. No
matter what you did or didn't do, God was going to come for you when
it was your time to go.

It was madness. Everybody knew it was madness. Still no one talked
much about the end of the war—and about how the DMZ between

North and South Korea was supposed to stop it. It was sheer madnesss to fight and kill for hilltops without end while "peace talks" continued. It was madness that the one thing an infantryman cared about when he crossed the LD, cared about more than anything else, was fire support. Artillery, airplanes, napalm . . . Throw fire and brimstone itself at the enemy if need be. Burn 'em, blow 'em up, shred 'em, send their shriveled-up little commie souls to the everlasting pits of Hell.

Utter madness.

Walsh was an ammunition bearer for the machine gun section. A big, young, strong Irishman. While each bearer normally lugged two cans of .30-caliber when his outfit kicked off, in addition to his pack and carbine, Walsh strapped *four* cans to his packboard and tucked *two more* under one arm. That left a hand free for his weapon. Just because he was a pack mule didn't exempt him from fighting when they went up the enemy's hill on the other side of this one and across a ravine.

He took pride in being the best ammo bearer in his section. First Sergeant Shoemaker, "Shoe," called him the "First Idiot Ammo Bearer."

Shoe came by now. The Top Sergeant was relentless. The old rooster cut slack for nobody. Ranting like always as he hopped from squad to squad, his mean little prune face was about to bust some veins as he declared his "shitbirds" to be lazy with bad breath and questionable parentage. He goaded them to check weapons and spare parts, making sure everybody had water and rations and ammo and grenades for when the push came.

"Whattaya think, ladies—there's gonna be room service up on that hill? When yens are out there, spread out and keep down, ya hear? Don't be no heroes, 'cause you can't tell no dead hero from dead chickenshit. You get drilled, it means somebody has to tote your fat ass back down the hill. If yens get shot, it's 'cause you been stupid."

Ranting. A tough old bird. Mean to the core.

"Any of yens get kilt out there, I ain't speaking to your sorry ass again."

Somewhere behind the trenches, on the downfield military crest of some other hill, a battery of 155 howitzers worked over the Red Chinese defenses, prepping them for the attack. Artillery rounds flying overhead sounded like giants hurling freight train cars through the air. They exploded on the enemy in thunderous crescendos of sound that clapped and clapped and clapped, echoing from hill to hill to hill and down valleys.

The hill the Chinks occupied rose high above all the others, and had been worked over several times. It should have been green this time of year, maybe even had a few young trees on its slopes that weren't big enough for villagers to cut as firewood. Instead, it was all gouged and pockmarked and scarred and red with inflammation and putrefaction.

Walsh wondered why anyone would want that hill enough to fight and die for it. There were enough hilltops to go around. Everybody could have his own and lift a beer to all the others.

"Nothing can live through that kind of pounding," Clouse said. Clouse was new to the hill game.

"They're still there," Walsh said. He knew that a lot of good men, and perhaps some not so good, were going to die before lunch.

Walsh remembered the first time he'd seen dead GIs, a sight he'd found strangely more surprising than sorrowful. He and other replacements had been trucked forward from the repo depot. The dead, a half dozen of them, were all neatly arranged and laid out side by side as though they were in a funeral parlor. Bodies once filled with vigor and life were wax dummies with pale faces and hands, blood spots staining their fatigues.

A lone rifleman guarded the dead. He knelt over them on one knee. Top Sergeant Shoemaker stood nearby. Helmet in hand, he shook his bare head sadly. Tears glinted in the old rooster's eyes. He looked up, suddenly aware of being observed. His fierce little eyes locked on the replacements in their clean new uniforms.

"What the hell is you boots looking at?" he snarled and stomped off.

A vague fear stirred in Walsh's heart. He suddenly felt mortal, fragile, his first recognition that life in combat might be very brief. He bowed his head and said a prayer for the souls of the departed, asking God to forgive them and take them in. That was when he was still thinking about becoming a Catholic priest. He had quit the seminary against his parents' wishes in order to enlist in the Army and do his patriotic duty.

He had seen many corpses since then, either lined up side by side for transport to the rear, or strewn all over the countryside.

The howitzers ceased firing, leaving sudden and startling silence. Clouse stared at Walsh. Walsh stared at Clouse. Their faces turned pale. Clouse's eyes shifted first. He pointed at the sky.

"It won't be long now," he predicted.

A trio of F-84s sliced down like sharp knives through the haze of smoke left shrouding the hill by the 155s. The top of the hill erupted as though every high explosive shell in the entire Eighth Army had landed on it simultaneously, resonating like deep thunder in ear-shocking waves.

Walsh and Clouse threw themselves on top of each other in the bottom of the gun pit to escape the concussion. When they looked up again, the F-84s had turned the enemy's terrain into a scorched charnel field trapped in an aura of crimson glow. The jets wagged wings as they flew off, their pilots pleased with themselves.

Shoe was out of his hole and scuttling down the line. "Listen up, shitbirds," he scolded.

That must mean the command to attack had been issued.

Walsh looked at his rough and begrimed hands. Less than a year ago they had been folded in seminary chapel prayer. Now, they pulled a trigger and turned knobs on a machine gun to traverse and search for communists to kill. His transformation from seminarian to soldier had occurred in stages, changing him from the godly to the deadly.

He doubted he would ever return to studying for the priesthood. War had changed him forever.

"All right, shitbirds! Get ready to move out!"

ARMY PRIVATE WALTER BROMWICH,
World War I, 1918

Rain fell steadily. It had been falling like that since late the day before. The sun had not seemed to rise this morning, not for the living, much less for the dead whose twisted corpses littered No Man's Land between opposing trench lines. In Private Walt Bromwich's state of mind, the lowest it had ever been, he thought the sun might never rise again.

Thousands like him on both sides hunkered down like rats in jagged trenches and took refuge from the weather in muddy bunkers gouged from the walls. The colonels and generals would probably not call for an action today. Soldiers—American and Hun alike—were too weary, their spirits drubbed by the incessant rain.

The war was one of attrition, not of huge strategies rendering glorious victories and devastating defeats. Each day was more of the same—shoot and be shot. Who was winning at any given time was anyone's guess.

Today, on such a dreary, miserable morning, it seemed no one wanted to die. Only the occasional sniper carried on the war with a desultory rifle shot, the general depression of the troops causing no response.

Private Bromwich was writing a letter home to his pastor in Pennsylvania. He used the stub of a thick lead pencil and a lined pad of paper that had been in his pack too long and showed it. The paper was damp and rotting, and he had to write carefully to prevent shredding it. He wrote with the pad on his knees, and his knees drawn up into the shelter of his shallow bunker. Runoff rain made a transparent curtain across the bunker's entrance. A little river of mud formed by water, blood, urine, feces, and other wastes oozed along the deep trough of the trench.

Directly across from him, a sentry on lookout stood on a parapet carved into the forward wall. He had turned his back to the wall and was facing Bromwich, holding his poncho away from his body so he could urinate into the trench. He seemed to have no eyes beneath his helmet because of the gray slant of rain and the way shadows pooled to make black empty holes of his sockets.

Dear Reverent, Bromwich began. *Here I sit in my little home on the side of the hill thinking of the little church back home.*

How did a man explain to his pastor about his doubts in an atmosphere so incomprehensibly horrible as war? He shifted his discomfort from one position to another. His boots and leggings felt heavy and soggy with mud. Behind him, his Springfield leaned against the wall of the bunker within easy reach, a balloon stretched over its muzzle to keep out water and mud.

It's a queer thing I can't explain, he went on, *that ever since I volunteered I've felt like a cog in a huge wheel. The cog may get smashed up, but the machine goes on, and I know that I share in the progress of that machine whether I live or die.*

He hesitated, then added with a quick, gritty scratch of his pencil, *and I can't feel God is in it.*

There. He had said it. Would the "Reverent" understand?

How can there be fairness in one man being maimed for life, suffering agonies, another killed instantaneously, while I get out of it safe? Does God really love us individually or does He love His purpose more? Or is it better to believe He makes the innocent suffer for the guilty and that things will be squared up some day when those who have escaped suffering here will suffer, or those who have suffered here will escape suffering? Sounds rather calculating, doesn't it, and not a bit like the love of a Father?

Thunder rolled across the scowling sky, startling the young private. His eyes darted upward. This might not be the time to harbor spiritual doubts.

What I would like to believe is that God is in this war, not as a spectator, but backing up everything that is good in us.

The lookout on the parapet finished urinating. Water drained from the edges of his helmet. He watched Bromwich writing his letter.

"Bromwich? Your sweetheart?"

Bromwich hesitated. "My pastor. Back home."

The sentry considered that. "Have him pray for all of us," he said.

That wasn't the way God worked. *He won't work any miracles for us because that would be helping us do the work He's given us to do on our own.*

"Bromwich?"

"Yeah?"

"Do you think praying helps?"

I don't know whether God goes forth with armies but I do know that He is in lots of our men or they would not do what they do.

"Bromwich? Do you think praying helps?"

A sergeant slogged by carrying his gas mask and rifle. "We have reports of mustard gas," he said. "Keep your masks handy."

The private closed out his letter with, *Remember me to all.* He carefully folded it for when the next time someone went to the rear with outgoing mail. The sentry was still watching Bromwich, his shoulders hunched up in his poncho and around his neck and helmet. He looked dejected, smaller than life as he waited for Bromwich to answer his question.

Bromwich looked around—mud and blood, dysentery and trench foot, hunger and fear, misery and loneliness and homesickness, the dead and the not-yet-dead. He stuffed his letter and pad of paper back into his pack and reached for his rifle and gas mask to rejoin the war.

"Yeah, prayer helps," he said. "It certainly can't hurt anything."

MARINE LANCE CORPORAL PAUL STEPPE,
Korea, 1951

War brings out both the best and the worst in men. Marine Lance Corporal Paul Steppe was reluctant to shoot his first man. The Chink was coming at him, stampeding up the hill with a horde of other guys in quilted uniforms and pith helmets, all of them yelling their lungs out and firing their weapons. Steppe drew a bead on his target. He hesitated.

It's either him or me.

It was *him.*

Killing was easier after the first one. Still, afterward, came the demons. Even chaplains, as Steppe soon learned, wrestled with them.

Christmas Eve of 1951 was white, bitterly cold, and miserable. The North Koreans launched a counterattack against Marine lines. Steppe heard a live grenade land in his trench with him. He dived for his bunker. Too late. A searing strobe of light and a crash of thunder shredded the night.

When he regained consciousness, some South Korean civilian laborers attached to his company had him on a stretcher and were preparing to carry him to the battalion aid station in the rear. He must have been out cold for some time; the enemy probe had been beaten back and, Steppe wryly observed, it was again a silent night, holy night.

The South Koreans lifted him out of the trench and started down the snow-covered slope of the hill toward the base and the aid tent. It was tough going both for bearers and the wounded Marine. Snow in drifts reached the Koreans' thighs in places and overlay a slippery base of ice. They kept losing their footing. Once they dumped Steppe in a drift and had to dig him out to get him back on the litter.

They finally arrived at the battalion aid station, a large general-purpose tent erected among others in a valley sheltered from the north wind. Medics wrapped Steppe in blankets and placed him near the wood-burning stove. Drowsy while he waited for treatment, he was dozing off when the battalion chaplain came by. He touched the Marine's shoulder. Steppe awoke in a cloud of strong alcohol odor.

"Are you comfortable, son?" the chaplain slurred, barely able to form coherent words. "Are you warm? Do you want anything?"

He swayed back and forth next to Steppe's cot. His hands were full of small whiskey miniatures of the type served on airlines. A number of the little bottles had obviously bit the dust already.

"Son, would you like a miniature?"

"No, thanks, Padre."

"I'll pray for you."

His features were drawn and worn with bags underneath his eyes, his nose inflamed and his face florid. He looked like a man too beaten by evil and depravity to stand up to it without an aid. He bowed his head to pray, weaving on his feet, eyes moist and pained.

Steppe felt *he* should be praying for the chaplain.

ARMY CAPTAIN LARRY NAUGHTON,
Vietnam, 1967

Larry Naughton attended seminary before he went to Vietnam, thinking he wanted to be a priest. "Thank God you were born into a Catholic family," a nun once exclaimed over him when he was in high school. "Now you're sure to go to Heaven."

As a combat commander in Vietnam, however, he thought little about God. God wasn't in this war, not for him. If he made it out of a scrape, the appropriate response was, *Oops, got out of that one.* If a time came when he didn't make it . . . Well, if such a place as Heaven truly existed, he figured he wasn't going to make the cut.

By 1967, he had had command time of two platoons and a company. He volunteered to take over leadership of an elite "Tiger Force" reconnaissance element of the 101st Airborne Division—about forty soldiers. Operating in I Corps, south of the DMZ around Dak To, Captain Naughton and his Tiger Force went out snooping and pooping in Indian Country for days at a time searching for bad guys and pinpointing them for action. This close to the DMZ, the enemy mostly consisted of trained NVA with a smattering of local VC guerrillas.

Battalion S-1 learned of an enemy command post using a village as cover. Gunships and artillery prepped the village prior to ground assault. Villagers and enemy combatants both scattered. It wasn't the optimum situation; Naughton preferred sweeping in by surprise and catching the gooks with their pants down, sending as many as possible to the Big Buddha in the sky or wherever their souls went.

A few grass-thatched huts still burned, black chimneys of smoke twisting and turning in the calm morning air, when Naughton's Tigers in Huey helicopters set down in a maze of rice paddies nearby. The paddies were almost dry this time of year. Scrub jungle and mangrove swamps fringed the rice fields. A narrow dirt road led through the settlement and toward a muddy brown river. Beyond the river rose a series of low, forested hills.

Alert and cautious, Naughton's boonie rats traveled in three columns along the road toward the river. The road ran straight over a little rise before sloping down to the stream. The commander and his command post, consisting of two radio telephone operators (RTOs) and a medic, walked the middle of the column between the point element and rear guard. Point leader, a staff sergeant, radioed back that he saw neither squat nor signs of squat.

"Keep on your toes," Naughton cautioned. "They're somewhere."

"Yeah. It's quiet. Too quiet," the staff sergeant replied in mimicry of Clark Gable or Van Heflin in some old African safari movie.

Captain Naughton rolled his eyes.

The long column of army green topped the rise and looked down upon the river. Naughton paused to scan the low surrounding jungle. It *was* awfully damned quiet.

Things could go all to crap suddenly and without warning in a war without front lines and where contesting parties shared the terrain and played games of deadly hide-and-seek. One moment you could be diddy-bopping along, minding your own business, the next you were the lightning rod of a firestorm.

From thick undergrowth on the opposite side of the river, less than two hundred meters away, a machine gun opened up on the paratroopers with a long and loud staccato burst. Bullets followed up the road, pluming dirt and chewing ground. The staff sergeant leading point pirouetted, shouting at his men to take cover. Like they needed encouragement. Grunts dived for the underbrush.

The sergeant failed to make it. The machine gun cut him down in a mist of blood. Remarkably, he was still alive and conscious. He started to crawl off the kill zone, but his legs were paralyzed and his progress resembled that of an insect tethered by a pin through his back. The machine gun blistered the road all around him, then moved off to flail the jungle, the enemy gunner apparently assuming this guy was done for.

Captain Naughton quickly assessed the situation from behind a vine-covered wall enclosing an ancient cemetery. His RTOs had disappeared into the shrubbery. His medic dropped on his belly next to the wall and froze there. The kid was about nineteen or twenty; this was his first time under fire.

"Get that man off the road!" Naughton yelled at him.

The poor medic appeared petrified with fear, unable to move. Fuming and impatient, Naughton cast aside his M-16 and snatched up the medic by the nape of his neck and his web gear. He ran out onto the road with him, the kid's arms and legs dangling or dragging and, under fire all the way, rushed him to the fallen element leader and deposited him there.

"Now, take care of him."

Unarmed, the CO took a knee and shouted for his men to provide suppressing fire. GIs launched a mad minute of shooting at everything on the far bank. Rollers of lead shredded undergrowth, liberating whirlwind clouds of clipped leaves and branches.

The enemy machine gun continued to fire. Rounds ricocheted all around Naughton, the medic, and the downed sergeant, slashing into trees and gouging at the earth. The medic recovered from his initial terror and jabbed a syringe full of morphine into the sergeant's arm. A bullet smacked his first aid bag with such impact that it knocked him off his knees onto his back.

"Sir, let's move him," the medic finally suggested when he was up again and checking the sergeant's wounds with newfound composure.

"Good man."

They dragged the element leader to safety. Somehow, all three survived the hail of machine gun fire.

A Phantom jet with the cool call sign of *Flash Gordon* burned out the machine gun nest with napalm. Captain Naughton took a deep breath after it was all over, and that was when he noticed how near he had come to losing his life.

A canteen on his belt had a bullet hole through it, as did his soft cap. Other bullets had sliced through the shoulder strop of his web gear and knocked a heel off his boot. Somehow, he came away unscathed, in spite of rounds zapping all round him and mangling his gear. Not even a scratch. Reflecting on it, he knew that this time it was more than another *Oops, got out of that one.*

Either the gook on the other side of the river was the world's worst shot—or somebody was looking out for him. God must be saving him for some higher purpose.

Captain Larry Naughton returned to Oklahoma after the war, rededicated his life to Christ, and started a music ministry.

ARMY PRIVATE ARTHUR "DUTCH" SCHULTZ,
World War II, 1944

In early 1944, as the troop buildup continued in Britain for the forthcoming invasion of Fortress Europa, paratroopers like twenty-one-year-old Private Arthur "Dutch" Schultz, 82nd Airborne Division, attended confession as often as possible since they had no idea when they would be called upon to go into battle. Roman Catholic doctrine offered a fairly straightforward proposition in this matter: a man who died in a state of grace with sins forgiven and absolution offered by a priest went to Heaven; a man who died out of grace went to Hell.

Private Schultz sometimes wondered if he was being hypocritical in making deals with God and the Virgin. After all, he openly acknowledged, he would probably return to sinning if he made it out of the war alive. Nonetheless, guilt and hypocrisy failed to deter him from attending Mass regularly. After all, it was commonly asserted that many soldiers got religious before a pending action.

Father Matthew Connelly set up for Mass wherever he could—in a mess tent, on the parade field with a folding table, on the hood of a jeep. Since Schultz had yet to see combat, a condition that made him self-conscious with veterans who had, he felt somewhat uncomfortable among men who had legitimately developed churchgoing habits because of their encounters with violent death.

Veterans came to Mass in their combat fatigues. Hard men who had witnessed hard things. They bowed their heads in prayer with the private. Like many of the men of the 82nd, Father Connelly had also seen his share of combat, having administered last rites under fire to the dying and to the severely wounded and traumatized. Thus combat-hardened, he prayed for the men kneeling before him.

"Take away from us our iniquities, we beseech then, O Lord, that being made pure in heart we may be worthy to enter the Holy of Holies."

Schultz worried that no amount of absolution could cleanse men who violated God's commandment against killing. Filled with his fears and misgivings, he thought he should get right with God as often as he could before the invasion, and worry about the sins of the battlefield afterward. Each time at Mass, he clung desperately to the plea for forgiveness.

"I confess to Almighty God . . . that I have sinned exceedingly in thought, word and deed."

It couldn't hurt. On one occasion, he went to confession and confessed the sin of fornication, expressing his regret and remorse for all six times.

MARINE LANCE CORPORAL ROBERT GADDY,
Vietnam, 1967

Y ou know they're in trouble when you hear Marines in combat singing
'The Hymn,'" said General Oliver P. Smith, 1st Marine Division.

General Smith's dispirited Marines spontaneously broke into "The
Marine Corps Hymn" as they withdrew under fire from Korea's Chosin
Reservoir. A couple of generations later, riflemen of Charlie Company
1/1 (1st Battalion, 1st Regiment) of the 1st Marine Division sang the
hymn in combat on a small jungle-ringed LZ in Vietnam.

The 1st Marines kicked off Operation Medina in October 1967
by deploying battalions in force on "search and destroy" missions in
the Hai Lang Forest southwest of Quang Tri City, where the North
Vietnamese Army's 9th Regiment was active. Captain Bill Major and
the 162 Marines of Charlie Company airlifted by H-34 choppers onto
a hilly LZ in the jungle to spearhead for 1st Battalion.

Point squad led off through a sea of elephant grass. Grass
soon turned into dense triple-canopy jungle, down through which
a light rain wept. The long green caterpillar that was Charlie Company wound its way up and down slippery mountainsides, treacherous with slime and mud. If it weren't for mud, complained Lance
Corporal Bob Gaddy, twenty-one, team leader for the company's
106mm recoilless rifle section, there would be no need for infantry. Infantry and mud went together like stink and hogs, like fleas
and dogs.

The company spent a miserable night bivouacked in the jungle,
hunched inside their ponchos in near-total darkness, listening to the
dreary drop of rainwater through the foliage. No matter what, Gaddy
couldn't get comfortable enough to sleep. Tree roots dug into his pos-
terior. Water seeped down his collar, chilling him to the marrow. His
spirits were as soaked as his feet.

"When I get back to the real world," vowed Private First Class Knobby Clarke, "I ain't never going out in the rain again."

The march resumed at dawn. Third Platoon led the way, hacking trail for the company. Gaddy's 106mm team accompanied the point element. Word was sent back down the column to Captain Bill Major that point had come across a wide footpath that appeared well traveled.

"Gooks," Gunny Thompson decided. "I don't like the idea of using that trail."

The commander liked even less the prospect of another night surrounded by visibility-hampering undergrowth and strung out in positions where superior firepower accounted for little. After consulting with battalion by radio, he decided the path was the surest way to their day's objective. Machetes disappeared into canvas scabbards. The green caterpillar picked up speed. Charlie Company proceeded rapidly through a silent green world that magnified the soft call of an occasional bird, a whisper, the clank of canteens.

At 1500 hours, the point squad of Third Platoon came upon a small hill where the trail twisted up toward the left and disappeared around an outcropping of brush. That was where, without warning, the green, silent world blew up.

Concealed in the jungle not more than five yards away from the leading Marines, heavy 12.7mm machine guns, AK-47 rifles, and concussion grenades suddenly hammered the point squad. Opening volleys of the ambush killed or wounded twelve Third Platoon Marines, including platoon leader Lieutenant Paul Nelson.

Because of the dense terrain, only point squad and parts of Third Platoon actually made contact and were pinned down alongside the trail. Lance Corporal Gaddy opened up with his M-16, firing blind since he saw no traces of the enemy. Standard operating procedure against an ambush called for immediate suppressive fire.

Grenades exploded. Bullets clipped down blizzards of leaves and limbs. Men were yelling and screaming from everywhere.

The enemy immediately broke contact, withdrawing from withering return fire. Captain Major sent Lieutenant Jack Ruffer's First Platoon to high ground beyond the hill. Lieutenant Bob Anderson's Second Platoon fanned out above a nearby draw. Third Platoon, now commanded by Platoon Sergeant Tom Livingston, rushed to form a defense to the front.

The diameter of the perimeter, where all weapons pointed outward like the horns of buffalo, measured less than fifty yards. Company engineers rushed into the center and began hacking at underbrush and trees to clear an LZ for medevac choppers. Wounded Marines made medical evacuation a priority.

Gaddy and his team stuck with Third Platoon, putting aside their recoilless rifles in favor of M-16s. A 106 was somewhat like the old bazookas of World War II, except heavier and more cumbersome. They were used primarily against targets such as fortified bunkers, buildings, and vehicles and were more or less ineffective in close-in jungle fighting.

All remained quiet except for the chopping of axes and machetes. One stubborn tree remained on the cleared LZ, a petrified giant stripped of all life, its bleached-bone branches gnarled in display against the reddening sky. It resisted all efforts to chop it down.

Unable to find clearance around the big tree in order to set down, an H-34 medevac helicopter flared above the upper trunk of the tree and bumped it several times with his right wheel. Finally, repeated impact splintered the dead giant all the way to its base. Branches flew like old bones as the tree crashed to the ground. Four of the most critically wounded Marines were ushered aboard. The helicopter lifted off on its way to the hospital.

More choppers arrived to ferry out the rest of the wounded; the dead would have to wait. By the time the last bird lifted off, the sky provided only enough light to illuminate clearings. Jungle became trapped in pools of darkness. From this black suddenly cackled a machine gun to let Charlie Company know the enemy was still out there and ready to fight. The machine gun spat streams of green tracers at the last medevac helicopter. Its door gunner replied with red tracers.

The H-34 disappeared over the horizon, following its mates to the hospital. Gaddy lay on his belly and peered into the jungle's gloom, feeling alone and abandoned. Obviously, Charlie Company must spend the night on this dreadful hilltop isolated from the rest of the battalion and surrounded by NVA waiting for nightfall to make their move. Before now, he had given little thought to God or religion or the ultimate destiny of his soul. He had had no reason to think about such things. After all, young men rarely think of their mortality.

Maybe it was time to start.

"Dear God," he began, but he was unaccustomed to praying and wasn't sure he should go on.

The enemy launched a ground probe against Third Platoon's sector, looking for weaknesses. Shadows flitted ephemeral and fleet among the trees. Muzzle flashes winked like swarms of fireflies. Gaddy fired and fired and kept firing into the hellish bedlam. A man fighting defensively like that in the dark felt utterly isolated. The fight turned surreal, a sound and light show of fantastic proportions.

"Dear God . . ."

Corporal Sherman Betts's machine gun section engaged two squads of NVA. "There's a pot full of them and they're coming this way!" he yelled.

The bright flash of an exploding grenade put the machine gun crew out of commission. Although wounded, Betts was the only man able to fight back. He picked up a discarded M-16 and drove the NVA back.

Minutes later, high-pitched whistles signaled a Red attack in force against Ruffer's sector. More whistles and the peal of a bugle announced a charge against Anderson's Second Platoon.

The Marines were now surrounded and in a life-and-death struggle that could have only one of two endings: either the enemy overran the Marines and wiped them out, or the Marines held—and held throughout the long night ahead. There was no middle ground, nowhere left to go.

Suffering from a brain concussion, Captain Bill Major stood on the exposed LZ directing the fight and maintaining commo with the battalion command post.

"We're being hit hard, sir," he reported. "Would like to know if you can send Delta Company to reinforce?"

A grenade bounced off a log behind Gunny Thompson while he was directing a 60mm mortar into position. He dived for cover. The concussion caught him in midair, shredding one arm and perforating his ear drums.

NVA killed or wounded every Marine in Corporal Jimmy Leonard's M-60 machine gun team. Leonard was hit three times. He fought on.

Ruffer's platoon held off the attack against the company's left flank by throwing teargas grenades.

Down by the ravine, sappers in ones and twos broke through Lieutenant Anderson's perimeter. A Marine shouted, "They're . . . in here with us!"

A shadow darted past Gaddy. He rolled to one side and fired.

More whistle blasts signaled additional enemy joining the fray. Outnumbered by at least four to one, Charlie Company was about to go under. The battle reached its most critical stage.

Bob Gaddy had no trouble praying this time. "Dear God," he murmured while firing at ghosts and crackling spears of flame, "please get me out of this. If not, Lord, please let me die like a man."

Just as annihilation appeared inevitable, from somewhere across that tiny, jungle-enclosed battlefield, above the staccato bursts of weapons and the rumble of exploding grenades and mortar rounds, a clear baritone voice began singing "The Marine Corps Hymn."

From the halls of Montezuma
to the shores of Tripoli,
we will fight, fight, fight forever
our country's battles
in the air, on land and sea.

"It's that crazy Lieutenant Ruffer!"

Other Marines picked up the chorus. It radiated around the perimeter until all able Marines, including the wounded, filled the night with the words of their brave fight song. Gaddy felt a surge of pride swelling his chest. They were the Marines, the badass, kick-butt Marines, and they could take anything the enemy threw and deal back double. He might die tonight, but God was granting him his request to die like a man. Like a United States Marine.

Amid the roar of battle and the overwhelming rough harmony of Marines, Lieutenant Ruffer's shouts of encouragement rang out: "Let's go! Let's go, Charlie! Let's go get some!"

Brandishing a .45 pistol, he charged, firing to either side and pulling other Marines along with him. A grenade bounced off his back while another landed in front of him at the same time. The explosions all but took his hearing. He and his band of warriors continued their counterattack.

The enemy withdrew from inside friendly lines, running for their lives against the disturbing presence of crazy Americans who sang as loud as they could while dealing death from both hands. The VC left at least a half dozen of their own dead on the LZ.

The battle went on for four hours without pause. The enemy hurled himself against one point in the line, then withdrew to attack another sector. Marines were beginning to run out of ammunition. Corporal Ken Chambers was down to a machete. Morale was nonetheless high, and every now and then a fierce voice broke out spontaneously with another verse of the hymn.

When Delta Company drew near to reinforce besieged Charlie, Lieutenant Ruffer volunteered to meet the relief force and guide it safely through to the fortified LZ. Fresh Marines shouted encouragement to their compatriots as they flowed into the perimeter to expand and reinforce defenses.

That did it. Enemy fire ceased abruptly. NVA companies melted away into the jungle, soundly drubbed by the crazy Lieutenant Ruffer and his equally crazy choir of fighters.

"If it doesn't rain now," commented Private First Class Chesty Story, looking up at the moon, "we'll make it after all. We can see them if they come back."

The rest of the night remained clear for the first time in two weeks. Moonshine brightly lit the makeshift LZ until 0500 when the eastern sky brightened into Friday the 13th of October.

"Amen," whispered Lance Corporal Bob Gaddy, who had survived the battle unscathed. "Dear God . . . thank You."

Of the 162 Marines of Charlie Company, sixty-four received Purple Hearts from that night's fight. Captain Major nominated twenty-three of his men for decorations ranging from the Navy Commendation Medal to the Medal of Honor. Corporal William T. Perkins, Jr., received the Medal of Honor (posthumously) for throwing himself on a grenade to save friends. Bob Gaddy, who like his buddies in Charlie Company fought valiantly to hold off overwhelming odds, now lives in Muskogee, Oklahoma.

9

WHY ME, LORD?

I watch, and am as a sparrow alone upon the house top.

—PSALMS 102:7

Ira Hayes, a Pima Indian from Arizona, was one of six soldiers depicted in the famous World War II photo of Marines raising the flag over Iwo Jima. Three of the six later died in combat on the island. Hayes and the other two survivors were sent home to capitalize on the photograph's fame and raise needed war funds.

"You're a hero," said President Harry Truman, praising Hayes at a White House reception.

Hayes responded, "How can I feel like a hero when two hundred and fifty of my buddies hit the island with me and only twenty-seven of us walked off alive?"

Ultimately, Hayes found himself unable to cope with survivor's guilt and the horrors in his mind of so many dead friends. He died facedown and dead drunk ten years later behind a barn at the age of thirty-two. One can't help but wonder if his last thoughts were: *Why me, Lord? Why did I live when so many others died?*

MARINE LANCE CORPORAL BOB GROSS,
Vietnam, 1968

Lance Corporal Bob Gross was an average eighteen-year-old grunt scared out of his wits half the time. The other half of the time he scratched jungle rot boils and parasite sores on his legs and buttocks. As a platoon radioman with Golf Company 2/5 (2nd Battalion, 5th Marines), he humped not only his ruck, weapons, and other combat gear, but also a heavy PRC-25 radio. Sometimes he felt like a pack mule.

Golf Company spent much of its time in the field patrolling the hilly red dirt country between Phu Bai and Da Nang, sweeping for bad guys and protecting friendly Vietnamese villagers from the VC. In June 1968, a few months after the New Year's Tet Offensive, Golf penetrated the foothills to "search and destroy" a suspected NVA hospital guarded by a large element of combat troops.

It was a clear day with a white-hot sky. A good day for another "walk in the sun." No one expected to find the hospital, since Charlie usually built his essential facilities in tunnels underground. Hilly terrain with steep grassy rises, jungle along streams in the lowlands, and a burning sun combined to tax the company's endurance. At about 1700 hours, the company climbed in staggered combat formation to the top of Hill 88, more weary than wary since it had encountered nothing more exciting than mosquitoes all day.

The hill was a former Marine outpost overlooking the grass-thatched roofs of a friendly ville nestled in a valley to the south. Old fighting holes and deteriorating sandbagged positions pockmarked the grass with red scars. Golf Company had passed through there a couple of weeks earlier on another sweep that had been as fruitless as this day's. It was familiar terrain.

Word came down the line from the platoon sergeants: "Dismount! Take ten!"

Gross needed the break. His green jungle utilities were black with sweat. He swung the radio off his back and stretched his cramped and aching muscles. About ten feet away on the crest of the hill, Lance Corporal Steve Molner didn't even bother removing his pack, he was so beat. He issued a weary sigh and dropped to the ground in place, leaning back on his ruck. Another lance corporal, Gene Butcher, grinned at him. They were buddies.

"Mind if I plop down?" Butcher said.

"Better on your ass than on your feet."

The enemy had a nasty habit of booby trapping any site to which he suspected Americans might return. Butcher was just about to sit when a grunt further up the hill triggered a Bouncing Betty. A Bouncing Betty was a live grenade stuffed into a tin can set on top of a spring. Once triggered by an unsuspecting victim, the can bounced into the air about waist high and the grenade exploded where it could do the most damage.

Marines nearest the booby trap watched in stunned horror as the grenade flew free of the can, releasing the device's handle with a startling *Ping!* They knew they were about to get it.

Instead, the grenade plopped back into the grass. A dud.

Platoon Sergeant Levi Jones started to shout a command. He meant to say, "Nobody move!" But he only reached "Nobody—" because Gene Butcher, who was already on his way to the ground when the Betty bounced, could not arrest himself in time. He sat down on a second booby trap.

This one was no dud. A fiery blast of smoke and dust knocked both Molner and him backward off the edge of the hill. Miraculously, Butcher's same heavy pack that set off the little bomb also absorbed most of the detonation and saved the two Marines from certain death.

Bystanders were a different matter. They had no time to react. A tiny piece of shrapnel stung Gross's belly. Lance Corporal Jesus Greco, who was standing next to him, let out a little groan and staggered, jolted by the concussion. But he remained on his feet. Although Greco was a Mexican-American and had been darkened by weeks of constant exposure to the sun, he turned suddenly and completely pale.

Gross reached for him. "Jesus, are you all right? What's the matter?"

"Oh, Bobby . . . I don't feel so good."

With those final words, he toppled over into the grass and died. A tiny piece of steel no larger than a pencil eraser had pierced his heart.

What explanation could there be for why Butcher, Molner, and other Marines were saved from certain death while Greco was chosen to die in such a freakish, haphazard manner?

Gross couldn't help feeling a certain guilt, one that plagued him for years afterward. Why hadn't he been killed instead of Greco? After all, they were standing side by side. Was it all chance? Fate? God's impenetrable will?

Maybe one day, he thought, *one day* he might find the answers.

Bob Gross returned from Vietnam, became a Christian, and now lives in New York.

ARMY AIR CORPS LIEUTENANT HAIG KOOBATIAN, *World War II, 1944*

Lieutenant Haig Koobatian* thought he would like the weather in Italy when he shipped overseas and was assigned to the 419th Squadron, 301st Bomber Group, as a navigator on B-17 Flying Fortresses. The Mediterranean climate of hot, dry summers and mild, damp winters was supposed to be similar to that of his home state of California. He began to have his doubts as a dreary gray rain drizzled down onto tent city and the airfield at Foggia Plains when he reported to the commander in March 1944.

He was assigned quarters in a tent with another replacement navi-

* See also chapter 14.

gator, a captain named Edwards, who had also just arrived. The two airmen trudged in the drizzle down the length of the airfield where Flying Fortresses, called "Forts" by those who flew them, were crewing up for a bombing mission. Tent city lay beyond in the mud.

"Welcome to sunny Italy," Captain Edwards commented sarcastically. "I suppose it's called liquid sunshine here."

The newcomers began setting up their "home," ripping apart bomb crates in order to use the wood as a floor to keep them off the mud. The squadron navigator came striding among the tents. He was in charge of scheduling flights for navigators of the 419th.

"Koobatian, get your gear together," he said. "We need one more navigator—and you may as well start today."

Koobatian sighed. He would have complied without further protest had Captain Edwards not stepped in. Edwards was a lean Texan with a drawl, but a forward manner.

"Koobatian just got here," he explained to the scheduler. "It's rainy and muddy and we're trying to arrange some comfort here. There are other navigators. Why don't you get one of them? They've had plenty of time to get set up."

The squadron navigator scowled, but the argument was too reasonable to refute. He went on and left the two new men to their task. Koobatian felt relieved that his first combat mission was being delayed for at least another day or so.

The bombing run took off in the rain. Pilots stood on their brakes while powering up, then released them suddenly to rumble down the steel matting before laboriously lifting their heavily-laden birds into the air, wings wobbling. B-17s circled in the sky, then maneuvered into formations before heading northeast in Vs. Today's target was a rock island off the coast that served the Germans as an air- and sea-drome.

Fresh to the war, Koobatian watched them leave, unaware of how arbitrarily fate made its selections. The roar of powerful engines vibrated the air long after the bombers disappeared.

Koobatian and Edwards were still working on their tent when they heard the aircraft returning. The squadron had had to abort because of cloud cover. Koobatian arched his back to watch the return. The giant four-engine bombers in formation were an awesome sight impossible to resist.

The first Fort dropped low on approach, buzzing the ground. The pilot had once been a hotshot fighter jock. As his wheels touched matting, he either did something dumb or his plane got caught in something unexpected. The B-17 suddenly swerved and skidded sideways before it exploded with a resounding boom and erupted in flames and black smoke. It pancaked down the runway, shedding parts and people along the way.

Every member of the crew perished in the conflagration.

Koobatian later learned that the navigator on the ill-fated bomber had been a last-minute replacement. He had been assigned in Koobatian's place—and lost his life because of it.

From then on, Koobatian refused to let any other airman substitute for him. He tortured himself, twinges of guilt sweeping over him at unexpected times.

"When you're exposed to danger and your life is at stake, you start thinking, *Why me, O Lord, what did I do to deserve this? Why him and not me?* I don't know how many times I've asked myself that. I can't help thinking the answers will come when you start asking on a deep enough level, when you have some spiritual base to build on. I can't help thinking that."

NAVY CAPTAIN CHARLES MCVAY III,
World War II, 1945

The sky was overcast and a slight chop riffled the seas on Sunday, July 29, 1945, as the heavy cruiser USS *Indianapolis* steamed from Guam toward Leyte in the Philippines. Aboard were 1,196 sailors and

Marines captained by forty-six-year-old Annapolis graduate Charles Butler McVay III, a distinguished-looking, balding man with graying sidewalls.

Two months earlier, VE (Victory in Europe) had been declared after Adolf Hitler shot himself in his Berlin bunker. Now, if everything went according to top secret plans, cargo delivered by the *Indianapolis* to Tinian would soon usher in VJ (Victory in Japan). After off-loading the several hundred pounds of uranium-235 from which Atomic bombs would be built, the cruiser continued on her way via Guam to rejoin the Pacific Fleet in the Philippines.

Chaplain T. M. Conway, a young parish priest from Buffalo, conducted Mass on the fantail of the *Indianapolis* that Sunday morning. Afterward, the ship's doctor, Lieutenant Commander Lew Haynes, and a few other officers helped him with Protestant services. They noted how the morning congregations appeared larger than normal.

Nightfall overtook the ship when she was still 250 miles from the nearest landfall. The Palau archipelago lay to the south, Leyte more than 550 miles to the west. Everything seemed secure underneath a cloud-scudded sky. Captain McVay retired from the helm and left the watch to his officer of the deck.

Most of the crew not on watch slept belowdecks while the cruiser steamed through the night at 15 knots per hour. Not far away, a lone Japanese submarine prowled the depths seeking prey.

The submarine struck a few minutes past midnight, ushering in Monday by firing six torpedoes at the *Indianapolis.* The first fish ripped off the cruiser's bow. The second ignited a massive chain of explosions in the warship's fuel tank and powder magazines.

Chaos reigned. Jarred out of peaceful slumber, panicked sailors, many of whom wore nothing but skivvies, struggled to reach open decks. Although taking on water, with fires blazing out of control, the ship continued to move across the sea from its own momentum, scattering survivors of the explosions widely across the water. Time did not allow a proper "abandon ship." By the time some men were fully awake, they were in the drink, slathered with fuel and half blinded, retching from having swallowed oil in their mad stampede into the water.

McVay had the presence of mind to dress fully. A wave washed him over the side of the ship and carried him out to sea. He struck out swimming in order to avoid being sucked under when the cruiser sank.

The hapless ship went under in 10,000 feet of water in less than twelve minutes. Its hull rose vertically against the midnight sky, hung there a minute, then slipped straight down out of sight. More than three hundred men were either killed by explosions, went down with the ship, or drowned shortly thereafter. Less than nine hundred were thrown to the sudden quiet darkness of the eternal sea.

Their heads bobbing in a blanket of fuel oil, survivors were soon widely dispersed by currents and wave action. Many who were critically burned or otherwise injured would never see Monday's dawn. Those who made it through the night were scattered into four main groups over a line of several miles, each out of sight and unaware of the others.

Captain McVay's group was the best situated. Shortly after being swept overboard, McVay ran into a crate of floating potatoes. He climbed astride it and soon salvaged a shattered desk. Hearing men calling for help, he spotted two inflatable rafts not twenty feet away. He swam to the rafts and clambered aboard.

By dawn, his group consisted of four rafts, one floater net, and ten men. Whereas the other groups had little or no food, McVay's survivors managed to salvage some fresh water from the rafts and a few survival crackers.

Commander Stanley Lipski, gunnery officer, was senior in the largest group of about two hundred men. However, he was dying from ghastly burns suffered during the explosions. By Monday night, most of the injured in this group would be gone, about fifty or so. Blind from the slick and nearly incoherent, Commander Lipski took off his life jacket and gave it to another sailor. Before sinking, he gasped final words into Doc Haynes's ear.

"I'm going now, Lew," he said. "Tell my wife I love her and I want her to marry again."

That left Doc Haynes senior man in charge. Other than a few inflatable life belts and various flotsam—a toilet ring, a lard can, ammunition cans—his group had only a long cork ring on a line formed into a circle to which the shipwrecked men clung.

Lieutenant Dick Redmayne's group consisted of about 130 men with three small rubber rafts, one floater net, a few ammo cans, and other flotsam.

Ensign Ross Rogers, with four rafts and nineteen men, including two Marines, made up the fourth group.

The remainder were isolated in small groups of two or three; they faced the most daunting obstacles to survival.

Although no one could be certain the ship's final radio SOS had gotten through, everyone figured help would soon be on the way. Surely Leyte would miss the *Indianapolis* when she failed to show up tomorrow and dispatch search and rescue planes and ships.

Incredibly, however, due to a number of oversights and plain neglect, the Navy, unbelievably, would not notice the disappearance for four long days. That meant survivors who went into the drink were on their own, left to endure one of the most savage ordeals in the history of seafaring.

Sharks appeared only a few hours after the *Indianapolis* went to her grave, telltale dorsal fins circling ominously. Radioman Jack Miner in Doc Haynes's group worked his way to the center, figuring it would take the predator fish hours to find their way to him. He prayed to God to pull him through.

A fin headed directly for Seaman John Bullard. It veered at the last moment and sliced toward a sailor who had drifted away from the others. The last anyone saw of the victim, the shark had him by the legs and was pulling him across the sea, his head skimming over the surface of the water like a fishing bobber pulled by a catfish.

One sailor saw another crate of potatoes floating by. He swam to

get it—and went under like a bug sucked down by a bass. His screaming head popped up one more time. Then he was gone in a swirl and
the splash of a black tail. There was nothing anyone could do.

Dark silhouettes below the surface percolated everywhere, nudging
legs, rubbing past and between terrified men who, like live bait cast
onto the water, could do little to protect themselves. Men beat the
water with their arms and legs and screeched pitifully in attempts to
drive them off. It only seemed to attract more. The fish fed, and fed
well.

Exposure and dehydration were almost as bad as the sharks. Most
of the men were covered in oil. The unforgiving sun blistered them
during the day. At night they shivered and prayed for daylight. Lips
cracked. Eyes puffed and swelled shut.

Slowly, the elements and predators weeded out the weak and injured.
Acting as coroner for his group, Doc Haynes gave the final check. If a
man was dead, he nodded. The man's buddies slipped off his life jacket
and passed it to a man who had none.

Father Conway wore himself out praying and attempting to help.
He collapsed into a delirium and died in Doc Haynes's arms.

Others simply gave up. "I'll see you, good buddies," said one sailor
as he swam away.

Men prayed constantly. At dusk each night, Captain McVay led the
men of his four rafts in reciting the Lord's Prayer. Bobbing, parched,
and frightened, some hallucinating, they bowed their heads together on
the lonely and unforgiving sea.

> *Our Father Who art in heaven,*
> *Hallowed be Thy name.*
> *Thy kingdom come,*
> *Thy will be done . . .*

Weak and dispirited, some survivors drank seawater, went into horrible
convulsions, and died terrible deaths. Others hallucinated. They saw a

nice little island within swimming distance, complete with hotel and airstrip. Some insisted the sunken ship was directly below them. Several drowned trying to dive down to it and get ice cream and other food. A few set out swimming for Leyte and never came back.

"Honestly, now," Lieutenant Charles McKissick demanded of a man who said he knew the hotel owner on the nearest island. "Is there really a hotel there?"

"Can't you see it, Lieutenant? It's right there!"

Men out of their minds accused one another of hoarding nonexistent food and water. After nightfall on Wednesday, someone in Doc Haynes's group sounded the alarm. "There's Japs on the line!"

Fighting broke out as hallucinating men battled among themselves with anything that came to hand. Fists, cans, teeth . . . A knife blade flashed, followed by a struggle over the victim's life jacket.

Survivors had been in the sea for nearly sixty-four hours when they finally received a stroke of good fortune at noon on Thursday. The pilot of a Navy patrol on a routine flight spotted heads bobbing in an oil slick. Only 316 men of the original 1,196 were plucked out of the ocean. Nearly three hundred had died during the submarine attack. Another six hundred who survived the sinking were either eaten by sharks, drowned, or died of dehydration and exposure.

As one survivor commented years later, "My life ended on that ship. I had such a difficult time understanding why the Good Lord let me live and not others . . . After that trip, my life was like nothing."

Captain McVay was court-martialed for negligence in the loss of his ship. His career was finished, even though the court-martial board recommended clemency and retention on active duty. He retired from the Navy at fifty years old on June 30, 1949.

He was haunted and despondent by the loss of his men and his ship and received hate mail from relatives of the sailors who died in the Pacific. Some accused him of murder, some of cowardice in not going down with his ship.

Captain McVay never recovered from the experience.

"I should have gone down with the ship," McVay said in anguish many times over the years. In 1968, he lay down on the grass outside his Connecticut home, put a revolver to his head, and pulled the trigger.

10

THE UNEXPLAINED

Behold, I shew you a mystery; we shall not all sleep, but we shall all be changed.

—I Corinthians 15:51

During the early days of World War II, a middle-aged widow in Ontario, Canada, was startled out of a troubled sleep. Awake, she suddenly saw her younger brother standing at the foot of her bed in the dim glow of her night-light. He was dressed in a pilot's flight suit and his face was deathly pale and solemn. She screamed—for her brother was in England serving with the Royal Canadian Air Force.

She was kneeling on the floor sobbing her heart out when her three children rushed in.

"He's dead! I know he's dead!" she wailed.

He was, in fact, dead, his Spitfire having been shot down over the English Channel on the same day and hour that the woman saw the spectral figure in her room.

While preternatural events like this do not happen every day, they occur more frequently than one would suppose, especially among those connected in one manner or another with combat and warfare. Warriors and soldiers since the beginning of time have had shattering glimpses into a strange world beyond the one perceived by the normal five senses. Plato described how a soldier killed in battle suddenly came back to life on his funeral pyre. The soldier, whose name was Er, said he was brought back as a messenger to tell humanity about the "other world."

Psychic phenomena, near-death experiences, and evidence of possible reincarnation provide tapestries of unexplained mysteries for the soldier in battle, or who has been in combat. Even though the Bible talks about both Heaven and Hell in an afterlife, no one can be *sure* what happens to us after death. Scientists like Doctor Jim Tucker, medical director of the Child and Family Psychiatry Clinic at the University of Virginia, are trying to find out through research into the spiritual and psychiatric realms of the human psyche. His only conclusion so far? "I became open to the possibility that we're more than just our physical bodies, that there is more to the world than just the physical universe."

Edgar Cayce, a sixth-grade dropout from Alabama who died in 1945, was a God-fearing man who read the Bible completely through each year of his life. He predicted every major world crisis from before World War I through World War II, diagnosed some illnesses and diseases more accurately than trained medical doctors, and spoke in dozens of languages while in his self-imposed "trances," even though he was unschooled. He introduced to the world in a very practical sense the "startling possibility" of reincarnation, the idea that the soul returns to earth in different bodies.

His life was so remarkable that statesmen, financiers, professors, scientists, and other accomplished people from around the world were drawn to him. His message was fundamentally one of hope and faith. Close to his heart was the universal quest of trying to understand God's purpose for man on earth.

In 1923, shortly after Cayce began using his gifts, a religious philosopher named Arthur Lammers engaged him in a sharp debate.

"What is the human soul?" Lammers demanded. "Where does it come from and where does it go? Is man but another of nature's creatures, put on earth for a brief cycle, then turned to dust like the fallen trees?"

"Try the Bible," Cayce suggested. "The answer for everything lies there."

MARINE SERGEANT GENE BECK,
Canada, 1982

Marine Sergeant Gene Beck fought in two tours of combat in Vietnam and suffered hardly a scratch. A bullet grazed his knuckles and a piece of shrapnel won him a Purple Heart. Neither was much more than a bug bite, simple occupational hazards. After all that, he ended up car-crashed in a ditch in Canada, unconscious and perhaps dying in the middle of the night while a Canadian captain ran for help and a sergeant stayed with him.

The Canadian sergeant was injured, too, but he possessed lifesaving skills and stayed behind to work on the comatose American. He thought it no use, but kept at it anyhow.

The accident occurred on the way back to the mountains. As senior enlisted instructor of the U.S. Marine Corps Mountain Warfare Center, Beck had been ordered on temporary additional duty to the Canadian Rockies to train that nation's airborne in mountain fighting. After graduating the last class, Beck and the two Canadians were returning to base from a crossroads pub out in the middle of nowhere. A deer darted into the headlights. The captain swerved his Toyota Land Rover and lost control. It sailed off a culvert and rolled, throwing out all passengers. That was the last Beck remembered of that night. Perhaps the Old Man Above and Beck's Guardian Angel had finally given up on him.

In 1968, Beck had been a team sergeant in the Combined Action Program (CAP) working south of Marble Mountain in South Vietnam's I Corps. CAP was part of the American effort to win hearts and minds in Vietnam, its purpose to help the indigents, not kill them—unless, of course, they were Viet Cong guerrillas terrorizing the neighborhood.

The CAP team consisted of fourteen Marines and thirty Popular

Force (PF) Vietnamese troops. They taught horticulture and animal husbandry while at the same time tracking down communists and exterminating them. Quite naturally, the commies resented the new guys on the block. The previous CAP had been sandbagged in an ambush and wiped out. Beck was determined that the VC would not do the same to his men and him. Nor would he and his men be run out of town.

He moved his men into a village called Qua Giang and set up housekeeping. He knew the VC were watching and listening. On the first day, he and his PF counterpart walked the entire area with loudspeakers, daring the enemy to come out and fight.

"We're here to stay," he blared. "If you want to take us on, come on out or you don't have a hair on your asses."

Nothing happened.

Beck and his men got with the village elders to build ponds for growing larger strains of fish. They introduced a new type of rice from the Philippines that doubled the single annual harvest. As the village prospered, VC in the area grew more resentful and hostile.

Living on the edge while conspirators schemed to assassinate him and Main Force VC tried to lure him into a trap, a man developed a Sixth Sense—that is if he wanted to survive. Beck was never sure he understood his mysterious and acute Sixth Sense, other than to realize that it derived not from his own efforts and talents. It had to come from God.

He was not a born-again Christian who went to church every time the doors opened. He wasn't even particularly "religious." He simply tried to live the Ten Commandments in his daily life in a world gone to crap, chatting with God as he might with a superior officer. The Lord sent a Guardian Angel to guide and protect him, who talked to him through his Sixth Sense. How else to explain the countless times some mysterious power intervened in his life?

Often, on a trail he had never trod, Sergeant Beck could see in his mind's eye exactly what lay around the next bend—a well, a house— and sure enough the enemy was always there. One evening, just as his troops were digging in their night defensive position, he clearly envisioned mortar rounds landing on them.

"Fill in your holes and saddle up," he ordered his men. "We're moving out."

Having patrolled all day, his weary men weren't happy with the decision. Nevertheless, they gathered their gear and moved out. They had just vacated the site when mortar shells began exploding on it. It scared the piss out of them. They never questioned their sergeant's premonitions after that.

Beck's Sixth Sense, his Guardian Angel, whatever it was, had shipped to Vietnam with him. Before CAP, while he was still a lance corporal, he and another Marine had been manning a nighttime listening post one night in an old French fortress outside the perimeter. He got off watch and leaned back against the mud walls to close his eyes for some shut eye while his partner took over. He dozed off. Suddenly, a voice spoke directly into his ear.

"Beck?"

He stirred.

"Beck? There's going to be a lot of fighting and dying, but just keep doing what you're doing and you'll be all right."

His eyes snapped wide. He sat up.

"What did you say?" he asked his partner.

"I didn't say nothing."

"You didn't hear that voice?"

The other Marine regarded him. "What voice?"

"Never mind."

Marines who went around hearing voices became candidates for a Section 8 discharge.

The Sixth Sense voice interceded more than once after that.

A month or so after this first "contact," he was standing outside a bunker watching an Air Force Phantom work napalm against an enemy force on an adjacent hill. The pilot's skills amazed him. The sleek Phantom jetted in upside down, its sonic boom resounding off the hills. It flipped rightside up at the last instant to dump its bombs and light up the countryside with fire.

The enemy responded by firing mortars at the entrenched ground Marines. Just as a round impacted nearby, a loud voice called out from inside the bunker. "Hey, Beck!"

Beck's head turned. A shard of burning metal struck the sandbags precisely where his head had been. It would have decapitated him had he not been warned. He ducked into the bunker where three other Marines were holed up.

"Thanks."

They looked at him, puzzled. None of them had called out.

His Sixth Sense kicked in once again at the Cam Ne bridge during the Tet Offensive. Sergeant Beck and his CAP Marines and PF linked up with grunts and a pair of tanks to hold the bridge against a battalion-size enemy force. Entrenched and surrounded south of the bridge, they held out for three days and four nights of fierce fighting.

AD Skyraiders dumped 250-pound bombs around the defensive perimeter to create barriers of fire and steel. "Irish" McClancy and Gene Beck clawed the ground in their common fighting hole as the earth shook underneath them.

Beck felt someone tap him on his right shoulder. At the same time, McClancy felt a tap on his left shoulder. Instinctively, they rolled away from the center just as a bomb shard the size of a football landed, hissing, between them. The two Marines looked at each other in astonishment, the same question on their tongues: *Who warned us?*

Now in Canada all these years later, God had finally had enough of Gene Beck's recalcitrance and abandoned him to his own human resources. More dead than alive, he was medevac'd to a local hospital, stabilized, then transferred to a major medical center in Ottawa where he remained in a coma for nearly six weeks.

He was unconscious but somehow not unconscious. At some point, he felt himself weightless and flying through the air without benefit of anything other than his own inner energy. The earth moved underneath him at a breathtaking clip. Towns, farms, meadows, trees, and hills flashed past.

He reached his destination very quickly. Early morning sunlight bathed the tiny Quonset hut chapel at the Marine Corps Mountain Warfare Training Center in California. He hovered above it a moment, then went inside directly through the roof. His Marine company was gathered in the pews, and Master Sergeant Hogan was leading a prayer service.

Beck couldn't hear what was being said—his world was totally silent—but he knew it was a memorial for a fallen Marine. He had attended functions like this before, especially in Vietnam. Never, however, had he attended in such an unusual manner, hovering out-of-body against the ceiling.

With a start, he realized the service was for *him*. He tried to attract the attention of his buddies, but it seemed no one could see or hear him.

Everything faded away in an instant. Somewhat later, exactly how much later he couldn't tell, for time had no meaning, he experienced a bright warm tunnel of light. Two faceless figures moved out of the tunnel toward him. The junior of the two, whom Beck assumed to be Jesus Christ, walked to the right of the Father and a step behind. As a military man, Beck understood the protocol.

Utter silence still prevailed. Nonetheless, the holy pair communicated with him in a sort of picture word dialogue that radiated within his body cells. In this manner, they reviewed his entire life for him, what he did and didn't do, his sins and his virtues, all the way from his childhood to the present time. The Holy Figures seemed pleased that he had tried with all his heart to help the Vietnamese people and that he continued to live the Golden Rule as best he could. But . . .

He found himself back in Ottawa at the hospital. He saw himself in bed surrounded by his mother, three doctors, and an attractive blond woman. His mother and the blond woman were holding his hands.

He opened his eyes and looked around. It must have been much later, for his mother was alone in the room with him now. Tears streamed down her cheeks.

"What's going on?" he asked. "Who was the gorgeous little blond holding my hand?"

His mother looked shocked. "How did you know that?"

"I—I saw her. I saw you, Mom, and I saw three doctors . . ."

She gripped his hands with all her might. "Darling . . . Darling, you couldn't have. You were . . . dead."

Sergeant Gene Beck flatlined twice in the Ottawa intensive care unit and was officially dead for several minutes each time. He was right about the blond and the three doctors. She was a U.S. Marine sergeant with the American embassy in Ottawa. He was also right about the memorial service being held at the Marine Corps Mountain Warfare Training Center in California. He surprised Master Sergeant Hogan and the other Marines by describing exactly where they were sitting and what they were wearing. He had no explanation for what happened. He still wonders why he didn't stay dead. Perhaps it was because God still had a mission for him on earth.

ARMY AIR FORCE LIEUTENANT JAMES M. HUSTON,
World War II, 1945

The slugfest for ownership of Iwo Jima and its neighboring islands of Chichi Jima and Haha Jima in the Pacific had been raging for two weeks when the escort carrier USS *Natoma Bay* launched four of its FM2 Wildcat fighters on March 3, 1945, to strike shipping in Chichi's Futami Ko Harbor. The Wildcats reached for altitude in a clear morning sky, circled once to form up over the *Natoma* and accompanying warships dotting the sea, and struck out at 300 miles per hour for the Japanese harbor.

This was Lieutenant James Huston's fiftieth and final combat mission. At twenty-one, the slender hotshot pilot from Pennsylvania had been with VC-81 squadron aboard *Natoma Bay* since October 1944. The Japs had shot down twenty-one of his fellow pilots during his time aboard the carrier, but so far he had not sustained so much as a single bullet hole in his fighter. A few more days and he would be on his way home, or at least to some cush job back in Hawaii. He volunteered for today's mission rather than ride out the rest of his time in relative safety.

From 3,000 feet, Huston and his wing mates, Lieutenants Jack Larsen, Bob Greenwalt and William Mathson, Jr., spotted Jap transports inside Chichi's half-moon harbor, some of which had apparently off-loaded under cover of darkness and were now attempting to sneak back out to open sea and hightail it to Japan to reload. Air antishipping strikes destroyed transports, docks, and other infrastructure the Japanese needed in order to resupply troops on Iwo Jima and keep them fighting. To the south, Iwo Jima remained eight square miles of foul-smelling volcanic ash and cinders consumed by clouds and chimneys of fire and smoke as Marines and Japanese went at it.

Antiaircraft fire punctuated the sky over Futami Ko Harbor with puffs of smoke, looking harmless from a distance, but extremely deadly. The four Wildcats tipped off one by one onto a wing and screamed in at wavetop level to deliver their bombs and .50-caliber swaths of death and destruction.

Lieutenant James Huston made his run last. He caught rounds in his engine as he streaked in low and fast through antiaircraft fire and tracers lashing up from the beach. The Wildcat exploded in a fiery burst, struck the surface of the sea, and skipped across it like a flat rock thrown across a still pond, shedding pieces of itself in all directions. A wing knifed the water and broke off. The fuselage sank immediately, pushed deep by its momentum.

Huston's wing mates flew back over to see if they could spot him, but he and his Wildcat were gone, vanished into the deep blue grave of ocean off the island's coast.

. . .

In February 2000, fifty-five years later, the parents of another James took their two-year-old toddler to the Cavanaugh Flight Museum in Addison, Texas. So enthralled was little James Leininger with the World War II exhibit that he fussed when he had to leave after three hours.

From the moment he could walk, even before, little James had been fascinated by airplanes. He spent hours playing with toy planes and shouted with excitement whenever he saw a real one. As he grew older, furniture in the Leininger home in Lafayette, Louisiana, took a beating as the boy crashed his toy aircraft into tables and chairs. The kitchen table served as his "flattop." He knew more about aviation than any child his age could reasonably know.

The visit to the Cavanaugh Flight Museum was the point from which James's parents realized their little son was somehow "different." Violent nightmares began to steal his sleep. He would kick and scream, hands thrashing at the ceiling as though trapped in a box.

"Airplane crash, on fire!" he shouted. "Little man can't get out!"

The dreams became more intense, along with James's obsession with the frightening event that generated the dreams. He provided details as he became older and more articulate. He told of how *his* plane took off from a ship on the water just before it crashed. When asked who piloted the plane, he replied, "James."

Questioned about what type of plane "James" flew, little James said, "Corsair."

A Corsair, he explained quite correctly, frequently had flat tires and had a tendency to yaw to the left.

What happened to the plane?

"Got shot."

Where?

"Engine."

Where did it crash?

"Water."

Who shot it?

"The Japanese."

He knew it was the Japanese, he said, because of the red sun on the enemy's planes and flags.

What was the name of the ship from which "James" flew?

"*Natoma.*"

He remembered a fellow flyer, he said, whose name was Jack Larsen.

One evening, James's father was thumbing through a book about the World War II Battle of Iwo Jima. James wriggled onto his father's lap and pointed to a map of Iwo Jima.

"Daddy!" he exclaimed. "That is where my plane was shot down!"

Certain food also sparked recollections of "the event." The first time his mother made meat loaf, James clapped his hands. "I haven't had meat loaf since I was on the *Natoma.* . . . We could have ice cream every day on the *Natoma.*"

By three years old, he was sketching crayon pictures of warplanes fighting in the air, complete with red suns on Japanese planes. He knew the types of planes he was drawing.

Concerned, his parents finally started investigating his claims. To their amazement, they discovered that almost everything little James said about the "other James" could be substantiated by hard fact. A Lieutenant "James"—James Huston—*was* stationed aboard the USS *Natoma* during World War II. He *was* shot down by the Japanese at the Battle of Iwo Jima, into the ocean where he perished; his wing mate *was* Jack Larsen . . . About the only thing little James Leininger of the twenty-first century had wrong was the type of Lieutenant Huston's aircraft. It was a Wildcat, not a Corsair. However, Huston *had* flown Corsairs off carriers prior to his death.

Carol Bowman, author of *Children's Past Lives: How Past Life Memories Affect Your Child,* explained to the Leiningers how reincarnation, or past lives lived, expressed themselves most commonly in children. She considered all the evidence and reasonably concluded that Lieutenant James Huston from World War II was manifesting his experiences through James Leininger.

Was James Leininger a reincarnation of James Huston?

"It's very hard to describe," said James Huston's sister, who was now eighty-seven years old, "but I just can't help but say it has to be true. He [little James Leininger] knows too much. For some reason, he knows these things."

Finally, little James named his three GI Joe action figures Leon, Walter, and Bill, the names of three pilots who had served with Huston and who were among the twenty-one killed in action while flying from the USS *Natoma Bay*. Lieutenant Leon Conner, Ensign Walter Devlin, and Ensign Bill Peeler. Asked why he named his GI Joes these particular names, James Leininger replied matter-of-factly, "Because they greeted me when I went to Heaven."

James Leininger no longer has nightmares. Even his memories are starting to fade. According to Carol Bowman, most children like James start losing memories of past lives when they reach age seven or eight. James's father is writing a book about his son and Lieutenant James Huston.

ARMY SERGEANT LLOYD KING,
Vietnam, 1968

As a platoon squad leader in Bravo Company 2/327 of the 101st Airborne Division, Sergeant Lloyd King always feared he might unintentionally submit to fatigue, let down his guard at a crucial life-or-death moment, and one of his men would be killed unnecessarily. For that reason, he drove himself mercilessly, constantly at the front of his squad wherever it happened to be.

His squad ran point for Bravo Company as it moved through the A Shau Valley, tracing a branch of the Ho Chi Minh Trail in an effort to shake out the enemy. Their mission was to find him, fix him, and kick his ass—search for him through treacherous rain-soaked jungles, up muscle-cramping hills, across fetid swamps infested with mosquitoes, leeches, and other pests whose sole purpose, it seemed, was to inflict torment on human bodies.

Crotch rot made testicles swell to twice their normal size. Intruders were cursed by the presence of venomous snakes and spiders, mazes of "wait-a-minute" vines, elephant grass like standing razors, backpack straps cutting into aching shoulder muscles from the weight of gear required to fight and survive, rain-soaked or sweat-encrusted fatigues . . . all stresses to test a soldier's patience and his fragile hold on sanity.

Fresh enemy signs were everywhere. The trail Bravo paralleled was almost the size of a single-lane highway. Bicycle tires and Ho Chi Minh sandals had packed the trail almost as hard as concrete. King's point found sniper loops at the bases of several trees. Later in the day, the squad came across freshly dug bunkers and camouflaged spider holes strategically placed along the crest of a ridge.

Sergeant King scanned a large opening in the jungle with his binoculars. He motioned Cowboy to keep watch over the spider holes while he turned back to the front to lead point across the clearing. At that moment, a black-clad VC guerrilla with his rifle at sling arms walked out from behind two trees directly in front of him.

"Hit it!" he yelled to warn Cowboy and Four Eyes, his radioman.

He dived to the ground and at the same time squeezed off three rounds from his M-16. The VC dropped as if he had been hit with a giant sledgehammer from the sky.

Only four months in-country and King was already accustomed to the presence of death and dying. On the other hand, Four Eyes was a more recent inductee into the sausage grinder and vomited all over the trail as he and his sergeant dragged the corpse into the forest, covered it with leaves and brush, then cleaned up blood and puke. Although other enemy in the area had undoubtedly heard the shots, King saw no sense in leaving a plain sign to advertise Bravo Company's precise location. The objective of combat patrolling was to find the enemy before he found you. Hide-and-seek with lethal consequences.

. . .

Dense fog rolled in shortly after Bravo settled into its night defensive perimeter (NDP). It was so thick by 1845 hours that Sergeant King could barely see the fingers on his extended arm. The CO detailed his squad to set up a night ambush farther along the trail; the enemy KIA earlier meant more VC lurked in the area.

The squad occupied a cluster of boulders to the right of the trail. By the time the last daylight vanished underneath the blanket of fog, members of the squad had set up trip flares, grenade booby traps, and claymore mines—and were settling in to wait for prey to come along. Fifty-fifty alert. Half slept while the other half kept watch. Then the halves switched every two hours. King took a central position among the boulders from which he could control any contact.

He could not sleep, no matter how fatigued. He couldn't take the chance. Typically, most men tended to get lax at the end of the day and to succumb frequently to the false sense of calm and nod off around midnight. At least the sergeant could be counted on to keep himself awake.

A full moon glowed through the veil of fog for a while. The fog thickened and the moon disappeared, replaced by the inherent emotion of Vietnam—fear. Reduced visibility in a pitch-black night would allow the enemy to be inside the kill zone before anyone spotted him.

Four Eyes made his radio check, breaking squelch twice. Distant artillery shells began exploding. Some other poor bastard outfit was being probed or attacked and had called in fire support.

The shelling soon ceased. It must have been nothing but H&I (harassment and interdiction) after all. Eerie night settled in. Harmless objects in the darkness took on formidable shapes as the human eye played tricks on the mind, causing danger to lurk in every shadow and shape.

Sergeant King's aches and pains and cramping muscles eased a bit. His abrasions and skin cuts stopped bleeding. His body and mind seemed to wither from exhaustion. Only the itching and burning rash on his butt and the ubiquitous presence of mosquitoes kept him irritable and on edge.

He made radio check at 0107 hours. Although it was time to wake Fast Eddie and Four Eyes for their turns on radio and trail watch, he let them sleep. He shivered in the cool, damp air and counted fallen leaves to keep his mind active.

The blanket of ground fog slowly dissipated. Soon, moonlight penetrated it again, splashing fantastic bands of light on both sides of the trail. Sergeant King watched in wonder and amazement as shreds of remaining mist swirled around the band of light and formed what appeared to be a stairway leading out of brilliant moonlight to the ground.

He shook his head. He must be hallucinating.

It was no hallucination. Maybe he was going crazy.

An image appeared in the sky at the top of the ephemeral stairway. He rubbed his eyes and squinted. The image remained and took on an angel's form of such feminine beauty and clarity that he caught and held his breath. Shock waves coursed through his body. He could not move. He merely stared in awe and disbelief, consumed by the display, heart pounding in his chest, breath raspy and startled.

The "angel" lifted a commanding arm, and the world seemed to stand still. Then she spoke in a soft voice, saying, "I bear news of sadness and bring you inner peace and solace to ease the burden of your loss."

The stairway and the angel vanished as quickly as they had appeared. Four Eyes grabbed King by his fatigue shirt, shook him hard and demanded in a subdued whisper to know why the hell he was talking out loud.

"Whattaya mean? I wasn't talking."

"The hell you wasn't, Sarge. You must be going nuts. I heard you say, 'Wait! Come back! Come back!'"

It had been so real. It was *still* real. King sighed. "Four Eyes, you wouldn't believe me even if I told you. I can hardly believe it myself."

. . .

Sergeant King remained awake the rest of the night, pondering the angel's message, wondering what she meant by "loss." At dawn, he pulled trail security while his squad disarmed and recovered early warning devices, booby traps, and claymores. He found it difficult to concentrate on anything except the angel and what she had had to say.

One of his squad members, Snake, whispered to him from out of sight behind a small mound to his rear. "I can't find the claymore you put out last night, Sarge."

King turned and in so doing exposed his head and shoulders above the web-tangle of tree roots he was using for cover. The sharp report of a nearby sniper's rifle shattered the morning quiet. The bullet clobbered King's helmet, somehow spinning it completely around on his head and knocking him flat on his back across the trail.

When he regained consciousness, his first thought was *Don't move!* One twitch and the sniper would drill him again.

Blood filled the palm of his left hand where it was pinned underneath his helmet. The steel pot kept his head cocked forward with his chin wedged against his chest. He cautiously opened his eyes, slitting them, and saw nothing but white.

Was this what the angel foretold? Was he in Heaven?

His vision cleared. He heard members of his squad calling out to one another as they tried to figure out what happened. Four Eyes and Snake hid behind the small mound to his rear.

"Sergeant King?"

He must still be alive.

The position of his chin against his chest caused him difficulty in breathing and restricted the movement of his jaw and vocal chords. He dared not move. Taking a deep, slow breath, he clenched his teeth and called out with minimal lip movement, like a ventriloquist, "Snake? See the smoke ring? Up front, left of trail?"

"Yeah, Sarge."

"I'm counting to three. I want the squad to open fire up in the trees. I'll try to get up and make it to you."

At the count of three, the squad discharged a mad minute of firing, shredding the foliage. Loss of blood made King dizzy. Fighting numbness and lack of control, he prayed for the strength to get up and run.

He lunged toward the small mound, collapsing at the last moment before he reached it. Hands grabbed his shoulders and yanked him to safety. From up the trail he heard the sniper crashing dead to earth from his hide in the branches of a tree. King looked up and saw Big Daddy and Snake, the platoon's soul brothers. He grinned at them.

"What the hell took you so long?"

The next time he regained consciousness, the platoon medic was working on the wound where the bullet had split open his scalp without penetrating or shattering his skull. Talk about luck. The curve of his helmet had deflected the bullet. The rest of his squad gathered round. Mex said, "The sar-hente, he eez one lucky sum-beech."

King thought of the angel. In less than twenty-four hours, he had killed a man, experienced some kind of heavenly vision, and now had been shot. By all odds, he should be dead. His surviving was more than luck. God *must* be looking out for him.

Bravo Company remained in defensive posture for the next two days. Fog lingered too thick to call out a dust-off to fly King to the battalion aid station.

On the third day, the company moved toward a pickup zone from which the wounded sergeant could be medevac'd. The company commander radioed King's squad.

"Two One, this is Bravo Six. A member of your element is going home on emergency leave. Over."

Sergeant King immediately understood why the angel came. After a brief hesitation, he responded with "Bravo Six, I have a good copy. When do I leave? Over."

As it turned out his brother Jeff had drowned in Lake Mead, Nevada, at almost the same time the angel appeared on the stairway in

Vietnam to bring him "news of sadness." When King arrived home in Louisiana, he discovered the second part of the angel's message. Not only had he been spared from the sniper's bullet, his wife had given birth to their son the day before, thus fulfilling the angel's promise to "bring you inner peace and solace to ease the burden of your loss."

King had never before believed in miracles and premonition, but from then on God had his undivided attention.

Sergeant Lloyd King returned to Vietnam to complete his tour of duty. He is now an accomplished poet and artist living with his wife in Louisiana. His book of illustrated poetry, From 'Nam With Love, *was published in 2006.*

MARINE LANCE CORPORAL CRAIG ROBERTS,
Vietnam, 1966

Survival in Vietnam depended upon luck, fate, chance, or predestination. You could be the most careful grunt in 'Nam, always doing the little extra things to keep alive, like keeping your rifle clean and oiled, digging your hole deeper, staying awake on watch, never taking unnecessary risks, playing it safe—and still some fruit jar filled with powder and nails would get you. Or a fourteen-year-old gook with a bolt-action rifle. Or an old French mine.

Lance Corporal Craig Roberts, 9th Marines, had arrived in-country in May 1965, eight months before. He seldom worried about being killed. His Guardian Angel named "Joe" took care of him. Joe had been his imaginary playmate when he was a kid growing up in Huntington Beach, California. He and Joe, playing Davy Crockett at the Alamo, defended the backyard fence during many a battle with Santa Anna.

Roberts could never explain how he knew Joe had shipped to Vietnam with him as his Guardian Angel; it was just something he accepted within his soul. While Joe might guard him against death, however, his protection failed to extend to injuries and wounds. Roberts's main concern was losing a limb or somehow ending up as a semi-vegetable.

In October 1965, Roberts stepped into a punji pit with its sharpened bamboo stakes greased with human excrement. By January, he could not walk without hobbling. Dark streaks of infection appeared and ran up his calf. Along with the inevitable infection came intestinal parasites and malaria, which made him run a constant fever and hallucinate at times. His leg stank of death and rot, like the remains of some VC left to bake in the tropical sun.

Doc Lindstrom, the platoon's Navy corpsman, did everything he could, but it wasn't enough to ward off encroaching gangrene. He kept sending Roberts to the company's chief corpsman with requests that he be medevac'd to Da Nang to see a doctor. The chief corpsman delayed until Roberts forced a confrontation.

That initiated a process that propelled Roberts to the Naval Support Activity near Marble Mountain, a *real* hospital housed in Quonset huts. When the ambulance stopped outside, Roberts grabbed his rifle and staggered out.

"Hey, we're supposed to take you in on a stretcher."

"I walked into Vietnam. I'll walk out."

Dirty and faded and perpetually fatigued from infection, fever, and parasites, he limped into the hospital. As he passed a window, he glimpsed through it and saw another harried-looking boonie rat with lines etched deeply around his mouth and into his forehead. The guy looked as though he'd lived at least thirty years of a hard life.

With a start, he realized he wasn't looking through a window. He was looking at his own reflection. He was down to 123 pounds and had aged by at least ten years.

Two or three doctors had a look at the wound. They took pictures and exclaimed, poked and prodded while Roberts grew increasingly uneasy. The doctors went into a huddle. Finally, one walked over to him.

"I think we can save the knee joint," he said. "We'll try to leave a few inches of leg below the knee for a prosthesis."

For a heavy moment Roberts felt too stupefied to respond. At nineteen years old, a man found it hard to face the prospect of losing part of his body.

"The knee?" he asked dully.

"Yes. I think we can save it."

"Save it?"

"You can have an artificial leg. It'll work almost as well as this one."

The message finally sank in. "No!" Roberts said.

"No? We don't have a choice."

A one-legged man named Craig Roberts was not going to totter off an airplane back in the United States.

"We always have choices," the corporal said.

His eyes fell on the grenades attached to his combat belt. Before the doctors could react, before even he realized what he was doing, he snatched up one of the little hand bombs and hooked his thumb through the arming ring. He thrust it toward the doctors at arm's length, the act of a desperate man. The doctors stepped back involuntarily, their eyes bulging.

"I am not going home with only one leg," Roberts vowed, darkly sincere. "I either *walk* home—or I don't go home at all."

"Go get the captain," one doctor whispered to another who, nearest the door, slipped out.

A silent standoff continued until he returned with a Navy captain. The captain was short with gray hair. Roberts thrust the grenade toward him. Tears burned his eyes. His hands trembled.

"He's gone crazy, sir," a doctor whispered. "We can't save his leg, sir. It's too far gone."

The captain stepped forward. "Put that thing down, son."

"Not until you promise not to cut off my leg."

The captain gestured. "Mind if I take a look?"

Roberts felt a little seepage of hope. "I'll jerk the pin if you try anything," he warned.

"I just want to look."

He poked and probed and sniffed and pressed while Roberts held the grenade and his ground. At last, the captain looked up with a smile.

"You aren't going to lose anything, son," he declared. "These new people don't know anything about tropical medicine. That's why they send us old salts over here."

Roberts later learned the captain had practiced his medicine initially as a young doctor in the Pacific during World War II. He issued a string of instructions on how to treat Roberts's punji wounds and his other ailments. Then he turned a sympathetic smile on the young leatherneck.

"Now, son, would you mind letting us take care of your weapons for you while you're here. You won't need them. I promise you."

Was there hope? Or was this just a ploy leading to his sedation and the ultimate loss of his leg?

"Sir, you're not bullshitting me?"

The smile turned a little sad. "Son, you'll be back humping the bush with your unit in no time."

Roberts lapsed into a coma from infection and a spike in his fever. The only thing he remembered from the following day was a visit from Joe, his Guardian Angel.

"This is not your time to go," Joe assured him. "Don't worry about it. There are other things in store for you. We'll talk to you later."

In 1997, Craig Roberts was an author, military historian, devout Christian and highly decorated former Marine when, both legs intact, he suffered colon cancer at the age of fifty-two. Chemotherapy and surgery to remove a section of his colon destroyed his immune system. He developed internal infections that resulted in a massive loss of blood. On a Sunday afternoon in August, he collapsed on the floor of his home in Tulsa, Oklahoma. By 6 P.M. he was in the back of an ambulance on his way to ICU at Saint Francis Hospital.

"This guy's not going to make it," he overheard one EMT say to another.

Doctor Craig Smith, Roberts's cancer surgeon, was waiting in the emergency room.

"We're running some tests," he said. "Do you have a living will?"

"What's that?" Roberts managed.

"In case you have to go on life support. We've already told your wife. You're not going to make it. We're going to lose you."

"Doc . . . I'll make it. It's not my time."

"You're losing all your blood. We have five doctors working on you."

Roberts rallied. "Right up front, Doc, let's get this straight. You have *six* doctors."

"Six?"

"God's here. He's in charge. You listen to Him and do what He tells you to do."

That stunned Doctor Smith speechless. He was quite young, early thirties. Pale and shaking, he looked as though this was the first time he had ever told a patient he was going to die. Finally, he said, "We're going to need all the help we can get."

An orderly entered ICU to intubate Roberts. He kept jabbing Roberts's throat until Roberts passed out from the pain. He had had enough. *I'm outa here.*

In a flicker of time, he found himself sitting in a huge dark room. The feeling was as if he had left one room in a house to go into another. Somehow, he realized he had departed his old life—but he didn't care. It no longer meant anything.

He sat there entirely at peace with himself. He felt young again, and in perfect health.

Someone stood behind him. Some entity with its hand reassuringly on his shoulder. Not touching in a physical sense, but nonetheless *there.* Immediately he knew who it was—his old imaginary friend from childhood, his Guardian Angel from Vietnam. Joe.

Joe's unearthly voice was saying, "Remember? I told you back when we were in the Legion [Marines] that it wasn't your time. A decision is now being made on whether to take you on from here or to let you go back."

Okay. Been there, done that. What's next?

Going on, it occurred to him, meant passing to either of two destinations. Somehow he knew loved ones were waiting for him if he entered the passageway to his right. At the same time, he became acutely aware that a hole might open in front of him and swallow him into Hell. It was a little daunting, a little scary, but he didn't feel threatened.

A decision apparently had been made not to go on. So he was to be sent back. Suddenly, all kinds of information and instruction were being downloaded into his mind—a kind of illumination, a user's manual of knowledge and wisdom he was to pass on to others once he returned to the previous room of his life.

Time had no meaning in this *other room*. Still, after what felt like only three minutes, he opened his eyes and found himself in Saint Francis's ICU surrounded by his wife, Angela, along with other relatives, friends, and Doctor Smith. The doctor was wide-eyed, disbelieving. Eighteen hours had passed.

"I don't know where you've been," Doctor Smith said, "but we lost you. You flatlined. You were dead. We gave up and started to unplug you—but then, after three minutes, we got a heartbeat again."

Craig Roberts is a retired Tulsa police officer now living near Locust Grove, Oklahoma.

11

PRESENCE

God is my strength and power.

—II Samuel 22:33

After the Battle of Resaca during the American Civil War, Union General O. Howard visited a division hospital headquartered in tents and a private residence. He came upon a teenage soldier wounded so severely that doctors expected his death by morning. The general knelt on the edge of the boy's blanket.

"Is there anything we can do for you, son?" he asked.

"Yes," said the dying soldier. "I want somebody to tell me how to find my Savior."

General Howard took out his Bible. He prayed with the boy. A peaceful smile touched the boy's lips before he died.

Soldiers in combat search the supernatural for understanding, comfort, and protection. Belief in the presence of God, belief that God is always *there* to listen and care, helps comfort combat soldiers in difficult situations, helps reassure them of order and reason in the madness of war.

A study during World War II asked troops in the European and Pacific theaters how much belief in prayer and the presence of God helped when things were tough. Seventeen percent of troops in the Pacific said it helped not at all; 83 percent said it helped a lot. Belief was even more widespread among U.S. forces in Europe: 94 percent said it helped a lot.

"The belief in a benevolent God was the single greatest sustaining factor in my life," said Lawrence Nickell, 5th Infantry Division.

Polls from soldiers in Iraq and Afghanistan in 2004 revealed much the same results. "I'm in God's hands even more than before and He will look after me," Marine Lance Corporal David Bryant wrote from Iraq in 2003. "A scripture that helps me a lot is: *I will not put more weight on your shoulders than you can bear.*' Every time I get the feeling that I can't go on anymore, I think of that scripture and I feel better."

ARMY MAJOR SULLIVAN BALLOU,
Civil War, 1861

Sullivan Ballou volunteered as a major with the Union's 2nd Rhode Island Infantry shortly after the outbreak of hostilities between the North and the South in 1861. Letters home to his wife, Sarah, expressed his love for her and his deep faith in the presence of God. One week before the first Battle of Bull Run, he wrote the following letter:

Dear Sarah:

The indications are very strong that we shall move in a few days, perhaps tomorrow. And lest I should not be able to write you again, I feel impelled to write a few lines that may fall under your eye when I am no more.

I have no misgivings about, or lack of confidence in, the cause in which I am engaged, and my courage does not halt or falter. I know how American civilization now leans upon the triumph of the government, and how great a debt we owe to those who went before us through the blood and suffering of the Revolution. And I am willing, perfectly willing, to lay down all my joys in this life to help maintain this government, and to pay that debt.

Sarah, my love for you is deathless. It seems to bind me with mighty cables that nothing but omnipotence can break. And yet my love of country comes over me like a strong wind, and bears me irresistibly with all those chains to the battlefield. The memory of all the blissful moments I have enjoyed with you come crowding over me, and I feel most deeply grateful to God, and you, that I have enjoyed them for so long. And how hard it is for me to give them up and burn to ashes the hopes of future years, when, God willing, we might still have lived and loved together, and see our boys grown up to honorable manhood around us.

If I do not return, my dear Sarah, never forget how much I loved you, nor that when my last breath escapes me on the battlefield, it will whisper your name. Forgive my many faults, and the many pains I have caused you;

how thoughtless, how foolish I have sometimes been. But, oh Sarah, if the dead can come back to this earth and flit unseen around those they love, I shall always be with you in the brightest day and the darkest night. Always. Always. And when the soft breeze fans your cheek, it shall be my breath. Or the cool air, your throbbing temple, it shall be my spirit passing by. Sarah, do not mourn me dead. Think I am gone, and wait for me. For we shall meet again.

It was Major Ballou's last letter. He was killed a week later at Bull Run.

MEDICAL TECHNICIAN JANICE HERMERDING,
Vietnam, 1970

Being an American alone in a city like Da Nang was never a good idea, even at noon. A war was going on, and it was seldom apparent who the enemy was and who he wasn't. Janice Hermerding had been warned never to venture out into the city without an escort. A tall, slender young woman with bobbed light brown hair and a loose midwestern gait may as well have been carrying a neon sign pointing herself out. All kinds of unpleasant things could happen, of which a simple mugging would be the least. She could be kidnapped by the communist Viet Cong. She could be *killed.*

Trained as a medical technologist at the University of Missouri, Janice had volunteered to come to Vietnam as part of the American Medical Association's Education Project at the Saigon Medical School, where she taught pathology. Saigon had seemed relatively safe. Other than the occasional street bombing, no significant action had occurred there since the Tet Offensive two years before. Da Nang, on the other hand, was Dodge City, what with the U.S. Air Force and Marine base nearby.

Assigned to teach at the Da Nang laboratory school for two weeks, Janice was a stranger in a bustling, filthy, Dog Patch of a city buzzing with pedestrians, bicycles, pedicabs, and Honda motorbikes. Streets were narrow ruts squeezing through a juxtaposition of tin, plaster, and stucco. Everything smelled of rotted vegetables, spoiled chicken and pig carcasses, and human wastes. It took some getting used to.

When classes at her laboratory closed at noon one rainy afternoon, Janice decided there was little risk in having her hair done at a nearby salon, after which she could readily catch a pedicab to her gated housing unit. She was still in the chair at the Vietnamese beauty shop when the monsoon skies opened up and poured down a flood as through a breached dam. Rain drummed hard on the tin roofs, rumbling like a continuous explosion and drowning out all other sounds. Torrents of floodwater washed through gutters and sewers reeking of garbage. Janice had heard of old people and children actually drowning in such downpours. Exposed babies were sometimes knocked unconscious by the force of falling raindrops.

Shops closed. Cabbies disappeared. Pedestrians fled to shelter. Janice fought back a rising sense of panic as she discovered herself the only customer in the shop. She looked out into a dark, roaring-rain afternoon that suddenly became ominous and forbidding. It was bad enough being the only American woman in this part of the city, but now she was stranded with no safe way to reach her housing unit. Once it started, the rain might continue like this all afternoon and throughout the night.

The Vietnamese hairdresser spoke no English; Janice's command of Vietnamese was less than skilled. Growing increasingly frightened, she attempted to get across to the shopkeeper her plight.

"See? This is the school where I teach. I live in this direction . . . this address. Can you tell me how to get there? Do you understand? No?"

Tears welled in her eyes. She prayed silently and fervently. *God? God, are You listening, sir?*

What was she expecting? That a divine guide or road map would appear?

She was cut off from all the people she knew and trusted, cast adrift in a dangerous city beset by monsoons and teeming with enemy guerrillas. Her parents might never see her again.

A pedicab driver pulled up in front of the shop and stopped. Janice shrank away from the window, although she knew he had already seen her. He sat out there on his three-wheeled bicycle, not moving, merely staring in through the rain-swept window with his hooded, expressionless gaze. He wore black pajamas. A flimsy shelter of sorts covered the driver's seat, but he was still soaked by the deluge. Canvas enclosed the passenger's seat behind him.

He waited patiently, like a predator at a watering hole. VC wear pajamas like that, Janice thought.

The beautician, closing her shop, gently took Janice's arm to hustle her out the door into the rain, but Janice drew away, afraid and shaking her head. If she got into that thing, she could vanish and no one would ever know what happened to her. The beautician insisted, smiling reassuringly.

What other option did she have? She had to trust in God. Still it took a great leap of faith for her to get into the pedicab. The strange, silent driver beckoned to her to come inside then zipped the canvas skirt. Rain attacked the cab, but it was dry inside. She thought to hide from weather and the outside world as the operator mounted and began to pedal through empty, drowned streets where no one would ever hear her scream.

With an effort, she forced herself to sit back and relax and let God handle it. As soon as she did that, a gentle wave of peace grew within her heart until she actually began to enjoy the trip.

All too soon, the driver stopped and unzipped the cab. She was astonished at how quickly they had arrived in front of her housing complex. She offered piasters for the ride, but the silent man in black refused them by smiling, folding his hands together as in prayer, and bowing three times, as though thanking *her.*

She observed him more closely now. He was not a young man. His face appeared weathered and wrinkled and he had a gold tooth in front. His kind brown eyes suddenly dimmed before he turned away to resume his business. The broad smile revealing his gold tooth faded. His face saddened.

Quickly, he climbed onto his pedicab seat and bicycled away, his head down against the rain as it ran down his back, leaving in his wake a plume of blown white water. Stunned by this simple act of kindness, Janice watched him until he disappeared into gray sheets of falling water. She could only speculate upon the circumstances that God may have used to send him to her in her hour of need.

Perhaps the sad old man had lost a family member in a similar situation, a wife or a daughter murdered by the VC? Seeing the young American woman through the shop window, seeing how scared she was, may have prompted him to make sure nothing happened to her before he got her home.

She would never know for sure. But for years afterward, especially when it rained very hard, she could feel her old rescuer's presence and the haunting, knowing way he looked at her.

ARMY PRIVATE FIRST CLASS GALEN KITTLESON,
World War II, 1944

Less than a year before, the war had been so far away from young Galen Kittleson and the farm country of Iowa where he was raised that it seemed almost unreal. Since then, however, the kid who once harbored the notion of becoming a high school coach had been honed into a deadly weapon of destruction with the Sixth Army's Alamo Scouts. He was forced to turn off emotion in order to meet the cold, hard demands of combat. Evil had to be conquered in the same way that God did his share of smiting in the Old Testament.

As lead scout for his company's movement, Private First Class Kittleson followed a jungle trail in New Guinea that twisted like a serpent beneath thick foliage. It was dank and dim on the trail. Jungle canopy absorbed sound so that any noise not dampened became louder than in real life.

Corporal Olsen covered Kittleson twenty to thirty yards back, moving nearer or farther as terrain dictated.

He saw Kittleson pause to peer into tropical growth alongside the trail. Sprawled on the forest floor lay a Jap skeleton, its bones picked clean by insects and scavengers and turning yellow and green-scummed from moisture and lack of bleaching sunlight. Scraps of uniform clung to the bones. It took tropical forest mere days to reclaim dead flesh.

It was the first enemy Kittleson had seen, not counting Japanese Zeros fighting in the skies with Yank Wildcats.

The skeleton was only bones with dark eye sockets and death-grinning teeth. A missing tooth must have affected his smile when he was alive. Kittleson wondered if he had had a lisp. Oddly enough, the nineteen-year-old scout felt only a mild curiosity at sight of the dead man. He murmured a brief prayer, "God have mercy on his soul." Then he moved off down the trail, tommy gun slung ready for use, right hand on the pistol grip, finger laid alongside the trigger guard.

The terrain opened into a wide grassy area splashed with sunshine at the base of a rise in the trail. Kittleson spotted movement on the other side of the opening. He thrust out a warning hand and dropped to one knee. Olsen passed along the warning. The column froze. Most of Echo Company remained in forest shadow.

Kittleson watched as the top of a gray-brown crush cap, bouncing with the head underneath, gradually appeared above the rise. Then came the shoulders with a long rifle slung across the back. The Jap looked no older than he did. He bopped along as merrily as Little Red Riding Hood on her way to Grandma's house. He had everything except a picnic basket and a summer's song on his lips. He was probably a runner delivering a message from one unit to another, and probably believed he had the woods all to himself.

Kittleson crouched in the open, as visible as a tree trunk. The Jap failed to see him until it was too late. Kittleson pressured the tommy's trigger, his left hand hard on the forward grip to control any muzzle rise.

The submachine gun burped. Little Red Riding Hood died without seeing the wolf. It was so sudden he didn't even look surprised. Heavy .45s stitched him from his belly to his face.

The first *live* enemy soldier Kittleson had ever seen close up—and he killed him cleanly.

It was war. He had trained for it. The only emotion he felt was that continuing mild curiosity. He approached the body cautiously, one eye on the trail beyond. The jungle was quiet and again motionless, not even a breeze. The dead Jap lay on his back. Most of his face was gone and there were bloody ragged holes in his guts and chest. A short, scrawny little kid. Kittleson wondered how long it would take the jungle to polish these bones.

He circled around the fresh corpse, watching ahead, concerned that more enemy might have heard the shots. Second Platoon leader Lieutenant Abbott came forward and motioned the scout to continue down the trail.

It was Echo Company's first kill. Kittleson became something of a hero.

"How does it feel to kill a man?" Olsen asked him later.

Kittleson thought about it. He said, "Are you going to eat them peaches?"

What he felt was between him and God. He would deal with his actions in his soul after the war ended.

Kittleson retired from the U.S. Army and returned to farm in Toeterville, Iowa. A gentle man of the soil in his final years, he "dealt" with war by becoming a devout Christian. He died in 2006.

NAVY CORPSMAN ROBERT H. DIRR, JR.,
Vietnam, 1967

Navy Corpsman Bob Dirr squatted on his heels in a foxhole on
the wire perimeter of one of a string of U.S. Marine fire support
bases (FSB) that occupied a ring of hilltops. Rain that morning left
an inch or so of water and mud at the bottom of his hole. The rest of
the day Dirr sweltered in triple-digit temperatures. But now the evening
breezes returned to make him shiver. It was late on Christmas Eve, a
time of reflection and homesickness for young men isolated, afraid, and
far from home.

Dirr leaned back against the muddy wall of his fighting hole but
remained on his heels out of the mud. He was on perimeter watch.
With him were his medical aid bag, M-16 assault rifle with three hundred rounds of ammo, six grenades, and the trigger clacker for a claymore mine set up in front of his position. Helicopters thumped overhead. Artillery at a distant firebase roared, followed by a brief staccato
of small arms fire. Then silence. Just another night in the 'Nam.

Dirr's eyes fixed on the North Star, the Guiding Star, the Christmas Star. His heart ached from loneliness on this special night. There
were no brilliantly garnished trees with gifts arranged beneath them.
No stockings hanging from mantels. No family or family friends. No
prayer of thanks over Christmas dinner tomorrow. The chaplain might
drop by the mess tent, but that wasn't the same as being home.

Sometimes Dirr thought he might never see home and Christmas
again.

He watched idly as a green flare streaked skyward through the mist
that obscured a distant FSB. Before the flare completed its arc across
the sky, another one shot after it. And then, to his astonishment, firebases all along the line, including his own, were popping flares, filling the heavens with them. Red and blue and yellow and green. They

charged the tropical sky with kaleidoscopic illuminations. Balls of light catapulted through the air from all angles and all directions.

Surprised and overjoyed, Dirr glanced at the phosphorus hands of his watch. One minute after midnight. Christmas!

Flares were just the beginning. Faintly at first, but then louder and louder as one firebase after another caught on, pulsing across the valley . . . from outposts and FSBs miles apart . . . a familiar harmony . . . *singing!*

Notes rang off bald hilltops. Over valleys and rice fields. Through forests and above grasslands. Waking villagers in their grass-and-tin hooches, disturbing Charlie VC wherever he crouched, bringing tears to the eyes of combat-toughened Marines. Picking up volume as it swelled nearer and nearer. As beautiful as the Mormon Tabernacle Choir.

The singing reached Dirr's outpost. Marines chimed in from foxholes and bunkers all around the perimeter. The flash of flares played from horizon to horizon. Tears carved streaks through the grime on Corpsman Dirr's cheeks. Reverently, he added his voice to Vietnam's Christmas carolers.

> *Silent Night, Holy Night.*
> *All is calm,*
> *All is bright.*
> *Round yon virgin,*
> *Mother and Child . . .*

ARMY SPECIALIST BILL MCDONALD,
Vietnam, 1967

Specialist Bill McDonald,[*] a helicopter door gunner for the 128th Assault Helicopter Company, had been shot out of the air three times, won the Distinguished Flying Cross and a Purple Heart for a

---

[*] See also Foreword and Chapter 14.

hand wound, and been nominated for the Silver Star medal. By the last two weeks of Operation Junction City, he looked beat, worn-out, as he stood in front of the commander's battered field desk. He had lost weight and had bags underneath his eyes big enough for a trip back to California.

"McDonald, I'm suggesting you take a few days in-country R & R," the CO said. "You look like you can use it."

A few lazy days sunning himself on the beach, swimming in the South China Sea, sleeping in a *real* bed.

McDonald hopped a chopper to the airbase at Nha Trang and caught a pedicab downtown. A Vietnamese cyclist took him to a small, clean-looking hotel away from the "Dog Patch" area of nightspots and whorehouses where most GIs hung out. He wanted to get as far away as he could from Army life and combat, never mind that he was probably staying right in the middle of a hive of VC. He was likely the only American in Vietnam dumb enough to sleep overnight in the city alone and unarmed.

His was a great room straight out of the French colonial period. Ceiling fans stirred the tropical air over a huge bed. A blue porcelain pitcher and a wash pan, looking to be from an ancient dynasty, rested on a nearby stand. The draped window even had a view. In one direction, a giant Buddha that also served as a temple occupied a hillside. In the other, gleaming white beaches edged the soft blue waters of the South China Sea. It was such lovely countryside in contrast to the war-torn interior where he had been living and fighting for the past months.

"I want to sleep for an entire year," he told the hotel's mamasan manager. "Don't bother me with anything."

She gave him a questioning look.

"No good-time girls," he emphasized. "Sleep is all I want."

Later, he might go out sightseeing and to the beach. Right now, all he wanted, *needed*, was to close his eyes and make the war go away. Fully clothed, he stretched out on the bed and slowly drifted off, thinking of home and watching the rotating fan blades.

A muted knock on the door disturbed him. He got up and cautiously opened the door. In the dimly lighted hallway stood a young Eurasian woman, a pleasing mixture of French and Vietnamese. She looked at first glance to be in her early twenties, near McDonald's own age. At the same time she looked ageless, timeless, somehow very *different.* Her skin appeared so white it almost glowed, as though made of porcelain through which shined an eternal light. An aura as soft and ethereal as a veil radiated around her body. She wore the traditional long wraparound.

McDonald blinked in astonishment, so overcome by her otherworldly beauty that he was unable to speak. She merely looked at him. She was silent, with demure almond eyes cast slightly downward. His first thought was *What is this gorgeous girl doing whoring GIs?*

He recovered with a rush of annoyance. He had specifically *told* the mamasan *no girls.* "I'm not interested in whatever you're offering," he snapped. "I'm not paying for anything. I want none of your services. Go away."

He slammed the door in her face, locked it, threw himself facedown on the bed and buried his head in his pillow. He went quickly to sleep.

His eyes sprang open at the touch of soft feminine hands gently massaging his back and neck. How did she get inside? He had left her standing outside with the door locked. He thought to throw her pretty ass out—but he couldn't seem to move. Still she said not a word.

A feeling of peace and well-being overcame his resistance. Mind and body completely relaxed as this woman's remarkable hands coaxed all the tension, anger, and depression from his body. In some surreal sense, he drifted into an altered state, neither fully asleep nor awake. He felt *loved* in an inexplicable spiritual way. It was similar to the feeling that overcame him after he fasted for long periods of time—lightheaded, floating in another world, an almost out-of-body experience.

He turned over to look at her. Sunlight shone through the window backlighting and blurring the gentle figure that hovered over him. She rewarded him with a soft, motherly smile before she rolled him back into position and continued to rub his back.

He needed to get a good look at this woman who brought with her such healing energy. He turned over again, but the room was empty.

Astounded, even a bit frightened, he leapt out of bed and searched for her. But she was nowhere in the room. He threw open the locked door, raced into the hallway, and looked in both directions.

No one there.

He must be going buggy. He ran down the stairs and out onto the street. "Which way did the girl go?" he demanded of the hotel bellboy.

"No one come out door."

"No one?"

"Not in boo-coo hours."

"Has anyone come in?"

"No one, *monsieur.*"

Confused and wary, he confronted the hotel mamasan. "Who did you send up to my room?"

She regarded him as though she thought he must be going buggy.

"Are you drink, boy-san?" she asked in pidgin English. "I send nobody. If somebody come or go the hotel, I see. I see no one."

He had not been drinking. Nor was he on drugs. Thoroughly baffled, he wandered back to his empty room. The girl's presence lingered there. The character of the room seemed to have changed, as though she had left love and peace behind when she departed so mysteriously. He was too tired to try to figure it out now. He simply lay down, and for the first time in weeks he was able to forget all about the war and sleep soundly.

McDonald awoke at twilight, feeling refreshed and reconnected to the world. He walked along the beach barefoot while the sun sank into the sea. He thought of the girl and wondered if somehow he might have concocted the whole thing in his mind.

But, no! She was as *real* as the ceiling fan and the bed and the blue water pitcher. As *real* as his two hands.

Warm water caressed his feet. He looked up as the first stars appeared. Suddenly God's love filled his soul, and he felt so exceptionally close to the Divine that tears filled his eyes. It was no longer necessary that he account for the beautiful woman in his room. Something special had happened that day. How else could he explain it? He had been touched by an angel.

Bill McDonald, who wrote the foreword to this book, is now a minister in California. His experiences in Vietnam influenced him to live a more spiritual life.

ARMY PRIVATE EDWARD A. PENICHE,
World War II, 1944

Operation Market Garden and the liberation of Holland were costly for the American airborne in its loss of paratroopers and equipment. After seventy-two days of combat, the 101st and the 82nd Airborne Divisions were pulled off the lines for refitting and outfitting. They had barely arrived in northern France when Germans broke through in the Ardennes Forest on Saturday, December 16, 1944, to launch what was later to become known as the Battle of the Bulge. Orders came down for the "Screaming Eagles" of the 101st and the "All Americans" of the 82nd to deploy to Belgium. Rumors were that this might be the toughest battle yet. And not the least challenge was that this winter was turning out to be the coldest on record.

Paratroopers, grumbling and bellyaching, loaded onto open, five-ton trucks to race across the frozen landscape to stop the Krauts. Attached to the 81st AT/AA (antitank/antiaircraft) Battalion, 502nd Regiment of the 101st, nineteen-year-old Private First Class Ed Peniche and his gunner, Corporal Darrell Garner, hitched their rolling 57mm AT gun to the bumper of a deuce-and-a-half truck and clambered aboard. GIs were packed in so tightly there was standing room only. If one man's butt itched, the man next to him had to scratch it.

Peniche was a diminutive Mexican immigrant, only an inch or so above five feet tall. Born in Yucatan, the eldest offspring of eight in a devout Catholic family, he came to the United States in December 1942 to stay with an aunt and uncle and pursue an education not available in Mexico. He finished high school in Paducah, Kentucky, and immediately enlisted in the U.S. Army on September 27, 1943, volunteering for the elite airborne. An altar boy back in Yucatan, he possessed an unshakable spiritual strength and a deep-rooted faith that God would take care of him.

Shortly after midnight on December 19, the 101st Airborne convoy passed through the Belgian town of Bastogne with a long rumble and roar and swirl of snow. By dawn, elements with attached AT/AA were setting up on the outskirts of Longchamps to block the main road intersection between Bertogne and Bastogne. Orders were clear: defend and hold the road at all costs.

The constant unnerving thunder of big guns from all sides and toward the front was sign enough that the Germans were near. As Garner put it, "The Krauts are on the way and, boy, are they pissed off."

Sergeant Joe O'Toole, squad leader for Peniche's AT gun section, placed his 57s on a farm facing the expected direction of the oncoming enemy. The farm consisted of a small rock-and-wood cottage and a barn. The owners had already cleared out. O'Toole warned his men to stay out of the house, but they could use the barn for warm-up. Garner and Peniche gathered straw to line the bottom and sides of their foxhole and help to ward off the terrible cold that, as much as the big guns and panzers, was Hitler's biggest weapon and ally in this fight.

All they had to do now was wait.

Corporal Garner took a stroll to expend nervous energy and keep up the circulation in his freezing arms and legs. He returned bubbling with excitement.

"Ed, praise the Lord!" he exclaimed. "We have a cross and crucifix in front of the house!"

Peniche scrambled from his foxhole. Sure enough, a crucifix of black metal attached to a four-foot-tall wooden cross stood in the front garden of the farmhouse. It had to be an omen. While artillery growled ominously in the background, Peniche knelt, mumbled a prayer, and made the sign of the cross.

The weather grew even colder and snow continued to fall. There was a snap to the air, as if it were freezing and breaking. Suspended ice crystals glistened. Paratroopers put on every scrap of clothing they possessed in an effort to keep warm. Fires were prohibited since smoke would give away their positions.

Snow fell heavily on the second night, big wet flakes the size of golf balls, so thick that visibility was cut to mere feet. It filled up foxholes. Walking through it knee deep, even to an adjacent foxhole, proved exhausting. A soldier threw up his arms and shouted in exasperation, "God, how I hate this miserable shit!"

Having grown up in sunny Yucatan, Peniche was afraid he would freeze to death.

Paratroopers situated around Bastogne to defend it fought a series of thrust-and-parry engagements against probing German infantry and armor. Americans in Noville, six miles northeast of Bastogne, stopped the 2nd Panzer Division dead, but then had to pull back to higher ground at the village of Foy, a mile nearer Bastogne.

Battles also raged in sectors around where Peniche and the other AT/AA gunners waited with the 101st Infantry. So far, however, they had little to do except potshot an enemy recon patrol now and then.

Then, suddenly, several German half-tracks and a line of infantry in winter camouflage emerged around a bend in the road several hundred yards away. Heavy American machine guns raked the intruders. Sergeant O'Toole issued the order to fire the 57s. The skirmish didn't last long. The German reconnaissance withdrew, leaving behind one of its half-tracks blazing so fiercely that it melted snow and ice for yards around.

"Touched by an angel," Army Sergeant Bill McDonald survived seventeen bullets that passed directly through his body. *Photo: Bill McDonald*

Navy Lieutenant Commander John McCain's plane was shot down over Hanoi, and he was captured by the North Vietnamese. He and an atheist guard engaged in conversations about the resurrection of Christ. *Photo: John McCain*

A heavenly voice saved Marine Lance Corporal Nathan Jones's life and changed it forever. *Photo: Nathan Jones*

An angel rode on the wing of the plane flown by Marine Lieutenant Colonel Neil Levin (right, being decorated by Group Commander Colonel Les Brown) during bombing missions over North Vietnam. *Photo: Neil Levin*

With God's help, Army Sergeant Terry M. Jorgensen went back to the field of battle to retrieve a friend in Vietnam.

Photo: Saints at War archives, Brigham Young University

Army Air Corps Chaplain George R. Barber landed on D-Day armed with only a Bible and a prayer.

Photo: U.S. Air Force

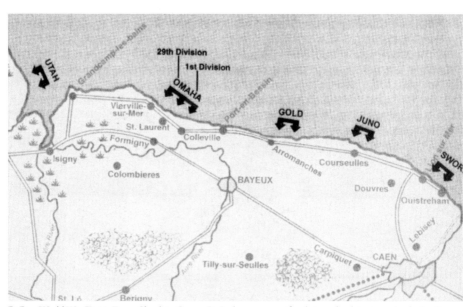

D-Day, World War II. Air Force Chaplain George R. Barber was one of only two chaplains to make the landing.

Army Chaplain Delbert Kuehl (shown being decorated by General Mark Clark) was the "Battling Padre" of the 504th Parachute Infantry Regiment, 82nd Airborne. *Photo: National Archives*

Army Private First Class Desmond T. Doss (shown being awarded the Medal of Honor by President Harry Truman) refused to carry a weapon and as a conscientious objector was branded a coward. Doss went on to win the nation's highest award for valor as a medic. *Photo: National Archives*

Surrounded in the jungle by North Vietnamese forces and cut off from reinforcements, Marine Lance Corporal Robert Gaddy and Charlie Company resorted to prayer and the Marine Corps Hymn. *Photo: Robert Gaddy*

Marine Lance Corporal Bob Gross pondered God's impenetrable will after the North Vietnamese killed his buddies. *Photo: Bob Gross*

Cast adrift after the Japanese sank his ship, Chaplain George S. Rentz led survivors in prayer and a hymn before he sacrificed his life so another soldier might live. *Photo: U.S. Navy*

An angel appeared to Army Sergeant Lloyd King in the jungles of Vietnam. *Photo: Lloyd King*

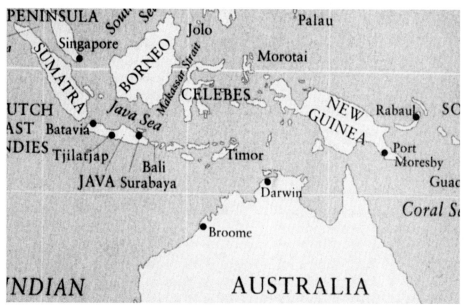

Java Sea, World War II. The USS *Houston* was sunk in the Java Straits. Navy Chaplain George S. Rentz sacrificed his life for his shipmates.

Army Air Corps Lieutenant Haig Koobatian saw a glowing presence in the sky that protected his aircraft from German fighters. *Photo: Haig Koobatian*

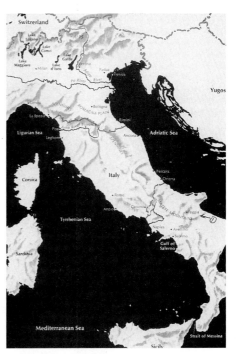

Italy, World War II. Lieutenant Haig Koobatian's 301st Bomber Group flew missions from the Foggia Plains over Germany.

ABOVE: Army Air Corps Lieutenant James Huston perished when his plane was shot out of the sky during the battle for Iwo Jima. Did his spirit appear in a two-year-old boy fifty-five years later? *Photo: National Archives*

RIGHT: What Army Private First Class Galen Kittleson (kneeling left, with other members of his unit) felt about killing in World War II was between him and God. *Photo: Galen Kittleson*

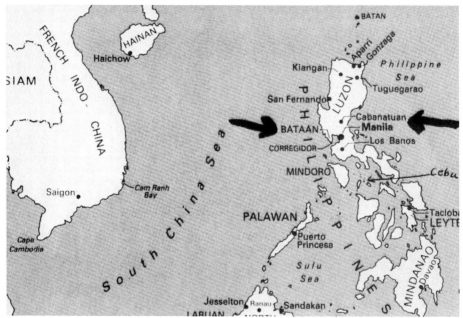

The Philippines, World War II. Some of the heaviest fighting occurred here at the beginning and end of the war. The USS *Indianapolis* was on its way to Leyte when a Japanese submarine sank it. Cabanatuan was where most of the survivors of the Bataan Death March spent their captivity.

Commander of the USS *Indianapolis* when a Japanese submarine sank it in shark-infested waters, Navy Chaplain Charles McVay III led survivors in reciting the Lord's Prayer. *Photo: U.S. Navy*

A near-death experience sent the spirit of Marine Sergeant Gene Beck flying back to a small Marine chapel hundreds of miles away. *Photo: Gene Beck*

Army Private Edward A. Peniche, a gunner during the Battle of the Bulge, was wounded and in great pain when he came upon a huge cross standing in a farm courtyard and appealed to God for help. Years after the war, he revisited the site and found the cross still standing. *Photo: Edward A. Peniche*

Marine Lance Corporal Leonel R. Perez, point man in the jungles of Vietnam, called out to God after being wounded in an ambush—and God answered. *Photo: Leonel R. Perez*

During the invasion of Bougainville, a torpedo from a Japanese bomber failed to explode when it bounced off the landing craft occupied by Leonard Owczarzak, or "Sack," (right) and his AA outfit. *Photo: Leonard Owczarzak*

Army Sergeant Marcus "Mike" Brune ripped sections from his Bible and handed them out to Korean orphans. *Photo: Mike Brune*

A helicopter pilot in Vietnam, Army Chief Warrant Officer Jim Eskildsen came under intense enemy fire while transporting lifesaving medical supplies to a unit trapped by the enemy. In pitch darkness, a "heavenly light" guided him to the rescue. *Photo: Jim Eskildsen*

Usually armed with a Bible and a guitar, the "Bible Answer Man," Navy Chaplain Brian Kimball, tended his Marine flock in Iraq. *Photo: MCRD Parris Island*

The Four Chaplains (left to right): Protestant Chaplain George L. Fox, Rabbi Chaplain Alexander Goode, Protestant Chaplain Clark V. Poling, and Catholic Chaplain John P. Washington gave up their life jackets to other men and went down with the ship, elbows linked while they prayed and sang hymns after a German torpedo sank their troop transport. *Photo: The Four Chaplains Memorial*

Even worse than the weather, if possible, came the daunting news that the 101st Airborne had been cut off and surrounded, trapped in a lumpy circle some five miles in diameter. Knowing that American supplies and ammunition were running low, Germans demanded the division's surrender.

Airborne commander General Anthony McAuliffe replied with one word: "Nuts!" At first, this singular reply baffled the Germans. Soon it would become famous to the troops and later to English-speaking people everywhere.

The paratroopers fought on.

White-clad grenadiers and white-camouflaged Panther and Tiger tanks of the 9th Panzer Division finally attacked Peniche's sector in force. The entire Longchamps-Monaville region exploded in bloody and ferocious fighting as Germans attempted to break through the American main line of resistance (MLR). All along the perimeter, American machine guns, mortars, ATs, and artillery sawed at the attack.

Peniche's heavy 57mm gun boomed until the barrel glowed with heat, delivering high-explosive and armor-piercing rounds on target at enemy armor both in the valley and along the road. Corporal Garner was a crack shot. His second round of the battle knocked the turret off a tank and put it out of action. Bursting shells destroyed another German tank on the road and damaged a third, which withdrew dragging one of its tracks.

Bullets thumped into the heavy double shield of Peniche and Garner's 57. Exploding mortar shells stomped all around. A piece of shrapnel caught Peniche in the left leg as he returned from a dash to the ammo dump near the barn to pick up more shells. Painful though the wound was, he still crouched behind his gun shield to fix fuses to the rounds so Garner could fire them.

German mortar fire homed in on Peniche's gun. An airburst over Sergeant O'Toole's foxhole wounded him severely and put him out of action. Simultaneous explosions knocked Peniche's gun out of commission, sending one of the wheels flying and slamming Garner to the ground. Peniche felt himself thrown through the air. He landed in the snow and couldn't get up for what seemed an eternity.

Groggy, his ears buzzing from the concussion, Peniche seemed to exist in a vacuum where he no longer felt afraid—sort of a momentary trance.

Reality gradually returned. He was in a bad way. His left shoulder was dislocated and twisted, his jaw out of place and swelling, shrapnel like fire burned in the muscles of his legs. Mud and blood were splattered everywhere on the snow.

Hearing O'Toole moaning, the injured Peniche pulled himself on his belly to the sergeant's hole and discovered him lying at the bottom with shattered bone sticking out of his right thigh and leg. He saw a syringe dangling from O'Toole's hand where he had stabbed himself with morphine. Although pale and on the verge of shock, O'Toole looked up and saw Peniche.

"Ed . . . Ed, stay down . . . Don't get hit."

Garner sat in the snow nearby, stunned and out in the open where bullets and mortar shells played deadly all around him. Peniche crawled over and helped him reach the cover of O'Toole's fighting hole.

Once his two wounded friends were relatively safe and out of the direct line of fire, Peniche took time to assess the gravity of their injuries. He had to make a decision. He could think of his own skin, stay hidden in the hole with them and perhaps let his buddies die—or he could make his way through the pounding barrage of German shells and seek aid for them.

Although in pain and consumed with terror, praying in both English and Spanish, Peniche set out crawling through the thick snow and slippery ice. Sheer bedlam reigned as he made his way toward the battalion command post (CP) located beyond the farmhouse on the lee side of a knoll. When he reached the large cross, he paused to ask for the Lord's help. Bullets thudded into the ground all around him and tore into the front of the house, but both he and the cross remained untouched.

While he prayed, he suddenly felt his panic subsiding. In its place was a sense of peace and well-being. His pain became more bearable. God assured him everything was going to be all right.

Bolstered by his moment at the foot of the cross, Peniche wriggled the rest of the way to the other side of the knoll, paying little attention to bursting shells, and quickly reached the CP.

"My buddies are hurt out there," he reported to medics. "God is protecting them until you can reach them."

Sergeant Joe O'Toole and Corporal Darrell Garner did survive. Upon hearing of her son's moment of solitude in front of the cross on the battlefield, Peniche's mother offered a simple answer: "Son, rest assured that that was the hand of our Lord blessing you and saving you. That is the only explanation . . . and there is no need for you to ever wonder."

PFC Ed Peniche was awarded the Bronze Star with "V" for valor for his heroism in seeking help for his buddies in spite of the danger and his own wounds. He became a U.S. citizen in 1953 and retired from active duty with the U.S. Army in 1970 after a combat tour in Vietnam. After completing the education for which he originally came to the United States, he became a college professor at Central Virginia Community College (22 years) and eventually a professor emeritus until he finally retired from teaching at the age of seventy-four. He lives in Kentucky with his wife, Deanie.

MARINE LANCE CORPORAL LEONEL R. PEREZ,
Vietnam, 1966

It was midday in Vietnam during one of the strangest wars ever fought by the United States. The game was simple, if deadly. Blindman's bluff and hide-and-seek played with live ammunition. An equal opportunity war in which everyone had pretty much the same opportunity to get killed.

Point team of Charlie Company, 1st Recon, 1st Marine Division, worked its way up a small hill through razorlike elephant grass five to six feet high. Point's job was to lead the way, clear the trail for the main element, and take the hit first if the enemy set up an ambush. If Marines were unionized, point men would draw top scale.

Lance Corporal Leonel Perez wiped the sweat from his brow using the tail of the rag knotted around his neck. As point team leader, he pulled double duty on the compass and map to keep the movement on course. He took a reading and rechecked his map. A few feet ahead of him, the grass stopped rustling as Private Jones took a knee and shot up a closed fist. *Danger!*

Perez passed the signal back to halt the company, then worked his way forward to see what had alerted Jones. He dropped on one knee next to the kid. Jones was peering through tall grass, craning his neck like a turkey, finger on the trigger of his rifle.

"Something in the weeds shines when the sun hits it just right." He pointed with the barrel of his weapon. "I can't tell what it is."

Perez edged past Jones to get a better look. It could be almost anything—moisture on grass, beads of water left over from last night's rain. Still, it was better to be safe than sorry.

Oh, shit!

A booby trap with the trip wire stretched through the grass. Where there was one, there were likely more. Maybe even a whole field of them. Gooks sometimes initiated ambushes built around booby traps.

"Let's get our sorry asses out of here," Perez said fast. "Jonesey, we're going back the same way we came in. Careful. Step in my boot-prints. Got it?"

Jones's eyes shone like silver dollars. He followed as Perez led the way, eyes darting, toes feeling for the tracks he made coming in. He took maybe four or five steps that way before the ground suddenly heaved out from beneath him with an ear-shattering *Bang!* He had stepped on a pressure-detonated device that he and Jones had missed going in. Sky spun above his head as the blast flipped his legs, spun him through the air, and deposited him on the ground like a thrown rag doll. He hit hard, momentum tumbling him downhill through the grass toward a tree line. Black powder and smoke bit his nostrils and throat.

He finally stopped rolling. But when he tried to get up, his legs refused to work. He wriggled around in the grass like a live insect pinned to a collector's board.

Run! Run! The bastards were probably all around him, as thick as fleas on a village cur.

His legs refused to work.

He pushed himself to a sitting position. Pain like burning pokers blazed through his groin all the way to his brain. He stared aghast at his legs. Little was left of them except two useless masses of mutilated flesh and bone with blood spurting from several veins, pulsing with the frantic beating of his heart. An ugly cavity in his left leg spurted even more blood. His right foot looked cloven right down the middle of his boot, as though split by an ax.

He was so scared.

Someone was screaming and screaming.

He looked around. There *was* nobody else. It must be *him* screaming. His mind recoiled. *I got to get outa here . . . I got to get outa here . . .*

Movement down by the tree line caught his eye. The VC were coming for him!

Oh, God, help me! Help me, please!

He didn't even realize he was calling out to God. He had never been much of a churchgoer, never thought much about the Creator or the hereafter. Until now.

Until now when the gooks were going to drag away his mauled ass to torture him for hours, skin him alive while he hung upside down in a tree. He had seen such victims after the VC got through with them. It took them hours and hours to die. They must have been begging for death's relief at the end.

Perez looked around for his rifle to fend them off. He couldn't find it. *I don't want to die like this. I don't want the VC to drag me away and kill me.*

He ripped a frag grenade from his belt and crushed it against his chest, thumb through the pin and ready to pull it. He intended to take as many as he could with him when he went. He closed his eyes against the pain and the reality.

His mind must have drifted for a moment. He was with his mom and dad and his brothers and they were all saying good-bye to him. *Sorry, folks. I guess I won't be coming home after all. God, please help me?*

A voice called his name softly. He thought it a whisper from Heaven, God answering him. *Huh?* A calm presence seemed to surround him. He relaxed. Tears ran down his grimy cheeks. Someone took the grenade from his hands. He drifted in and out of consciousness. He thought he heard a medevac helicopter flaring in. Then he knew it was a chopper, that it was here, coming for him. *Like an angel.*

An *angel* had come for him. *God loves me! God loves me! I'm going home!*

Leonel Perez lost his right foot. He now lives in Los Angeles, California.

ARMY CORPORAL LEONARD OWCZARZAK,
World War II, 1945

Corporal Leonard "Sack" Owczarzak, nineteen, received a letter from his ten-year-old brother, Arthur, back in Detroit as the U.S. Army's American Division island-hopped its way across the Pacific: *I pray six rosaries for you. I pray for you, and so does Spot* . . . Of course, his mother would be on her knees every night, too, adding her voice to Arthur's and little dog Spot's.

Prayer must be working, Sack figured, considering how many times fortuitous intervention saved his raggedy butt. His good luck and his "little voice" that always seemed to warn him became things of both wonder and good-natured banter among his buddies of the 746th Antiaircraft (AA) Battalion, for which he was a .50-caliber machine gunner.

"Sack, what's your little voice telling you this time?"

"It says keep your ass down and your eyes open."

"Talk directly to God, do you?"

"My mama does, my kid brother does, and his dog does . . ."

It had to be more than dumb chance and blind luck that Sack and everybody around him could wade through shit up to their necks, as Sack's buddy Fritz Schultz put it, and still come out smelling as sweet as roses.

During the invasion of Bougainville, a torpedo from a Jap bomber failed to explode when it bounced off the landing craft occupied by Sack's AA outfit. Ashore, an incendiary bomb lit up the AA site, exposing the gunners like roaches in a slum house when the lights come on. Glare from the flames blinded the soldiers as a Japanese Zero screamed out of the black sky to obliterate the position. At the last moment, for no apparent reason, the fires extinguished themselves. Blinded by the return of darkness, the Zero pulled up without firing a shot. As soon as the sound of its engine faded, the fire caught and again blazed brightly.

"It's a miracle!" stunned gunners exclaimed. "Sack, whatever it is your mama, your brother, and his dog are doing—tell 'em to keep doing it."

In March 1945, the 746th received orders to use the pinpoint accuracy of its big 90mm AA guns to blast Japanese out of caves on the Philippine island of Cebu, where they were holding up the advance of the Americal Division. An overnight LST voyage from liberated Leyte disgorged the battalion and its weapons and gear on the docks of Cebu City. The settlement had been almost demolished in fighting to free it from Japanese occupation. Nonetheless, the grateful local population thronged the Americans as their trucks and vehicles rumbled through town.

At dusk, the heavy convoy pulled off into a pineapple field and fanned its trucks into a defensive position similar to the way early American settlers circled their wagons against Indian attacks. A narrow dirt road junctioned off from the main highway and stretched across fields toward the Japanese-held hills several miles away. Orders came down from the commander to dig in. An enemy attack was always possible.

The soil on Bougainville had been volcanic and easy digging. The earth here was so hard it bent the edges of shovels and entrenching tools. Tropical nightfall caught Sack and his buddy Fritz Schultz still working on their foxhole behind their five-ton truck. Sack finally threw up his hands. His tall, skinny body had aches that had their own aches.

"To hell with this. I'm beat. I'm sleeping on the front seat of the truck."

Schultz looked doubtful. "That might not be the smartest thing you've ever thought of, Sack."

At almost the same time that Sack sprawled himself across the seat of the five-ton on one side of the convoy's perimeter, a Filipino farmer wearing a straw hat and carrying an armload of firewood approached a sentry on the other side. It was past the 7 P.M. curfew. In broken English, the peasant explained that he was on his way to market with his firewood and knew nothing about a curfew. The sentry finally allowed him to go on down the road past the bivouacked convoy toward Cebu City.

Hardly had Sack closed his eyes to sleep than they snapped open again. A voice in his head warned him to get out of the truck immediately and back into the foxhole with Schultz. He never questioned such premonitions. He simply obeyed.

"Honey, I'm home. Move over, Fritz."

"You hearing voices again, Sack?"

The sentry had made a big mistake in allowing the "peasant" to pass through. The guy was actually a land-borne *kamikazi* with his firewood hollowed out and filled with dynamite. Sack and Schultz were still trying to get comfortable together in their shallow excavation when the night exploded in lightning and thunder.

Glass, metal, and other debris sliced through the air, clanging off trucks and guns and skipping across the ground. Sack buried his head next to Schultz's as deep in their hole as they could get until crap stopped raining out of the air. After the all-clear, they discovered that a chunk of shrapnel had busted out the windshield of their truck and slashed completely through the seat where Sack would have been sleeping had not his little voice urged him to *get out now!*

Thank you, Mom. Thank you, Art and Spot. Thank You, God.

. . .

The 746's 90mm guns proved effective against Japanese entrenched in caves. The enemy fled to the northern part of the island. The battalion with its AA guns and water-cooled .50-caliber machine guns moved into the defense of strategic roads across the island. Six or seven gunners from Sack's D Battery erected a roadblock next to a culvert over a small jungle stream. The rest of the battery blocked a second road about a half mile away across a hill and through heavy rainforest. The roads were main connections between Gogo, San Remigo, and other villages around Cebu City.

It was cush duty. There was fresh water for drinking and bathing and a little native hut that provided shelter. Villagers passed each day on their way to market. The young soldiers teased and laughed with the young women and bought chickens and eggs and other produce. Although six or seven thousand Japanese still lurked thereabouts, the only sign of them was a dead Jap found decayed and fish-nibbled upstream from where the Americans normally bathed and got their drinking water. Life returned to normal and was good, however, once the corpse was dragged away from polluting the stream.

One afternoon, Schultz decided to cook some old-fashioned chicken soup. Several chickens were butchered and soon bubbling away in a five-gallon coffee can over an open flame. Tantalizing aromas wafted across the hill to the nostrils of the men at the other roadblock. The portable field phone buzzed.

"What are you guys cooking over there? It's driving us wild over here."

Sack undertook the humanitarian mission of delivering soup. He filled up a discarded coffee can, snapped a clip into his M-1, and set out through the cane brakes. Halfway there, that old feeling of imminent danger overtook him. His little voice shouted in his ear. He stopped in his tracks, turned around, and went back. His instincts had served him too well to go against them now.

"Whassa matter, Sack? Chicken out on catering the chicken soup?"

Shortly thereafter, a Filipino farmer charged up to the roadblock, breathless, wide-eyed, and excited, saying in broken English, "Japs in my house. Japs in my house!"

Once the Americans succeeded in calming him, he related how a half-dozen or so Japanese troops came down from the hills and ordered him to leave his farm. He felt fortunate indeed that he and his family had not been murdered.

An American patrol rushed the farmhouse and killed seven Japanese after a fierce firefight.

Had Sack continued his errand of mercy with the hot chicken soup, he would have passed directly in front of the house full of enemy occupiers. Undoubtedly, they would have ambushed and killed him—to steal the chicken soup if nothing else. Once again he had been miraculously spared by a presence that seemed to guide him. Owczarzak knew its identity.

After all, wasn't his mama, his little brother, and Spot praying for his safety every day?

Corporal Leonard Owczarzak survived many close calls during the war and returned home after VJ Day.

12

THE BIBLE

The grass withereth, the flower fadeth: but the word of our God shall stand forever.

—ISAIAH 40:8

The Bible has gone to war with the American soldier from the day of the nation's birth, providing comfort and inspiration and sometimes a shield against the physical and mental horrors of combat. General George Washington carried his Bible with him throughout the Revolutionary War. He urged his men to attend religious services and to seek solace, wisdom, and strength from reading the Bible. In this he set a precedent of bonding American military men with God's Word.

Bibles accompanied the Continental Army and the Grand Army of the Republic. Western settlers took them in their covered wagons through hostile lands. The bluecoats who held Cemetery Ridge and the graycoats who charged it depended on the comfort of their Bibles. Chaplains and commanders handed out pocket Bibles in Belleau Wood of World War I, to dogfaces in World War II and to the "Battling

Bastards of Bataan," to Marines during their retreat from the Frozen Chosin, to grunts and boonie rats in the jungles of Vietnam, to infantry and Marines in Kuwait and in Tikrit a dozen years later . . .

Army Sergeant Brice Coleman went to war twice with a Bible given him by his preacher—to Korea in 1950 and then to Vietnam in 1967. His son Mike took the same Bible with him to the Iraq War thirty-seven years later. "When I was going, my mom mentioned the Bible and asked if I wanted to take it with me. 'Yeah,' I told her. 'I'm going to need all the luck I can get.'"

"Men and women didn't set aside their religious convictions even though they were carrying rifles and machine guns," said Professor Dennis A. Wright of Brigham Young University. "They still found time to read their scriptures, take the sacrament, pray and share the Gospel with others. In the most trying of circumstances their spiritual life did not end; in fact it became a sustaining factor."

NED THE BEE HUNTER,
the Alamo, 1836

Colonel David Crockett and his party of eight frontiersmen bought horses, tack, and supplies at Little Rock, Arkansas, on the morning of November 13, 1835, and set out for Texas. They took lodging at a tavern in Fulton just before they struck the Red River lowlands. It was there they met a barrel-chested young man of twenty-two who introduced himself as "Ned." A cheerful man full of laughter and joking, Ned had black hair and wore clean ornamental buckskins.

"I never seed a hunter so clean," Crockett declared.

"My clothes are new," Ned conceded, "but I'm a *bee* hunter. Their wax is worth more in Mexico for church candles than their honey."

Thimblerig, a member of the party, slapped Bee Hunter's back and said, "Come to Texas with us, Ned. The world's biggest game is due there any day."

Ned accepted the invitation to fight the Mexicans in Texas, even though he said he would miss his sweetheart, Kate, who lived in Nacogdoches. An affectionate and religious girl, Kate gave Ned a Bible before he left home in hopes that it would help keep him safe and true. Every night, he read from his Bible before falling asleep.

"He never drank more than just enough to prevent his being called a total abstinence man," Crockett observed in his journal. "Then he is the most jovial fellow for a water drinker I ever did see. . . . He keeps everyone in good heart with his songs and his jests. . . . His gun is first rate, quite equal to my Betsy, though she had not quite as many trinkets about her."

Crockett's group reached Bexar, Texas, in February 1836, just in time to confront General Santa Anna's army of approximately 4,000 soldiers. As Mexican infantry, artillery, and cavalry appeared on the horizon, about 150 Texicans, including Crockett and his men, garrisoned in the Alamo, where they had already stored provisions, arms, and ammunition. The Bee Hunter burst into song as the U.S. and Texas flags were raised over the old mission on February 23.

> Up with your banner, Freedom.
> Thy champions cling to thee;
> they'll follow where 'ere you lead 'em,
> To death or victory.

General Santa Anna sent a message to the Alamo demanding its unconditional surrender. Colonel William Travis, who commanded the defenders, responded with a cannon shot. The Mexicans initiated the siege with a barrage of artillery.

Even though Travis dispatched a runner to Goliad to ask for reinforcements, it was soon clear his little band was on its own. They put up a determined and valiant fight. The walls of the citadel were thick and sharpshooters inside the fortress struck down the enemy at great distances. Ned the Bee Hunter nailed eleven Mexicans at such long ranges that Crockett noted, "We all thought it would be a waste of ammunition to attempt it."

Crockett himself was no slouch with a rifle. He recorded in his journal how he engaged in "a little sport this morning before breakfast."

> The enemy had planted a piece of ordnance within gunshot of the fort during the night, and the first thing in the morning they commenced a brisk cannonade, point blank against the spot where I was snoring. I turned out pretty smart and mounted the rampart.
>
> The gun was charged again, a fellow stepped forth to touch her off, but before he could apply the match, I let him have it, and he keeled over. A second stepped up, snatched the match from the hand of the dying man, but the Juggler, who had followed me, handed me his rifle, and the next instant the Mexican was stretched on the earth beside the first. A third came up to the cannon. My companion handed me another gun and I fixed him off in like manner. A fourth, then a fifth seized the match, who both met with the same fate. Then

the whole party gave it up as a bad job, and hurried off to camp. . . . I came
down, took my bitters, and went to breakfast.

Santa Anna lost three hundred soldiers the first week of the siege. Reinforcements, however, were constantly arriving to replace casualties. The small garrison inside the Alamo was completely surrounded and harbored little hope of either defeating the enemy or cutting through opposing lines to escape.

On February 26, the Bee Hunter led a small party out of the fortress to gather firewood and water. A larger body of Mexicans discovered him. A skirmish ensued, during which Ned and his scroungers beat the enemy off after killing three of them.

That night, when Ned opened his Bible to read before going to bed, he discovered that a musket ball had lodged in the Bible during his afternoon's encounter outside the walls. Had the Bible not been in his breast pocket, the bullet would have pierced his heart.

"See here, Colonel," he remarked to Crockett, "how they have treated the valued present of my little Kate of Nacogdoches."

"It saved your life," Crockett marveled.

The Bee Hunter looked grave. "True," he said. "But I am not the first sinner whose life has been saved by this book."

Ned the Bee Hunter was killed on March 4, 1836, on another foray outside the walls. On March 6, Santa Anna's army attacked and overran the fort, slaying all its defenders.

ARMY SERGEANT GORDON MADSON,
Korea, 1951

During the last of May and part of June 1951, the Red Chinese Army marched more than one hundred American POWs back and forth along its rear lines. Sergeant Gordon Madson, an assistant platoon sergeant with the 2nd Infantry Division, whose platoon had been cut off and overrun by the enemy, concluded that the display was a propaganda ploy by the Chicoms to bolster the courage of their soldiers and the civilian population. *Look. Americans are flesh and blood and can be killed and captured.*

The original one hundred rapidly dwindled in numbers. Diseased and filthy, plagued with body lice and other parasites, hands tied behind their backs, barefoot in the springtime freezes, surviving on a daily handful of "bug dust" rice, millet, wheat, and whatever water they could find in streams or rice paddies, men dropped out and were never heard from again. Sometimes a rifle or pistol shot sounded from the direction of someone who fell out along the way from exhaustion and starvation. Sergeant Madson, who was not a big man to begin with, quickly dropped thirty pounds.

At a rest stop where the prisoners spent several days, two Americans were too weak to get up off the cold ground. Blowflies buzzed their mouths and eyes, sucking out what little moisture remained. A tall, gaunt man attended them, a young buck sergeant named John Wheeler.

"Can't you put something on your faces to keep off the blowflies?" Wheeler asked them.

"I'm sorry," one responded in a hoarse rasp. "*What* can we use? Besides, I'm too weak. I can hardly lift my arms."

Wheeler took his own life in his hands and approached the Chinese commander. "Can't you do something for them?" he pleaded. "They're going to die."

"Later."

That was always the answer: *Later.*

Maggots hatched and squirmed around in the ill men's eyes, noses, and ears. The men promptly died.

Sergeant Madson dropped down next to where Sergeant Wheeler was reading a small pocket Bible. Wheeler looked up as he carefully rewrapped the Bible in a shred of oilcloth and tucked it back inside his tattered trousers.

"They let you keep your Bible?" Madson asked in surprise.

"It's my most valuable possession," Wheeler said, not bothering to add that it was his *only* remaining possession. "I try not to let them see me when I'm reading. It's a great comfort in times of tribulation."

"They took mine."

"We can read mine together if you want."

That was the beginning of a friendship forged in hardship, deprivation, and uncertainty.

Two days later, Madson and Wheeler were separated from the main body of POWs. Their hands were bound behind their backs and four guards escorted them into the mountains. Madson feared they were going to be shot for some slight or unknown infraction of the rules.

It seemed, however, that the Red Chinese had other plans for the two sergeants. After several days of walking, they climbed a winding mountain footpath to where some Korean baked-mud houses were arranged around a clearing. They were the only Americans present.

The purpose of the long hike soon became clear. Chinese officers from the various units in the vicinity rotated into the little settlement to ask the prisoners thousands of questions concerning their families, homes, and life in the United States. "They're using us to practice their English on," Madson decided.

In between "English lessons," the "teachers" were used for slave labor. "No work, no eat," guards constantly reminded them.

Throughout the summer, the two Americans hauled logs on their backs and dug bunkers for the Chinese. Frequently, under guard, they made runs down the mountain twenty-five miles away to haul back rice and sorghum and other camp supplies on their shoulders. Their boots soon wore out. The Chinese had no rubber tennis shoes big enough for Wheeler's size-twelve foot. He wrapped rags and pieces of canvas and anything else he could find around his feet to protect them. Madson's feet at size eight made him luckier in the footwear department.

Madson's weight dropped to ninety-five pounds. The larger-framed Wheeler weighed not much more. Both grew so weak they could barely walk. Wheeler contracted a skin disease. His hands, nose, ears, and face turned a muddy brown color, crusted over, and oozed a yellowish pus.

Chinese doctors gave him a small tube of sulfa salve captured from Americans. The rash dried up, but returned more aggressively than ever as soon as the salve ran out. The Chinese refused to provide more.

Surprisingly, Wheeler was allowed to keep his Bible, probably because guards didn't know what it was. The only other reading material available were the *Daily Worker*, published in New York, and *People's Daily World*, from San Francisco. Copies of these two American Communist Party periodicals magically showed up in most Korean POW camps, where they were used as propaganda to persuade prisoners that communism was the hope of the future. Wheeler shook his head sadly over the fact that *Americans* were giving support to the same enemy who tortured and murdered other Americans.

Then he and Madson would read his Bible together.

One day in August, guards informed the captives that Sergeant Wheeler would be taken to a place where many other American soldiers were kept. Good Chinese doctors with proper medicines would take care of his deteriorating health. A pall of despair enveloped the sergeants the night before Wheeler's departure. They had become as close as brothers over the months since their capture.

They read the Bible together. Wheeler looked up. His face was filthy, bewhiskered, and resembled a skull covered by ravaged, pus-draining, yellow-brown skin.

"We'll never see each other again," he said.

Madson tried to keep up their spirits. "Of course we will. You'll get well there with other Americans."

"You'll be alone with the Chinese, with no one to talk to," Wheeler lamented.

With that, he lovingly wrapped his Bible in its scrap of oilcloth. He cradled the book in his bony hands while both men bowed their heads in prayer. Then he passed the book to Madson.

"I can't take your Bible!" Madson declared.

"You must. There'll be no one with you to help remember all the wonderful things we love about America. The Bible will comfort you. You need it more than I."

Wheeler was willing to give away his most valued possession. The gesture deeply moved Madson.

At the first light of dawn, Sergeant Madson clutched the precious Bible inside his shirt and watched three guards lead Sergeant Wheeler away. Wheeler turned back once before he disappeared, managed a wan smile of farewell, and then was gone, leaving Madson alone with the enemy. Tears welled in his eyes. He had never had a truer friend or known a better man. He dropped his chin on his bony chest and wept bitterly.

In November 1951, Sergeant Gordon Madson was transferred to the same POW camp to which John Wheeler had been taken in August. There he learned that Wheeler had died in the "hospital." Madson was released in 1953 through a "prisoner swap." He penned a letter to Wheeler's mother and sister, relating the friendship of the two men and the story of the Bible.

"I still have with me John's Bible," he wrote, "and I would like to send it to you as a dear remembrance. I have read it through many times and it was a constant source of inspiration and strength to me. . . . I have kept it in excellent condition, always keeping it wrapped to protect it from the elements."

ARMY SERGEANT MARCUS "MIKE" BRUNE,
Korea, 1951–52

Allied forces had finally stalled the communist advance and started pushing the enemy back north. Staff Sergeant Mike Brune's combat engineers of the 7th Infantry Division packed their shovels and picks in five-ton trucks and headed to the front, their mission to repair roads and bridges to keep the advance moving.

Brune, twenty-five, had been drafted at the end of World War II as an aviation engineer; he was discharged in 1948 without seeing action. Recalled for Korea, the six-footer from Oklahoma saw more action this time than he bargained for. In addition to building and repairing roads, constructing airfields and buildings, and patching just about anything else that came along, engineers also laid and retrieved land mines and frequently contributed their trucks as hearses and ambulances.

Brune and his men of Charlie Company, tasked with the unpleasant chore of hauling off enemy corpses before they started stinking, pitched them unceremoniously into the beds of trucks and hauled the grisly masses to the rear, where they were dumped into massive trench graves and covered with dirt. American dead, on the other hand, were layered on stretchers for transportation and delivered to grave registration centers.

One afternoon, an infantry outfit came under such heavy mortar fire that it had to pull back. GIs stampeded to the rear across a field, skipping and dodging exploding shells. Pieces of the more unfortunate were being thrown about like old doll parts. Brune's Third Squad helped retrieve the wounded while the field was still under fire. Running about, trying not to intersect a round, engineers grabbed mangled soldiers and dragged them, carried them in blankets or on their backs, coaxed them—anything they could to get them off the kill zone and back to their trenches.

One kid had two broken legs and his belly split open like a too-ripe watermelon. His intestines spilled out on the ground. Brune and Sergeant Scott Collins ran to him.

"Oh, God!" the soldier sobbed. "The pain! I can't stand it. Shoot me! *In the name of God, please shoot me!*"

"We're getting you out of here," Sergeant Brune promised.

He and Collins spread their fingers wide on either side of the boy and scooped steaming guts back into their cavity. They rolled him onto a blanket, picked up the ends of the blanket, and dashed to the rear with him. A medic joined them. He tried to sedate the soldier and get some blood into him while they were running. That wasn't easy. Shells continued to bang all around and they had to hit the ground each time they heard a shell coming in close. After it went off, they would scramble to their feet again and continue their mad rush, the injured GI's butt in the blanket bumping against the ground.

The boy was still screaming and begging to be put out of his misery when Brune and Collins pinned him to the skids of a bubble helicopter and sent him back to a MASH unit for treatment. Brune never heard if the kid made it or not.

As American soldiers had done even before the Revolutionary War, Sergeant Brune took refuge from the carnage and hardship in his Bible. He had started out as a Lutheran in World War II, then switched to the Baptists after his recall to Korea. Each of the two denominations in his hometown sent him a Bible. He kept both in the event he should need a spare. Good engineers always keep spares of everything.

Whenever conditions permitted—a lull in the fighting, a temporary stalemate—Brune broke out a Bible and gathered with other weary GIs to read from it. Frequently, he ran into some soldier whose unit was returning from patrol or from an encounter farther up the line.

"We having services tonight, Sarge?" the infantryman might ask.

"Anytime is a good time."

"I'll pass the word, Sarge."

Five or six filthy, unshaved dogfaces would huddle after nightfall in a muddy trench or a musty old bunker once occupied by the enemy while Brune read from the scriptures by the dim light of a flickering candle. Lines of pain and worry gradually smoothed from combat-hardened faces. The sergeant ended each session with "Let us pray."

Wherever American troops went, Korean kids followed, begging for handouts. Most were orphans whose parents were either killed or turned up missing when the North started its burning-earth march to conquer the South. Crops, livestock, *everything* had been destroyed as completely as though a plague of Old Testament locusts had swarmed over the land and left its inhabitants starving.

The hollow-eyed, sunken-cheeked little faces of hungry children could not be resisted. Like most GIs, Brune doled out C-rations, Life-Savers candies, chocolate, anything he could spare. Children often joined Brune's circle of GIs when they gathered in the candlelight to read. Although they understood little English, they seemed to take comfort in the gatherings and begged to know more about the Book that was the apparent source of that comfort.

Sergeant Brune, who yearned to share the Bible and its message with everyone, found a use for his spare Bible. He ripped sections from it and handed them out to the kids, urging them to pass the chapters around. Proverbs to one, Psalms to another. John, Mark, Luke . . . The little Koreans didn't quite understand what they had, but they appeared to revere the gifts and held on to them.

"Mike, these tykes can't even talk English, much less *read* it," Sergeant Collins pointed out.

"Somewhere down the line, someone will explain it to them," Brune said.

Winter set in. Sergeant Brune and his platoon, driving a convoy of trucks loaded with tools and construction materials, rumbled through a village composed of a dozen or so mud huts dissected by a rough ribbon of road. Driving the lead truck, Brune braked to allow a villager carrying an old woman on his back to cross the road ahead of him. The old woman appeared dead.

As he sat at the wheel waiting, he looked down and spotted a tiny waif of a boy about eight or nine years old standing barefoot and shivering in the cold and looking up at him. The kid was dirty, snotty-nosed, with long, uncut hair, wearing ragged peasant trousers and a thin shirt that hung on his bony shoulders. The sight was enough to tear the heart out of any man with even a spoonful of compassion.

"Me name Kim," the boy introduced himself. "No mamasan. No papasan. Me go with you? Make good houseboy."

Brune looked down into brown eyes that seemed to encompass all the suffering that had befallen this poor country and its people. He thought of his baby daughter, Carla, back in Oklahoma. That decided it. He jerked a thumb toward the bed of the truck.

"Get in," he offered.

That night when the convoy bivouacked, Brune took a pair of old scissors and cut Kim's hair. Lice infested the boy's head, some so plump that the scissors cut them in half. The sergeant broke ice in the river, scooped up a helmet full of water, gave Kim a bar of GI soap, and ordered him to scrub. The skinny little creature shivered like a stray dog in snow.

Brune then rounded up the smallest uniform he could find. It hung loosely on the little boy's frame. The sleeves and trouser cuffs had to be rolled up. A pair of too-big boots on his feet made him look like a miniature circus clown. Sergeant Collins had to laugh at the picture Kim presented, but the little boy was so proud of his new wardrobe that he strutted about like a prince.

"Your little son is looking mighty good," Collins teased.

Brune repaired the framework of an old army cot so Kim would have a bed. From then on, the boy slept on his cot right next to his adoptive GI. Whenever the sergeant returned from a job or a night patrol, Kim was always up and had hot rations waiting. The boy squatted on the ground after Brune went to bed, carefully disassembled the soldier's M-I Garand, and cleaned every part before putting it back together. He even shined the cartridges before starting in on Brune's web gear and other equipment.

He faithfully attended every Bible reading, asking so many questions afterward that Brune, tired and sleepy, finally had to tell him to hush and go to sleep. Kim's most treasured possession was the chapter of Matthew torn from Brune's spare Bible. It contained the Sermon on the Mount.

The GI sergeant and the little Korean boy were together for nearly three months before close fighting and harsh winter conditions forced Brune to send him to the rear. The boy burst into bitter tears and clung desperately to his foster father. He had to be physically untwined from the sergeant's legs and taken back on the next resupply convoy. Brune turned away so the kid wouldn't see his tears. He prayed for Kim's safety and for a day when the boy might find peace and happiness.

Brune missed the boy, but the war went on. The killing, the misery, the horror. Months passed.

In early summer, Sergeant Brune's company was relieved off the line and sent to the rear for refitting, repair, and rest. As the engineers drove back through the layers of support units, Brune asked everywhere about Kim. "His name is Kim. He's about this tall. The bravest, sweetest little boy you've ever seen."

"Sarge! They're all named Kim, and they're all brave and sweet."

Brune had almost given up on ever seeing the boy again. One afternoon, he was sitting on the running board of his five-ton truck reading his Bible when he heard his name called in a high, boyish voice. "Sarge Mike! Sarge Mike!"

He looked up in astonishment. Kim came running. The kid was all cleaned up with a fresh haircut and a new little uniform cut down to fit him. Some support outfit had taken him in.

"Sarge Mike!"

Sobbing with joy, he threw himself into Brune's arms. In one hand he clutched his worn chapter of Matthew.

Sergeant Mike Brune wanted to adopt Kim and bring him back to the United States. That proved impossible under wartime conditions.

13

CHAPLAINS

He gave some, apostles; and some, prophets; and some, evangelists;
and some, pastors and teachers.

—EPHESIANS 4:11

General George Washington placed chaplains throughout his army during the American Revolution and had the government pay their salaries, a precedent that extended into the twenty-first century. His intent was to make the American army worthy of God's favor. His orders stated:

> *We can have little hopes of the blessing of Heaven on our arms if we insult by*
> *our impiety and folly. Let vice and immorality of every kind be discouraged,*
> *as much as possible, in your brigade: and as a chaplain is allowed to each regi-*
> *ment, see that the men regularly attend divine worship.*

Over two centuries later, in 2003, seven members of the 372nd Military Police Company were accused of abusing Iraqi prisoners of war at

Baghdad's largest prison, Abu Ghraib. During the investigation of the scandal, which resulted in several MPs being convicted and sentenced for crimes, George Washington's position that chaplains discouraged vice and immorality in the armed forces echoed with ironic resonance.

Chaplains at Abu Ghraib had been ordered to stay out of the way of soldiers and not intrude upon their lives. They were to stand by on the periphery and let soldiers come to them. As a result, they exerted virtually no moral or spiritual presence or influence upon the prison camp. Chapel attendance was low, sometimes attracting only a scattered handful of worshippers. A number of MPs didn't know who the chaplains were. Some didn't even know there *were* chaplains at Abu Ghraib.

Chaplains of the unit that replaced the disgraced 372nd were told *they* would be an active influence upon their MP soldiers, that *they* would be present at prisoner interrogations, at shift changes, and in the daily lives of soldiers. The entire atmosphere at Abu Ghraib changed, replacing darkness with light. Chapel attendance jumped dramatically. The prison became a model operation.

"THE FOUR CHAPLAINS,"
World War II, 1943

The United States pressed every available ship into service to carry supplies and troops to the war front in Europe. More than 16 million men and women were transported in this monumental effort. Shipping routes to England led first to Greenland via the Strait of Belle Isle between Labrador and Newfoundland, a treacherous stretch of sea known as "Torpedo Junction" because of prowling German submarines. Enemy wolf packs were sinking Allied shipping at the rate of one hundred vessels per month.

On January 23, 1943, three freighter troop transports loaded to capacity with young soldiers departed New York Harbor bound for England under the armed escort of three Coast Guard cutters. All amenities were removed from the transports in order to get as many fighting men as possible on each voyage. Cots were crammed into every available space. Designed to hold fewer than four hundred people, the aging luxury liner USAT *Dorchester* set sail with 920 soldiers aboard.

Listed on the *Dorchester*'s manifest were the names of four chaplains. Rarely were so many transported together on a single troop ship. These four had attended Chaplain School at Harvard in 1942 and had been close friends for more than a year.

Rabbi Chaplain Alexander Goode was an expert in U.S. and Middle East history and had served in a York, Pennsylvania, synagogue before volunteering for the Army. At thirty-one years old, he was the married father of a three-year-old daughter. He spent two days with his family prior to receiving debarkation orders. Hours before the convoy set sail, he wrote a quick letter to his wife, Theresa:

Just a hurried line as I rush my packing. I'll be on my way in an hour or two.
I got back yesterday afternoon just before the warning. Hard as it was for us

to say goodbye in New York, at least we could see each other before I left. Don't worry. I'll be coming back much sooner than you think.

At age forty-two, Protestant Chaplain (Methodist) George L. Fox was the oldest of the four. Abused by his father as a child, he ran away from home at seventeen and lied about his age in order to enlist in the Army. He served as a Medical Corps assistant in World War I, winning the French Croix de Guerre and the Silver Star for valor. He became a minister after the Great War ended, then reenlisted after Pearl Harbor on the same day his eighteen-year-old son joined the Marine Corps.

"I know from experience what our boys are about to face," he said as he kissed his wife and seven-year-old daughter good-bye. "They need me."

Catholic Chaplain John P. Washington, thirty-three, bespectacled and mild-mannered, did not appear the sort to go to war. Although a sensitive man who loved music and art, he was as tough as green oak inside. Once the teen leader of Newark's South Twelfth Street Gang, he received a calling from God and returned to Newark as Father to other people of the streets. He left eight brothers and sisters behind in New Jersey.

Chaplain Clark V. Poling, thirty, was the youngest of the four and pastor of a Dutch Reformed Church in Schenectady, New York. The son of Doctor Daniel Poling, a well-known radio evangelist, he seemed determined to enlist in the Army as a regular fighting soldier rather than as a chaplain.

"I'm not going to hide in some safe office off the firing line," he insisted.

"Don't you know that chaplains have the highest mortality rate?" his father countered. "As a chaplain, you'll have the best chance in the world to be killed. You just can't carry a gun yourself."

Reverend Poling ended up attending Chaplain School with Goode, Fox, and Washington, leaving behind an infant son and his pregnant wife. He asked his father to pray for him just before he boarded the *Dorchester*.

"Not for my safe return," he explained. "That wouldn't be fair. Just pray that I do my duty, never be a coward, and have the strength, courage, and understanding of men. Just pray that I shall be adequate."

The worst winter storm to hit the Atlantic in half a century froze decks to crystal ice and tossed the convoy about in a giant washer of churning waves. Frightened soldiers, most of whom had never been to sea before, were seasick most of the time. The stench in steamy bays and holds was almost unbearable.

Midafternoon of February 1, seven days out of New York and still one hundred miles short of Greenland, the skipper of U.S. Coast Guard cutter *Tampa* signaled the other craft that he had picked up disturbing sonar signals.

"We are being followed. Submarines estimated in our vicinity. Inform all ships to close up tightly and stay close for the night."

Dorchester's Captain, Hans Danielsen, got on his PA system. His voice spilled into crowded holds: "Every soldier is ordered to sleep with his clothes and life jacket on."

Most of the troops belowdecks disregarded Captain Danielsen's order. Hot and sweaty, they cast aside bulky life jackets and elected to sleep in their skivvies. The four chaplains were the most conspicuous exceptions as, fully dressed in fatigues and wearing life preservers, they circulated among the nervous troops doing what military chaplains do during times of threat: reassure men that the Lord watches over them.

Most of the soldiers were sleeping fitfully by midnight. The chaplains ventured onto the main deck to pray together. The transport carried no running lights in such dangerous waters, and they could make out nothing in the night, not even the horizon. Freezing rain and sleet pelted their exposed faces as they huddled together and bowed their heads.

Afterward, Chaplain Fox suggested they get some sleep themselves. "God will watch over us."

The attack occurred at 12:55 A.M., February 2. Submerged beneath the black chop, a German U-boat released three torpedoes. Two missed their target, but the third struck the *Dorchester*'s engine room with a blinding flash, knocking out the ship's power and instantly killing one hundred men. The transport rolled precariously to starboard as cold salt water poured into the vessel through its awful wounds. It immediately began to sink.

Panic and darkness engulfed terrified soldiers belowdecks. Ammonia fumes and spilt oil burned lungs and eyes. Injured men cried out. Frightened survivors screamed in horror as they groped frantically in the darkness to find exits. Piles of discarded clothing and unclaimed life jackets were flung about. Many men who reached the slanted, icy decks wore nothing more than underwear.

Water was flowing across the main decks within ten minutes. Icy waves broke over the railings, tossing men into the sea, many of whom had ignored the captain's warning and were without life jackets. Flames licked up through the decks from the engine room. Wind made the flames roar and flap like dragons, their light illuminating the horrible pantomime of frantic and desperate men.

Some lifeboats were frozen in their rigging. Others floated away empty. Panicked survivors capsized boats or sunk them by loading them beyond capacity.

Fully dressed and wearing life jackets, the chaplains could readily have saved themselves. Instead, working together, they organized escape efforts in the holds and directed soldiers to exits with calm words of encouragement, bringing some order to the bedlam.

On the main deck above, shouting to be heard above the chaos, they passed out spare life vests from deck lockers as frightened soldiers pressed forward in ragged lines with the seas already sucking at their ankles. A Merchant Marine seaman, dazed and confused and reeling from the cold, headed back to his cabin.

"Where are you going?" Rabbi Goode asked.

"To get my gloves."

The rabbi peeled off his own gloves. "Here. Take mine."

"I can't take your gloves."

"Why not? I have two pairs."

The seaman accepted the gloves on those terms and rushed off to assist in freeing one of the last remaining life boats.

Rabbi Goode continued to hand out life jackets with his bare hands; he actually had no spare gloves. Soon, the deck lockers were empty. No more life vests. Soldiers still in line realized they were doomed. They would be frozen and unable to swim within minutes after they went overboard unbuoyed.

Chaplain Fox stripped off his own life preserver and thrust it to a boyish-faced kid with blond hair. "God bless you, son," he said.

Rabbi Goode put his vest on a soldier suffering from a broken shoulder, using the laces from his own boots to tie it around the injured man.

Chaplain Poling and Father Washington likewise relinquished their life jackets and thus their only hope of survival.

Ragged lines remained before the empty lockers, still hoping, but there was nothing else the chaplains could do for the doomed remnants of their flock except pray. Remaining soldiers crying out in terror were swept into the sea. Orange flames leaping into the superstructures backlighted the last men left aboard the rapidly sinking ship—the four chaplains. Up to their thighs now in black water, they clung to the railing on the tipped deck. Their strong voices lifted in the cold, dark night above screams of pain and fear.

"*Shma Yisrael Adonai Elohenu, Adona Echad . . .*"

"Our Father Who art in Heaven . . ."

"Hallowed be Thy name . . ."

"Thy Kingdom come, Thy will be done . . ."

The four men of God had saved as many men as they could. They braced themselves against the railing and one another, arms linked together, and prayed and sang in a valiant final declaration of faith. The fine, clear tones of Father Washington's singing carried across the sea—and then all went silent. The *Dorchester* with the chaplains still at the railing sank to her watery grave in the North Atlantic. They had sacrificed themselves that others might live.

Of the 920 aboard the USAT Dorchester who left New York, 690 either died in the explosion or were lost in the frigid waters, the third-highest loss of life at sea during World War II. But for the chaplains, the toll would have been much higher. In 1948, the U.S. Postal Service issued a special stamp commemorating the brotherhood, service, and sacrifice of Chaplains Goode, Washington, Poling, and Fox. In 1960, the U.S. Congress authorized the Four Chaplains Medal. Inscribed on it in relief are the Star of David, the tablets of Moses, the Christian cross, and the names of the four heroic men of God who went down with their ship after midnight on February 2, 1943.

ARMY SENIOR CHAPLAIN DENNIS GOODWIN,
Iraq, 2004

On April 4, 2004, Brigade Chaplain Dennis Goodwin of the 30th Brigade Combat Team, 1st Infantry Division, got together with Baptist Chaplain Darrell Brumfield and Presbyterian Chaplain Kevin Wainwright to conduct Palm Sunday services on the big parade field of the Kirkush Military Training Base, Diyala Province, Iraq. Even just after sunrise, the weather was dry and hot, the sand already burning through the soles of boots. Some 150 soldiers from across the brigade gathered under the Iraqi sun to witness the baptism of eleven of their number.

Chaplain assistants had constructed the baptistry. It was a huge wooden box with a plastic liner to hold water, wooden steps up one side, and camouflage netting around it. From his open-air pulpit, Chaplain Goodwin delivered a short sermon in which he explained how baptism signified the washing away of one's sins and rebirth into a new life as a Christian.

The eleven soldiers awaiting baptism stepped forward. They came from a wide range of backgrounds, male and female, black and white, officer and enlisted. Their common denominator was combat boots, cammie uniforms, and a desire to serve God. The shortest soldier was barely over five feet, the tallest was six-eight.

A woman soldier with a lovely voice sang "Down to the River to Pray" from the soundtrack of the movie *O Brother, Where Art Thou?*

Chaplain Brumfield began baptism by immersing two men, one of whom was the six-eight soldier. Only five feet six, Chaplain Brumfield elicited a trickle of laughter from the congregation at his efforts to maneuver the tall sergeant into the tank and dunk him.

Chaplain Wainwright had never immersed anyone before. He made the rookie mistake of failing to hold the noses of his first two parishioners and almost drowned them. They came up sputtering and coughing.

He did much better on his next two.

Chaplain Goodwin conducted the final immersions. "I baptize you in the name of the Father, the Son, and the Holy Ghost . . ."

Someone pointed out that some of the new Christians had lived lives not completely acceptable by traditional standards.

"Those who have sinned the most often provide the most fertile field for spreading and sowing the Gospel," Chaplain Goodwin responded.

It was a significant day for the chaplains of the 30th Brigade Combat Team. Eleven children went down to the river to pray—and eleven brothers and sisters joined the Body of Christ.

On the following Sunday, over two hundred Easter sunrise worshippers packed the room that served as chapel. There was standing room only, even though attendance was not mandatory. The chain of command from the general on down attended. The walls of the building vibrated with the singing of hymns.

NAVY CHAPLAIN BRIAN KIMBALL,
Iraq, 2004

Navy chaplains have served in war and in peace with the U.S. Marine Corps on land, sea, and air for nearly 230 years. On a typical day at the Al Taqaddum Air Base, forty-five miles west of downtown Baghdad, home of 3rd Battalion, 24th Marines, Chaplain Brian Kimball rose at precisely 0600, shined, shaved, and showered, then grabbed his trademark guitar and went to work.

Stocky and fit, the twenty-seven-year-old lieutenant, with buzz-cut brown hair, rimless eyeglasses, and open smile, was the youngest Navy chaplain in-theater, as well as the most recognized figure on the airbase. After stuffing down breakfast in the chow hall, he started his daily rounds to visit every work area on the base. Far from waiting for parishioners to come to him, he went to them, walking with a loose, merry gait, sometimes whistling to himself, often plucking a few chords on the strings of his guitar to announce his arrival.

Daily temperatures averaged 100 degrees plus, up to 115 degrees. The air was always so gritty with sand that no one ever felt clean. However hot and miserable the weather, grease monkeys in the motor pool, grunts preparing for patrol, sentries in guard towers called out to the chaplain with smiles and laughter of recognition. "Hey, Padre!" He responded by clutching his Bible and whanging on his guitar.

The Bible Answer Man. That was what troops called him.

"Chaplain, I got a question for you. What do you think God meant when He said, 'Thou shalt not kill'? We're Marines. We break things and kill people. That's what we do. Does that mean we're going to Hell?"

Many Marines who had time on their hands took to reading the Bible. Chaplain Kimball always took the opportunity to answer their questions, whatever they were, quoting scripture to support his responses, showing them where to read further.

"Everything you do every single day *matters*," he said. "Each of our days here is more important because of the uncertainty of tomorrow. God helps us to learn to enjoy each and every day, regardless of circumstances. Come to chapel Sunday morning. We'll discuss it more in-depth."

Not much older than most of the Marines to whom he ministered, he related to them as a big brother as much as a chaplain. A big brother with answers to their spiritual questions. Sometimes late at night he was still answering questions, counseling young men and women with marital issues, acting as go-between with the Red Cross concerning emergency leaves, handling the other problems faced by young people far from home in a combat environment, making rounds to check on *his* people. Whatever happened, he always left troops chuckling and in good humor—plucking out a Weird Al Yankovic song on his guitar and singing the lyrics before packing up his Bible and guitar and moving on, like a wartime Johnny Appleseed sowing his seeds of faith.

Sunday church at his makeshift on-base chapel offered more than a sermon and a prayer. He recruited other Marines with musical talents and formed a worship band that played and sang with him during services. Shortly after the Abu Ghraib prison scandal, he performed at the EPW camp with his band as part of the armed forces' effort to make chaplains and their influences felt among the troops.

"Is this a great country or what?" he would sing out in imitation of Weird Al. "Let us pray."

While this might be the chaplain's *typical* day at Al Taqaddum, a combat zone produced dreadful atypical days as well.

Marine duties at Taqaddum included road patrolling the area surrounding the airbase. Chaplain Kimball commonly chatted with patrols, sometimes praying with them, before they donned their battle-rattle (combat gear), fired up their Humvees, and departed through the wire. Most of the time, security patrols were routine with few incidents.

Routine was broken, however, in mid-April just before Easter Sunday when a homemade IED detonated next to a patrol's lead vehicle. Iraqi terrorists in hiding opened up with RPGs and small arms fire.

Corporal Billy Willis, manning the grenade launcher on the turret of his hummer, was knocked off his mount and to the ground by the force of the initial explosion. His face, neck, and arms were bleeding from shrapnel wounds. He scrambled back to his perch and opened grenade fire at ambushers occupying two mud houses about four hundred meters away.

"Willis, you're losing blood!" another leatherneck yelled at him.

"I ain't got time to bleed!" he shouted back.

Enemy bullets sang all around the squad, thudding into the ground and ricocheting off armor plating. RPGs hissed smoke in erratic patterns as Marines took cover behind nearby mud walls and houses and returned fire.

A bullet punctured the helmet of Lance Corporal Curtis Hensley as he scurried for the wall, lodging in his brain and knocking him unconscious. Navy Corpsman Greg Cinelli braved the fusilade of hostile fire to drag the downed gyrene to safety.

The firefight continued unabated until a helicopter gunship and a mobile quick reaction force swept to the rescue. Terrorist attackers fled to melt back into the city's population. Willis and Hensley were the only friendly casualties this time.

Chaplain Kimball was waiting at the gate for the blooded patrol when it returned to base. There would be more questions for the Bible Answer Man, circumstances having impressed upon each Marine the reality that each passing day might be his last.

Lance Corporal Curtis Hensley and Corporal Billy Willis recovered from their wounds, although Hensley lost his right eye. Chaplain Kimball returned to the United States to become a civilian minister.

ARMY CORPORAL DAYTON KANNON,
World War II, 1944

As an ordained minister, Dayton Kannon could have sought a clergy deferment or requested to enter the Army as a chaplain. Instead, he chose to enlist as an ordinary infantry private.

"I'm no better than the other boys," he reasoned.

Soon enough, he was carrying a new Browning automatic rifle (BAR) in the jungles of New Guinea, rooting out strongholds of recalcitrant Japanese. Fellow GIs nicknamed him "Preacher," appropriately enough since he *was* a minister. He carried his BAR and his Bible.

The New Guinea rain forest was some of the darkest, most inhospitable geography on the entire planet. Blistering sun. Rainwater down the back of the neck and the crack of the buttocks. Wet and freezing at night. Exhausting treks through solid jungle teeming in the dark with shadows and silence. Swarms of bugs biting and sucking. Always craving fresh water, a break from what was treated in canteens to kill germs. Foot rot, coughs, and dysentery. "Oh, no! I've crapped my pants again!"

"Who cares? You already stink."

By May 1944, war for most of the U.S. Sixth Army in New Guinea consisted of mopping up what advancing forces had left behind. It was more skirmish than set-piece battle. Reverend Kannon's war was like that. And for several days, Kannon enjoyed the luxury of bed and real sheets in a rear hospital while being treated for minor shrapnel wounds. Although not fully recovered, he joined a group of eight soldiers headed back to his battalion with a load of ammunition. The BAR across his shoulders and pouches of ammo hanging off his frame were heavy enough to stagger an Aussie mule.

The jungle path serpentined beneath thick foliage. The trail was dimly lighted and the triple-canopy forest absorbed sound. Kannon lagged behind, weaker than he expected. Another GI dropped back to help him. At just that moment, Japanese ambushed the patrol with a rattle of machine guns and rifles that no amount of jungle canopy could absorb.

Machine gun slugs ripped a swath through the foliage and stitched Kannon from groin to ankles, knocking him flat on the trail. The other GI literally exploded at the waist, ripped into two parts. His top half flew one direction. His legs, still kicking, went the opposite.

Then, silence. Kannon had no way of knowing if the other Americans were dead or alive in hiding. He did know, however, that Japs always approached their victims to finish them off with bayonets and knives. A single movement of his pain-wracked body was sure to invite another volley of shots.

He had fallen with his BAR pointed in the direction of the ambush. He cautiously felt for the trigger. Then he waited, playing dead while inside he trembled with rage, terror, and anguish.

Turning to God, as he did in times of need, the minister-turned-warrior prayed silently and fervently. "Oh, God. If You get me out of this, I'll do anything You say for the rest of my life."

Leaves and bushes rustled. He heard stealthy footfalls approaching. His heart pounded against the jungle floor as, through slitted eyes, he watched enemy soldiers advance toward him. Gradually, they assumed human form against the foliage, their long rifles pointed, bayonets glistening like slivers of ice.

He dared wait no longer. He squeezed the trigger of his BAR, raking the flaming muzzle of the .30-caliber automatic rifle back and forth, spraying the Japanese, making them convulse and jerk in their tracks before heavy slugs slammed them to the ground.

An enemy sniper hiding in the top of a distant tree reacted to the slaughter of his comrades. His first shot punctured the muscles of Preacher's left arm with a numbing blow. A second and third shot followed immediately, the reports from the rifle blending and ringing. One bullet gouged a bloody hole through Preacher's neck. The second pounded his steel helmet like a sledgehammer driving a railroad spike through his brain. He went deaf. His eyes blurred, went almost blind.

He knew he had to be dead. A man couldn't live with a bullet through his skull.

So this was what it was like to be killed?

The Jap sniper must have been astounded beyond words when the "dead" GI suddenly came back to life and snaked away through the brush, low-crawling as fast as he could. By the time the sniper regained his senses, he was too late to score further. The rest of his shots went wild.

Kannon tumbled out of sight into a shallow gully, the bottom of which was already occupied by another GI survivor of the ill-fated ammo patrol. This guy had been nailed through the heel of his foot and was hysterical with fear.

"I've lost my helmet and they're going to kill me!" he howled.

Preacher thought he was probably dying anyhow, what with bullets through his arm, neck, hips, legs, and head. He took off his own damaged steel pot to give to the other soldier. That was when he discovered that the sniper's slug had miraculously glanced off his helmet liner rather than continuing into his skull.

As the Japanese quickly withdrew, knowing that American reserves would be rushing to the scene, Preacher Kannon rolled over onto his back and, thankful to be alive, peered groggily up through where stray, thin shafts of sunlight penetrated jungle tops.

"Thank You, Lord . . ."

Unbelievably, Dayton Kannon's numerous wounds proved superficial. True to his promise to serve God, he pastored churches for the next thirty-five years of his life.

ARMY SERGEANT JEFF STRUECKER,
Somalia, 1993

In 1993, Mogadishu, Somalia, was a shot-to-pieces dirtbag desert city on the northeastern tip of Africa where warlords had been fighting one another for power for three years. By the use of guile, terror, and drug dealing, Mohammed Farrah Aidid, a notorious warlord, struggled to the top of the trash heap. He dominated Somalia's capital by starving half the population into submission and doping up the other half to fight his rivals for him.

UNOSOM II (U.N. Operations in Somalia II) dispatched troops consisting mostly of U.S. Rangers and Special Operations soldiers to end Aidid's reign of terror and bring him to justice. Operating from a secure airfield and soccer stadium, U.S. Task Force Rangers conducted six raids into the dusty, chaotic city as of the first of October, nabbing key players each time.

On Sunday afternoon, October 3, the task force commander received intelligence that Aidid's henchmen were holding a high-level meeting in a three-story building on Hawlwadig Road. In the middle of the day when the hostile streets were packed with people was no time to launch a raid. Nothing drew crowds faster than a fight. But in a situation like this, peacekeepers had to strike when the iron was hot.

The mission was hastily organized. It called for Army Rangers to fast rope in to secure the building on all sides, while Green Berets and Delta Force roped out of Black Hawk choppers onto the flat top of the building to make the snatch. A convoy of twelve Humvees and five-ton flat-beds for hauling out captives set out ahead of time from the airport en route to downtown Mogadishu. Sergeant Jeff Struecker's ten-man squad of the 3rd Ranger Battalion led the procession in two Humvees.

Things went horribly wrong almost from the beginning. A young Ranger named Todd Blackburn fell from one of the Black Hawks during the rappelling, and critically injured himself. Armed Sammies—as soldiers called the Somalis—rallied to the target site in overwhelming numbers and opened fire on Americans with AK-47s and RPGs from every window, rooftop, and alleyway. The prisoner transport convoy was still blocks away when sounds of the fierce battle reached it.

As soon as the convoy arrived, the Ranger commander ordered Sergeant Struecker and his squad to escort the injured Blackburn to the field hospital at the airport. Struecker's much-truncated cavalcade now consisted of three Humvees and fourteen soldiers.

Private First Class Jeremy Kerr drove the lead vehicle with Struecker in the front seat with him, Sergeant Dominick Pilla and Specialist Tim Moynihan in the backseat behind the metal protection plate, and Private First Class Brad Paulson at the trigger of the .50-caliber machine gun in the turret.

The rest of Struecker's squad, another five Rangers, followed in the second hummer, while the third cargo Humvee carried Blackburn, a medic, and a couple of other Rangers from Blackburn's unit.

By now the entire city seemed to have exploded. Hammered from every angle, Struecker's little band wended its way through narrow, sandy, garbage-littered streets cluttered with signs of previous gunfights— burned out vehicles, piles of old tires, broken furniture, and wood scraps. All of these could be set ablaze to block streets and attract more fighters. The din of battle was terrifying, maddening. Sammies darted everywhere in bunches, firing as they ran. Roadblocks belched black smoke to mark the convoy's route and summon Somali reinforcements.

"Paulson, you take the left side," Sergeant Struecker directed. "Pilla, you take the right."

Rangers fought back with everything they had—M-16s, carbines, submachine guns, .50-caliber heavy machine guns. Paulson swung his machine gun from side to side, thumping targets from anywhere and everywhere.

The three Humvees stormed through five blocks of pure hell before breaking out onto National Street, a four-lane boulevard that led back to the airfield. Miraculously, the squad had so far sustained no injuries.

Dom Pilla spotted a gunner in the mouth of an alley leveling an AK-47 at him when Kerr, at the steering wheel, whipped the hummer around a corner. He fired his M-16, answered at the same instant by the Sammie. The two blasts resounded simultaneously, covering each other.

Moynihan screamed, "Pilla's hit! My God, he's shot in the head!"

Struecker twisted around to look into the backseat past the metal plating. Sergeant Pilla, a big man with a big laugh from "New Joyzee," was slumped over into Moynihan's lap. The bullet had entered less than an inch above his left eye, just below the rim of his Kevlar helmet, and blew off the back of his head upon exiting. Blood was splattered all over the back of the Humvee, as though someone had taken a bucketful and splashed it.

Sergeant Dominick Pilla was the first American lost in combat in Mogadishu.

The tiny convoy reached the airfield after the most intense forty minutes any of the Rangers had ever experienced.

Square-jawed and good-looking with an iron physique and so much bottom that he never seemed to tire, Jeff Struecker had enlisted in the Army in 1987 at the age of eighteen. Wanting to be "the best," he volunteered for airborne and the Army Rangers. By 1991, he was already a combat veteran, having shipped to Iraq for Desert Storm, the first Iraq war.

Struecker was also a devout Christian, having committed himself to Christ when he was thirteen years old, then recommitting himself after he became a Ranger. In the rough-and-bang culture of the Army's elite branches, a Christian soldier was automatically considered weaker because of his compassion and expressed love for his fellow man. Struecker never saw it that way.

In his opinion, a soldier with a moral foundation was stronger than one without, as he had proved many times so far in his leadership, devotion to duty, and stamina. While combat soldiers formed bonds as tight as brothers, the Bible stated in Proverbs how Jesus Christ "sticks closer than a brother."

Sergeant Struecker and his squad were shook up over Pilla's death. Nonetheless, they received orders that would throw them back into "the Mog's" fiery maw. Two Black Hawk helicopters had been shot down in the city. A rescue effort was being organized to reach the birds and their crews.

Before leading his men back into the fight, Struecker bowed his head and prayed. "God, I'm in deep trouble, as You can see. I need help. I'm not saying You should get me out of this. I just need Your help. My Father! If it is possible, let this cup of suffering be taken away from me. Yet, I want Your will, not mine . . ."

Twice during that long and bloody African day and night, Struecker and his squad fought their way through the streets of Mogadishu in efforts to rescue helicopter pilot Mike Durant and his airmen. But U.N. forces reached the crash site too late. Durant had been taken captive and his crew killed.

After daybreak, Struecker's worn and grimy squad straggled back to the safety of the airbase. Two members of the squad—Paulson and Specialist Bonnett—had been wounded, but the remaining seven were all right. The soccer stadium and the airport were gory scenes of death and human destruction. Shot-up helicopters and wrecked vehicles full of bullet holes were strewn about. More corpses were being brought in, extending the line of body bags on the tarmac. Eighteen Rangers and SpecOps would eventually be listed as killed in action.

Doctors and medics hooked up IVs and tended dozens of wounded. Helicopter rotors churned air constantly between the soccer field and the airbase as the more seriously wounded were airlifted to the field hospital. Some seventy-three soldiers would be treated for injuries ranging from minor to critical.

Stunned soldiers clustered around TV sets in hangars as CNN ran endless clips of jubilant Somalis dragging mutilated bodies of Americans through the streets. Weary and heartsick to the point of numbness, Sergeant Struecker went to his cot in the hangar to await further orders. He sat down, exhausted, face in his hands.

Soon, other Rangers confronting hard facts about their mortality and about life here and hereafter began to drift over to his cot. They knew Struecker had declared his Christianity. Now, they had questions.

"Jeff, why would God let this happen? If He had wanted to keep us from getting hammered so bad, He could have stopped it."

Lines of soldiers with such questions approached Struecker's cot one after the other throughout the rest of the afternoon and evening. Nearby, Sergeant Kurt Smith, a Christian friend, counseled other soldiers. The task force chaplain was also busy at the other end of the hangar. Combat and death forced warriors to look beyond the slender threads of life that anchored them to today.

"Jeff, I got questions. I need to talk to somebody."

"Sit down here with me, man."

"What I want to know is, where's Dom Pilla now? What's happened to him? And what's going to happen to me if I get sent out there, and I get blown up? Then what?"

Struecker gave it to them straight as he understood it. "What I know is what the Bible says about all this. It is destined that each person dies only once and after that comes judgment. If a guy has put his faith and trust in Jesus Christ, he goes to heaven. If not—unfortunately, he doesn't."

"Man, that stinks, doesn't it?"

"I don't make the rules, you know. I'm just trying to give you the Bible answer to your questions. Jesus is the only one good enough to deserve Heaven. He made it possible for us to ride His coattails, so to speak, if we'll turn from our sins and ask him to take us on. That's the amazing offer of grace He extends to us."

A number of tough Rangers in the hangar at Mogadishu that day knelt to recite the sinner's prayer and invite Jesus into their hearts.

Sergeant Jeff Struecker made the decision shortly after returning to the United States from Somalia to become a military chaplain. He completed college in his off-duty time to earn his degree. On April 16, 2000, he mustered out of the Army as an enlisted soldier and immediately rejoined the Chaplain Candidate Program. In March 2001, Chaplain (Captain) Jeff Struecker took his first ministry assignment with the 82nd Airborne Division at Fort Bragg, North Carolina, and is still on active duty.

ARMY CHAPLAIN DELBERT KUEHL,
*World War II, 1944**

After battling its way up the boot of Italy—Sicily, Salerno, Anzio—the 504th Infantry Regiment of the 82nd Airborne Division retired to England to refit and recuperate. It had been so shot up that Eisenhower held it in reserve on D-Day. By September 1944, however,

* See also Chapter 6.

the regiment was ready to fight again. It became part of the ill-fated operation known as Market Garden, the largest parachute attack in history.

After four days of intense fighting, British airborne troops trying to secure the bridge at Arnhem needed immediate relief. The 82nd Airborne was assigned to take a pair of side-by-side bridges, one a railroad, the other a highway, in the vicinity of Nijmegen. The seizure of these would allow British tanks to cross over and head up the road to relieve besieged paratroopers at Arnhem. General James Gavin, commander of the 82nd, came up with the idea of sending the 504th across the Waal River from the south to attack the bridges in open daylight. The maneuver had to be done swiftly and violently to prevent Krauts from blowing up the bridges if they concluded they could not hold them.

The display of might preparing for the daring mission was something to behold. Brits brought up their own forces to attack the southern ends of the bridges as soon as the 504th forded the river and moved against the northern ends. Day and night, British infantry and mechanized vehicles of all types and sizes moved up and into place— tanks, armored cars, half-tracks, mounted artillery pieces . . .

Regimental Chaplain Delbert Kuehl, twenty-seven, circulated among the soldiers of the 82nd on the afternoon of September 18, the day before the next morning's attempt to cross the Waal, stopping here and there to chat or to pray with GIs. He had been with the 504th since before North Africa in 1943. Rather short and slight of build with boyish features, Kuehl belied in action his mild appearance. The rowdy paratroopers to whom he ministered knew him to be as tough as they. Armed only with his Bible, a cross, and a prayer, the little chaplain had already made two combat parachute jumps and accompanied his GIs all the way across Italy. He contributed whatever he could as spiritual guide to bedraggled soldiers and as stretcher bearer, medical assistant, and "mule" for transporting food, water, and supplies.

He approached a wooded area next to the main road leading toward Nijmegen and the two contested bridges. There, several officers of the

3rd Battalion were discussing how the regiment would cross the river and take its objective.

"Brits are bringing up the boats," one officer commented.

"I hear there aren't enough boats for everybody to cross at once," said another. "We'll have to do it in waves."

"My God! In the *daylight*, no less."

Boats still hadn't arrived. How would they ever get here in time? Chaplain Kuehl expected large armored craft with powerful gasoline engines. After all, the river was wide with a strong current. The bridges were each 1,500 feet long, a span of over a quarter mile.

British trucks arrived at daybreak the next morning, each stacked with boats almost as flat as sheets of plywood. Officers and men alike stared with surprise and consternation as twenty-six flimsy craft were off-loaded and hurriedly assembled behind a berm out of sight of the river and Germans on the other side.

Each boat was nineteen feet long with collapsible canvas sides and a flat plywood bottom. Sides were held up by wooden staves that measured a scant thirty inches from floor to gunwales. Fifteen paratroopers with weapons and battle gear would be jammed into each fragile craft.

Chaplain Kuehl did the math. At best, only four hundred fighters could be sent across in the initial wave, against an enemy force that numbered several thousands massed along the river banks, at the bridges, and inside Fort Hof van Holland on the flats a short distance back from the river. At least that many paratroopers could *start out* from this side of the river. How many reached the other side was in God's hands. What remained of the boats would have to come back across for second and subsequent waves.

Watching the boats being assembled, Chaplain Kuehl shook his head. "How are they propelled?" he asked.

"Canoe paddles," came the reply.

"It's a suicide mission," an officer gloomily predicted.

Another officer took out his cigarettes and lighter and hurled them as far as he could. "I won't need them," he said. "I have no chance of getting across."

Kuehl decided to accompany H and I Companies of the 3rd Battalion in the first wave. As regimental chaplain, he didn't have to go on the mission. But if ever there was a time when his men needed a chaplain, this was it. He declined to advise the regimental commander of his decision; he knew Colonel Reuben Tucker would disapprove.

Lying on his belly behind the river berm with the sounds of maritime construction behind him, he cynically surveyed the river bathed in morning sunlight. Battle plans called for H and I Companies to cross the river, attack the dikes and sweep over flat terrain to neutralize and bypass Fort Hof van Holland. Then they were to seize the railroad and Nijmegen-Arnhem highway junction, and, finally, drive southeast along the highway to take the north ends of the bridges. A tall order for GIs fortunate enough or blessed enough to survive the blanket of fire from Germans dug in along the dikes.

Chaplain Kuehl closed his eyes and prayed silently for the paratroopers.

British Typhoon attack aircraft prepped the objective a half hour prior to the assault, strafing the entire north bank with bombs, rockets, and automatic cannon fire. German AA saturated the sky with black puffs of exploding shells so thick it seemed the crossing might be better accomplished by walking on them rather than floating the river.

Allied artillery took the last punch with HE and white phosphorus to lay down a smoke screen on the river. At 1500 hours, the 3rd Battalion's CO blew his whistle. Paratroopers grabbed the gunwales of their assigned boats and rushed up and over the embankment to reach the river. Erratic winds dissipated the smoke, denying the boats cover, and exposing them to German fire from the other side.

It took the Gemans a few minutes to recover from their surprise, during which time not a single shot was fired. Then they opened up with everything they had: machine guns, 30mm flak cannon, mortars, artillery, small arms. Shells exploded all along the bank and among the frantic Americans as they launched their boats. Small arms fire and shrapnel agitated the surface of the river like a hail storm. Men, screaming and crying out, were falling all around. Chaos and confusion reigned. A living nightmare.

Chaplain Kuehl tumbled headfirst into a boat with Major Julian Cook, the battalion commander, and a dozen other GIs. Another soldier reached for the gunwale, cried out in pain, and immediately sank in a swirl of bloody red water. Machine gun fire shredded an adjacent boat, sending men flying and reducing the craft to a piece of floating junk. One paratrooper got stuck in the mud and couldn't extricate himself, becoming a stationary target for enemy sharpshooters.

Frantically paddling men strived desperately to get across the Waal before they were killed. Some paddled with the butts of their rifles, others with their hands, anything to keep the defenseless boats floating across and downstream toward the north shore. Blood and water rose knee deep in some of the boats. Large numbers of men fell over onto the knees of their friends. Bodies floated on the river or hung over the sides of the craft.

Chaplain Kuehl paddled with his hands. He heard Major Cook's loud, quivering voice repeatedly reciting a cadence for the efforts of his paddlers: *"Hail Mary, full of grace . . . Hail Mary, full of grace . . ."*

The chaplain repeated his own phrase. *"Lord, Thy will be done . . . Lord, Thy will be done . . ."*

Thirteen of the original twenty-six boats and somewhat over half the initial first wave of men made it to the other side. Men more dead than alive scrambled over the dead and dying to reach the embankment. Fighting grew even more brutal as paratroopers caught their breath and headed up the banks to attack machine gun nests.

Carrying a first aid kit, Kuehl joined the brawl as part medic, part stretcher bearer, and part chaplain, working on the wounded and disregarding his own safety. Hearing a loud grunt, he glanced over his shoulder and, to his horror, saw a GI with his head completely blown off.

A mortar round exploded behind him as he tended a kid with three bullet holes in his belly. Shrapnel sprayed his back and knocked him forward. The frightened kid, though critically injured, cried out in alarm, "Oh, God! Chaplain, they got you, too!"

"I'm all right, son," the chaplain responded. He felt blood trickling down his back.

He spent four hours on the beach under constant automatic weapons and sniper fire. He seemed to be everywhere he was needed. Again and again he ranged the battlefield to bandage and comfort the wounded and carry them to the remaining boats for evacuation. It was later estimated he personally carried more than thirty-five wounded men to safety.

The 504th finally took the bridges. As the action subsided, an officer landing on the north riverbank surveyed the scene of devastation and soon encountered a bloody and injured young chaplain.

"What the hell are you doing here?" he cried in amazement.

Chaplain Kuehl replied with a simple "This is where the men are."

Chaplain Delbert Kuehl remained on the front lines with the 504th until the war ended. He received a Silver Star and two Bronze Stars for valor, a Purple Heart, and three Presidential Unit Citations. He returned to his native Minnesota in 1946 and married. His wife, Dolores, and he later went to Japan as missionaries and had five children, four of whom became Christian missionaries. In 1981 he retired to Lake Louise, Minnesota, where he still lives with his wife.

14

DIVINE INTERVENTION

Except you see signs and wonders, ye will not believe.

—Saint John 4:48

A loaf of bread and fish compounded to feed multitudes. Water turned into wine. Walking on water. Resurrection of the dead. Healing the mortally afflicted . . .

Were these true miracles performed by this man Jesus in the name of God, or were they misunderstood natural phenomena, even fables propagated by an illiterate and superstitious folk? What a historian, naturalist, or anthropologist might conclude about "divine intervention" in the petty affairs of men, and what the witness or survivor might believe are two very different things.

For most people, religious experiences are confined to no more than "give us this day our daily bread." Rare indeed do events in ordinary life rise to the point of being considered miracles. Yet no one will ever convince combat soldiers who undergo extraordinary religious or spiritual episodes that God does not still intervene in man's behalf and perform miracles.

In Iraq, an enemy rocket smoked through the window of a Humvee occupied by five Marines and exploded inside. By any logical consideration, every Marine in the vehicle should have been killed or at least seriously wounded. Not one was even *scratched*.

During World War II, Lieutenant Ed Hurd's P-47 was running out of gas and shot all to pieces on a bombing/strafing mission over Japan. There was absolutely *no way* the plane could have stayed in the air, yet it brought him safely home nonetheless.

"If you want the real story," Hurd said, "*God* brought me back."

After the terrorist bombing and collapse of the World Trade Center on September 11, 2001, two Port Authority policemen, John McLoughlin and Will Jimeno, were pinned down inside the rubble with escape or rescue virtually discounted. Fifty miles away, former Marine sergeant Dave Karnes listened to God. Answering the call, he rushed to New York and continued the search for survivors alone after everyone else gave up—and found the two cops alive.

Exactly why God might intercede on behalf of one person and not another is one of those unfathomable mysteries of the universe. Nearly three thousand died in the collapse of the trade center—yet God intervened to save McLoughlin and Jimeno. God spared five Marines at the epicenter of a rocket explosion inside their Humvee—while an identical occurrence the next day claimed the lives of every Marine involved. Lieutenant Hurd made it safely back from Japan in his P-47 while other pilots whose planes were in better shape than his crashed and the men inside perished. Why?

President Ronald Reagan may have supplied the answer to why God seemed to intercede in such an arbitrary manner. After he survived the assassination attempt against him in 1981, he told his daughter Maureen that God had spared his life for a purpose, that God was not yet through using him on earth.

"Whatever happens now I owe my life to God and will try to serve Him in every way I can," he wrote in his journal. Then he added, "Whatever time I have left belongs to the Big Fella upstairs."

ARMY SPECIALIST LEE DAVIS,
Vietnam, 1965

More than a dozen UH-I "Huey" helicopters swarmed out of the red of the rising sun, their rotors chirring and pulsing like a plague of impossibly giant green locusts. A company-sized element, about two hundred men, of the "Big Red One" Infantry Division was on the move to search and destroy, to track down Viet Cong that infested the region—and kill them.

The start of an operation like this was always the tricky part. Clearings large enough to accept a mass helicopter assault were rare in the AO. The enemy liked to stake out those few potential LZs that existed and wait in ambush when they thought the Americans were due to start a new offensive. What was intended to be a routine insertion by helicopter could well turn out to be the proverbial hornets' nest.

Army Specialist Lee Davis leaned forward on the web seating attached to the rear firewall of his chopper and looked out the open cargo door and down at the terrain unreeling below. He hadn't realized until he arrived in Vietnam that there could be so many shades of green.

As squad leader, he was responsible for the men in his "chalk," for getting them out of the bird and off the LZ quickly when it touched down. Rucksack snugged against his back, M-16 rifle gripped between his knees, he turned his gaze from the jungle below to Kettlebinder and Johnston and the other members of his squad. They grimly returned his look from beneath the brim edges of their snugged-down helmets. It was going to be another walk in the sun, he had reassured them before the company loaded up and lifted off. They would land, tramp around for a day or so, see nothing, then be lifted back into base camp. Charlie could be an elusive little bastard when hunted.

Davis thrust out his palm with splayed fingers: *five minutes!*

At twenty-two, the squad leader was an athletic black man slightly under six feet tall, with high cheekbones and a medium brown complexion. He had been a firefighter for the Oxnard Fire Department near Los Angeles when he became one of the first in his area to be drafted into the Army and sent to Vietnam. His mom and his church back home promised to pray every day for his safety. Skeptical at first that prayer had anything to do with who got it and who didn't, he was beginning to wonder if God might not really be with him after all.

On Davis's very first day in-country, Private Luis Miranda and he were digging in at a firebase when he climbed out of the partially completed fighting position and went back to the CP for supplies. While he was gone, a VC sniper shot and killed Miranda.

That was the first of several times when roles could have been reversed and Davis been the one wasted. Was it all mere coincidence, pure dumb luck—or was it something more?

He developed appendicitis and had to go to the rear for surgery. The guy who took his place got blown up by a road mine.

His foxhole buddy and he were squatting together heating a Charlie-rat (C-ration) for dinner when a tracer round fired by a lone sniper lashed out and smashed the buddy in the chest, knocking him back and killing him almost in Davis's lap.

It was enough to make a man paranoid.

"When the Old Man up there draws your billet number," Kettlebinder had philosophized, "it's your turn, ready or not."

In Vietnam, your turn could come up almost at random.

Abruptly, the pitch and attack angle of the Huey flight changed. The choppers had gone on final approach for landing. Davis looked out and saw the clearing directly ahead. Dense jungle surrounded it on all sides. Plenty of cover if VC were hiding there and waiting.

"Get ready!" Davis warned his squad. He had to shout to be heard above engine noise. In the netting across from him, Kettlebinder took out his canteen and sucked a long swig. Cottonmouth. Everybody had it.

Following some scheme of their own, Hueys flared in fast all over the field. Rotor wash flattened short tropical grass. Birds hovered ever so briefly to disgorge rushing men in green, all at about the same time.

"Go! Go! Go!" Davis shouted, then leapt out behind his squad, not bothering with the skid step, simply throwing himself out to hit hard and roll on the ground.

Relieved of their loads, choppers sprang back into the air, taking with them their engine roar and sense of last-moment urgency. The insertion was complete in less than a minute, men on the ground and helicopters aloft and scuttling back to base camp.

The enemy could be disciplined and patient. As soon as the Hueys were back in the air, intense crescendos of machine gun and rifle fire erupted from the forest all around the clearing. Charlie hadn't wanted the helicopters; he wanted the soldiers they contained, wanted them boxed in and unable to get away. Hot LZ! Today was the hornets' nest.

Muzzle flashes speared from the enveloping foliage. Tracers whipped back and forth at knee level. RPGs inscribed smoke trails in the air before exploding in clumps of fire, smoke, mud, and grass. The clamor of so much firepower unleashed all at once was deafening, rattling, echoing across the clearing.

Men trapped in the open were crying out or screaming in pain and terror, falling here and there, some wounded, some dead, some trying to crawl underneath blades of grass.

"Jesus!" Davis couldn't be sure if it was an exclamation or a plea.

Every man jack in the company was going to eat his fill of lead this sultry tropical morning unless he got the hell off the LZ and reached the cover of trees and jungle. Davis was yelling at his squad, urging his men to keep moving. Crawling and crawling himself, belly flat on the ground, chin digging into the earth.

Machine gun fire chewed a swath through his squad, bullets pluming, kicking up dirt. Green tracers flashed above his head. A slug whacked his ruck where it stuck up above the grass. The impact was hard enough to knock the breath out of his lungs. He shed the pack so it wouldn't continue to give him away. Then he rolled away from it and kept crawling, like a crippled lizard. The machine gun moved on to work over some other group of poor bastards.

The jungle's edge was at least fifty yards away, an impossible distance under the circumstances. Davis accepted the inevitable. He would never make it off the LZ alive. He was going to die this morning on a hellish piece of forgotten real estate in a shitbag country he had hardly even heard about until he got drafted. Kettlebinder was right: when your billet number came up, it was *up*.

And then something amazing happened that he could never explain—and even if he could, no one would believe him. Everything changed in an instant. It was like a hole in the universe opened to swallow time and alter forever Davis's perception of life and the corporeal world around him. It happened in the literal bat of an eye, in such a flash that he was left stunned, bewildered, a little dizzy, and more than a little awed.

One moment he was caught without cover in the middle of a deadly hailstorm of lead and steel and fire and smoke. He was already contemplating and accepting his prompt demise. He blinked, and the next moment he found himself in the trees at the edge of the jungle, somehow transported from one place to the other with no effort of his own.

"Oh, my God!"

He almost expected God to answer him. The first thought that entered his mind after he recovered from confusion was that his mom and his church must be praying for him today.

Lee Davis now lives in Sacramento, California. He still finds it difficult to explain what happened that day more than forty years ago on a hot LZ in Vietnam. "Perhaps it was a way the Spirit devised to accelerate my spiritual life."

ARMY AIR CORPS LIEUTENANT HAIG KOOBATIAN,
*World War II, 1944**

The typical mission day for pilots and crews operating B-17 Flying Fortresses out of Foggia Air Base in Italy started at 0330. A big breakfast came first; after all, it might be the last. Formations took off around 0530. By 0930, the planes were over their targets and bombing it. Flights returned to base around 1300 for a late lunch. Crews caught up on reports and housekeeping until dinnertime, after which they tipped a few at the makeshift clubs before retiring to their tents to rest for the next alert.

Earlier in the war, airmen had to complete thirty missions before maxing out and being reassigned either back to the States or to less hazardous duties. By 1944, that magic number had climbed to fifty missions for most combat aviators due to loss of aircraft and men. Fifty living nightmares over enemy railroads and depots, oilfields and refineries, communications facilities and airfields. Being a member of a bomber crew meant hours aloft in freezing drudgery followed by harrowing minutes over a target.

Late on an April afternoon in 1944, loudspeakers mounted around tent city at Foggia announced the posting of tomorrow's battle orders at the ready room. Lieutenant Haig Koobatian, a twenty-two-year-old navigator with crew-cut brown hair and a thoughtful grin, joined the rush to check his fate.

His squadron, the 419th, was assigned to bomb an aircraft engine plant in southern Germany. Koobatian would fly as lead navigator. His bombadier slapped him on the back. "Glad to have you aboard, Haig," he said. "We don't feel right when you're not with us. Everybody's noticed that when you're in a plane, nobody on it gets hurt."

Koobatian always felt that *somebody* was looking out for him.

---

* See also Chapter 9.

. . .

Twenty-three Flying Fortresses took off from the steel-mesh airstrip in the predawn, the awesome roaring of their mighty engines making the black sky throb. First planes in the air circled the field and waited until every aircraft reached altitude before the squadrons formed up and headed for Germany with their payloads of bombs. They flew in staggered combat box dispersal, each B-17 covering any other with its .50-caliber Browning machine guns mounted in the nose, tail, dorsal, waist, and belly. Ten men made up a bomber crew, twelve bombers and 120 men comprised a squadron.

At altitudes of 20,000 feet or more, temperatures in cockpits and crew stations commonly plummeted to 20 degrees *below*. Airmen wore oxygen masks above 8,000 or 10,000 feet. Heated flying suits with wires in the boots kept airmen reasonably comfortable.

As navigator, Koobatian twisted himself into the cramped nose bubble. The sun rose in a glorious spectrum of color, turning the earth into a translucent ball and transforming engine vapor trails into iridescent patterns etched against deep blue. The unobstructed view took his breath away, what with clear glass all around except to his back. He had the feeling of floating in space, a detached observer of earth and its puny inhabitants. God Himself must enjoy such a view.

Crews had little to do for the first three hours. Koobatian took care of his navigator duties with map and pencil, marking off landmarks and keeping the plane on course. Pilots switched out on their controls. The rest of the crew kicked back and ate cheese sandwiches and drank milk if it wasn't already frozen.

The atmosphere changed once the formations neared Germany and expected enemy contact. Tension grew as watchful eyes scanned the skies for enemy fighters.

Soon enough, welcoming committees of Focke-Wulfs and Messerschmitts would arrive to make their high-speed strafing passes, zipping down seemingly from nowhere, whipping through the formations like sharks loosed into a school of yellowtail. The trouble with a nose cone was that while it provided an unparalleled view of God's creation, it also thrust the observer into the same unobstructed view of hell once the air battle began.

First sightings of the enemy always chilled Koobatian's blood. He was busy with his calculations when an excited voice burst over the radio net: *"Bogeys at one o'clock high!"*

Koobatian glanced up in time to catch sight of a German fighter slashing past, guns flickering. Bombers replied with their formidable .50-cals. The nose gunner in the bubble with Koobatian slung red tracers. The B-17 shuddered in recoil.

The crew of the plane on the right flank suddenly began bailing out of every shattered orifice. They were so near that Koobatian could almost see the eyes of men he knew, buddies tumbling through the frozen air, then streaking toward earth, down and immediately out of sight. The B-17 that was their platform tipped into one smoke-trailing wing and plunged after them.

Enemy fighters inflicted what damage they could, slashing, ripping, and tearing. Then they pulled off to allow ground-based antiaircraft batteries to take over.

Ahead appeared fields of individual storm clouds of black smoke jagged with orange blasts of lightning from exploding 88mm shells. B-17s had to enter the tempest and survive it in order to reach their target. Airmen in a high pitch of excitement and fear yelled and screamed warnings and entreaties, prayers and death rattles over the radios as they were buffeted and rattled about in their metal coffins, flying through deafening thunder and blazing balls of light. Shrapnel piercing thin aircraft skin made distinctive sounds and left gaping holes. Oil leaking from damaged engines misted in the air, clotting on other pilots' windscreens.

Koobatian watched as a Flying Fortress detonated into blue windwhipped flames. A second bomber trailed thick black smoke from both starboard engines. Fire suddenly enveloped it. Crew in flak suits abandoned ship, leaping into space. Some of them were in human flames, burning through the air like Roman candles at an Independence Day fireworks show. Koobatian couldn't hear them screaming, but he knew they were.

Stuck out there in his box seat, alternately praying and trembling from fear, Koobatian could do little except stare in mesmerized horror. Great gaps and spaces appeared in the formation as plane after plane succumbed to the devastating AA barrages. At this rate, none of them would ever make it to the target.

Somebody might be looking out for him, but it seemed that that *Somebody* was looking the other way this morning. Koobatian resigned himself to his fate. Time sequences lost all meaning. Everything was *present* with no past, no future, merely a vast existing vacuum of *now.* He wondered how anyone could keep his wits when the world was going mad.

"We can't make it!" a pilot shrieked over the air, his voice strained and terrified. *"We'll never get to the target. There are no planes left."*

Perhaps what Lieutenant Koobatian witnessed next occurred as a result of extreme fright when a man's eyes focus outside his normal sphere, and he sees things the average person cannot see. Some higher consciousness. All he knew was that he *saw* what he saw. He experienced it—and no one could tell him he didn't. Whatever it was, he believed it saved his life and the lives of his fellow airmen.

A fire, suspended in the sky, suddenly appeared. It was like an enormous bonfire that discharged wonderful sparks leaping through the air. The fire grew until it filled up the universe, warm and glowing, and not terrifying at all. From Koobatian's perspective, it seemed an all-encompassing *heavenly* light, the eternal assurance of God's presence.

The thought crossed his mind that everything was going to be all right, that that *Somebody* who looked out for him had pulled a protective shield around his Flying Fortress. He relaxed. Fear drained away completely. He felt *safe.*

"Turn back!" the mission commander ordered through the radio net. *"We can't make it through. Turn back!"*

Koobatian's pilot immediately took up the call. "Reverse one-eighty," he shouted at his navigator through the plane's intercom. "Give me directions home."

Lieutenant Koobatian's Heavenly Light vanished as suddenly as it had appeared—but he still felt safe all the way back to Italy. Only six B-17s of the original twenty-three that set out on the mission returned. All the others were either shot down or forced to make emergency landings. Koobatian reported what he had seen during an intelligence debriefing back at Foggia. Surely others had witnessed the phenomenon.

Surviving airmen stared at the young lieutenant as though he had been hallucinating or was stone cold insane. Koobatian let it drop. They didn't have to believe him. He knew what he saw.

Somebody was still looking out for him.

Now eighty-seven years old, Haig Koobatian lives in California. He devoted his life after the war to exploring his personal spirituality. "It may sound crazy," he wrote in a letter, "but all one has to do is to read stories of men in action, under severe mental strain, to realize there are some unanswered questions over which we should brood, questions about the validity of some of our conventional thinking."

GENERAL GEORGE WASHINGTON,
French and Indian War, 1755

Even though English settlements in the New World were primarily along the eastern seaboard, English kings held that the voyage of Sebastian Cabot had given them lawful right to America from the Atlantic to the Pacific. The French began connecting their widely separated interior colonies by constructing a chain of forts along the Ohio and Mississippi Rivers to divide the American continent and erect a barrier against English advancements. Fort Duquesne, at the fork of the Allegheny and Monongahela Rivers, occupied the power center of this barrier. In 1754, the French and Indian War pitted the British with their American colonists against France and her Indian allies.

In late April 1755, General Edward Braddock set out to seize Fort Duquesne from the French with about 2,000 English soldiers, including one hundred Virginian provincials and some 250 workers and axmen. With him as his aide went twenty-three-year-old then-Colonel George Washington. Washington's mother, who feared for his safety, tried to persuade him not to go.

Washington responded, "The God to Whom you commended me, madam, when I set out upon a more perilous errand, defended me from all harm, and I trust He will do so now."

Nearing Fort Duquesne, Braddock left most of his heavy baggage and wagons behind with a 600-man escort and proceeded more rapidly with 1,300 select troops. On July 9, the British army forded the Monongahela River only ten miles from the French fort. Decked out in their crimson uniforms and waving banners gaily, the companies marched through the forest to the cheerful beat of martial music. Washington described the spectacle:

> Every man was neatly dressed in full uniform. The soldiers were arranged in columns and marched in exact order; the sun gleamed from their burnished arms; the river flowed tranquilly on their right, and the deep forest overshadowed them with solemn grandeur on their left. Officers and men were equally inspirited with cheering hopes and confident anticipations.

Outnumbered as the French commander was with only 855 fighters, of which 637 were Indians, he employed "Indian tactics" rather than wait to be attacked behind his own walls. He laid an ambush for the approaching British about seven miles from the fort.

At 1 P.M. on July 10, Colonel Thomas Gage's forward detachment of 350 soldiers and 250 laborers crossed a shallow ravine dominated on the other side by a hill and dense undergrowth to the right and a dry streambed to the left. General Braddock followed less than a hundred yards back with columns of artillery and the main body.

An engineer out front with a few scouts marking the road spotted Indians running through the woods. Before he could warn Gage, however, the French and Indians triggered their ambush, catching Gage's element between the wooded hill and the dry streambed. Dead and dying Redcoats littered the ground within a few minutes. The screams of wounded horses pierced the ears of wounded men as the suffering animals plunged mindlessly through the trees, trampling both the living and the dead. The unceasing rattle of musketry reverberated wave after wave.

Braddock charged forward to the rescue. Retreating in panic, Gage and his men collided with the main force, mixing the two elements and throwing the entire army into confusion. Frightened soldiers huddled in the ravine, firing at random while unseen attackers continued to play havoc with them. It was butchery rather than battle.

The frontier-savvy Virginians accompanying Braddock fought according to backwoods custom, hiding behind trees and rocks to pick off whatever enemy presented himself. General Braddock, furious at such "cowardly" tactics, issued stern orders that his troops would fight in regular platoons and columns according to the rules of established military tactics. He rode furiously among his Redcoats, using the flat of his sword to beat any soldier who attempted to take cover behind trees or fallen logs.

Braddock lost five horses shot out from underneath him. Washington lost two mounts to gunfire as he rallied troops to the defense and relayed the general's orders to all parts of the battlefield. Musket balls tore holes through his coat, but his flesh remained untouched by bullet or bayonet, arrow or tomahawk, even while hundreds fell dead and wounded all around him. French and superstitious Indians alike became convinced that an Invisible Power protected him.

"I expected every moment to see him fall," a Frenchman said. "Nothing but the superintending power of Providence could have saved him."

"Washington was never born to be killed by a bullet," asserted an

Indian leader in the attack. "I had seventeen fair fires at him with my rifle, and after all could not bring him to the ground."

An Indian chief named Red Hawk, an expert marksman, also singled out Washington for a target, shooting at him eleven different times before he gave up, convinced that the Great Spirit protected him.

In a letter sent to his brother afterward, Washington himself confirmed that "by the all powerful dispensations of Providence I have been protected beyond all human probability or expectation."

The massacre lasted for over two hours. Colonel Washington remained one of only a few officers left unscathed. Even General Braddock fell mortally wounded. Rallying the remnants of the defeated army, Washington organized and led the retreat. Of the original force of 1,300 men, 740 were killed and most of the others wounded. Scarcely thirty of the original one hundred Virginians remained alive.

Fifteen years later, in 1770, Washington and a close friend were exploring uninhabited regions near the Ohio River when a party of Indians led by an old and respected chief approached them. The chief used an interpreter to address Washington around a council fire. He said he had been at the battle of Fort Duquesne and had now traveled a long journey in order to speak to Washington about it.

"I am a chief and ruler over my tribe," he said, as recounted by Christian historian David Barton. "My influence extends to the waters of the great lakes and to the far blue mountains. I have traveled a long and weary path that I might see the young warrior of the great battle. It was on the day when the white man's blood mixed with the streams of our forest that I first beheld this chief. I called to my young men and said, 'Mark yon tall and daring warrior. He is not of the Red Coat tribe. He hath an Indian's wisdom, and his warriors fight as we do. He himself is alone exposed. Quick, let your aim be certain and he dies.' Our rifles were leveled, rifles which, but for you, knew not how to miss.

"'Twas all in vain; a power mightier far than we shielded you. Seeing you were under the special guardianship of the Great Spirit, we immediately ceased to fire at you. I am old and soon shall be gathered to the great council fire of my fathers in the land of shades; but ere I go, there is something bids me speak in the voice of prophecy. Listen! The Great Spirit protects that man [pointing at Washington] and guides his destinies. He will become the chief of nations, and a people yet unborn will hail him as the founder of a mighty empire. I am come to pay homage to the man who is the particular favorite of Heaven and who can never die in battle."

MARINE ANONYMOUS,
World War II, 1944

The U.S. Marine Corps has passed on a legend from World War II about a lost Marine and a spider. The name of the Marine and even the location of the drama have been forgotten, but it is assumed the action may have taken place during the invasion of Saipan in 1944.

According to the legend, U.S. Marines of the 2nd and 4th Divisions assaulted beaches on the southwest coasts of Saipan on June 15, then pushed inland toward high ground. A young leatherneck got separated from his unit in the smoke and crossfire during the 2nd Division's attack up the slopes of Mount Tapotchau. Alone in the jungle and hearing enemy soldiers coming, he scrambled to a high ridge and crawled into one of several small caves to hide.

The cave was narrow at the mouth and no more than ten or twelve feet deep. He huddled in the dark at the back of the den, his M-1 ready, and tried to make himself invisible. Rifle shots rang out in the jungle below the ridge. Japanese patrols shouted and raged as they hunted down American stragglers and executed them.

Sounds of the blood hunt drew near as Japanese climbed the ridge toward the caves. The Marine knew they would soon discover him. He might nail one or two, but in the end they would kill him. He began to pray.

"Lord, if it be Your will, please protect me. But whatever Your will, I love and trust You. Amen."

His entire body trembled with fear as he crouched in the cave listening to the enemy's approach.

Well, I guess the Lord's not going to help me out of this one.

He expected to see a Japanese face block out the light at the narrow entrance of the cave at any moment—or to have a grenade tossed in on top of him.

In his terror, his gaze focused on a hardworking spider as it stretched a thin strand of silk across the entryway to the Marine's hideout. Busily at work, it connected other threads to this anchor. God did have his ironic side, His sense of humor.

Lord, what I need is a brick wall—and you send me a spiderweb!

The leatherneck heard Japanese searching neighboring caves as they worked their way toward his. Finally, their shadows stretched across the entrance to his little sanctuary. He gripped his rifle, aiming it at the opening, resigned to the inevitable.

The spider had almost completed its project, its web glistening in the sunlight and blocking the cave's entrance. Enemy soldiers took one look at it and kept going, logically assuming that no one could be hiding inside since the spider's web appeared undisturbed.

The young Marine collapsed in disbelief and wonder. "Lord, forgive me," he prayed. "I had forgotten that in You a spider's web is stronger than a brick wall."

ARMY CHIEF WARRANT OFFICER JIM ESKILDSEN,
Vietnam, 1968

UH-1 "Huey" helicopters served as lifelines that supplied food, water, and ammo to troops humping the bush. They also served as air cover with their machine guns and rockets, as medical evacuation ambulances for the wounded, and frequently as a grunt's ride into hell and out again. Even the single Huey could be heard coming when it was still a tiny speck against the horizon, pulsing, throbbing, its rotars beating the stagnant tropical air of Vietnam. *Whop! Whop! Whop!* Getting louder and louder, bringing hope to foot soldiers in the jungle.

By the time he turned twenty-one, CWO Jim Eskildsen had already logged over six hundred hours as a Huey pilot and aircraft commander with the 1st Infantry Division. Often, as today, October 5, 1968, he preflighted his bird by flashlight. Sixteen different mission sheets meant he had to hustle to get his work accomplished before nightfall. Most were "ash and trash" short-range resupply missions, which meant hovering the chopper above the forest canopy and kicking out bundles to brief glimpses of GI faces looking up through treetops whipped into a frenzy by massive blade downwash.

CWO Fred Peters, who flew as Eskildsen's 2P, his co-pilot, was also about twenty-one, Vietnam-lean and intense, like most men who had been in-country a few months. He was still yawning and slapping at mosquitoes.

Crew Chief John Wilson, a Speedy Four (Specialist Fourth Class), was a skinny farmboy from the Midwest. He took good-natured verbal jabs at Corporal Samuel Jacobs, door gunner on the M-60 machine gun. Jacobs was a brown-skinned black man known as "Samson" because of his muscular build. Only months before he had been a star athlete in high school.

The chopper lifted out of its home base at Phu Loi at the first hint of light in the eastern sky. A temperature inversion capped the weather, turning the air hot and stagnant, like baking in a giant oven. Artillery fires and local peasants slash-and-burning to open up more farmland shrouded the terrain in a smoky haze. Dense scrub brush jungle covered the hills as thick as fur on a village dog. The only substantial clearings were scattered farms and bomb craters.

The firebase near Lai Khe was Chief Eskildsen's last stop of the day. He dumped cargo and took back to the air promptly, flying home against a hot setting sun diffused by smoke and haze into a gigantic orange ball.

"Bulldog Three-Three, this is flight operations. We have another mission for you."

"This is Bulldog Three-Three," Eskildsen snapped into his mike. "Are you joking? We've been out all day. The sun's going down. Can't Night Standby take this mission?"

Night flights multiplied combat flying's inherent dangers and risks by a factor of at least a hundred. Pilots dreaded them and flew after dark only when absolutely necessary.

"Negative, Bulldog. We have an emergency resupply mission and you're the closest."

"Bulldog Ops, disregard my last transmission. What have you got?"

"Return to Lai Khe and meet the lieutenant on the Red Ball pad."

The lieutenant waiting at Lai Khe explained in grim terms how a battalion of the 1st Infantry had been in sporadic heavy battle with a larger enemy force all afternoon about thirteen miles west of the firebase. Ammo had been redistributed among the troops, but the grunts were down to their last few rounds.

"We know the risk and this is not an order," the lieutenant stressed. "These men need resupply ASAP—but you can turn down the mission and no one will think the less of you."

It was something that had to be done. These guys couldn't be left out there to be massacred.

"We're wasting time," Eskildsen said.

The lieutenant went along as extra crew. Reloaded with ammo and water, the chopper struggled off the pad and hooked straight west into the thin retreating light of day. Eskildsen and Peters scanned for the north-south river that junctioned with a smaller tributary to pinpoint the besieged battalion's location. By the time the Huey reached it, the tops of trees a thousand feet below were a sea of black. Darkness, smoke, and haze smudged out the horizon. There was no moon.

Darkness was a chopper's best cover. Eskildsen extinguished all navigation lights and dimmed the red instrument panel to prevent making the Huey an easy target. Night flying with visual reference to an almost invisible horizon could easily create spatial disorientation. Vertigo. It was a suicide-prone condition while flying or attempting to hover above the tops of jungle trees. "Seat-of-the-pants" flying in the extreme.

After several attempts under forbidding circumstances, Eskildsen located the battalion by using the bleached skeleton of a long-dead tree as a geographical marker. It stood out ghostlike against the darkness. Since it was considered humanly impossible to maintain control of a hovering helicopter without an outside reference, Eskildsen also used the tree for that purpose while his crew kicked out resupply. Helicopters were inherently unstable, even under the best conditions. Hovering was like balancing a BB on top of a bowling ball.

Enemy machine guns from three separate locations no more than one hundred yards out pecked at the sound of the chopper. An RPG missed it by less than three feet. Chief Eskildsen issued a long-suppressed sigh of relief when the job was finally over. He lifted his bird back into the night sky and sped away toward Lai Khe to drop off his lieutenant passenger. Tonight had by far been the most hazardous mission he had ever attempted.

The night wasn't over. Another lieutenant in a jeep was waiting for him when he landed at Lai Khe. The first lieutenant spoke to the jeep lieutenant, then returned to Eskildsen. His face was so pale it glowed in the night.

"The guys on the ground have two men critically wounded," he reported, his voice wavering. "Medics think they might be able to save them if they can get some whole blood and surgical instruments. God, man . . . I don't feel right about asking this. Hell, I was just out there with you, but . . . but I've been instructed to ask. Will you . . . ?" He swallowed. "Will you try again. Will you go back out there?"

Chief Eskildsen blanched. He put the question to his crew. "Guys, I can't order you to die. You know the risk as well as I do. The odds are against us—but I'd like to give it a shot."

Somber looks passed among Peters, Wilson, Samson and the lieutenant. Samson spoke first. "What are we waiting for, Mr. E?"

Five normally sane men volunteered to risk their lives again to save two others about whom they knew nothing except that they were comrades-in-arms.

A cardboard box about two feet cubed and wrapped in green duct tape was loaded aboard the Huey. Attached to it was a rope that would allow it to be lowered through jungle canopy to troops on the ground. It couldn't be kicked out of the helicopter like ammo and C-rations; it had to be handled carefully.

The Lai Khe fire control center contacted Eskildsen on his flight out: "Bulldog Three-Three, be advised artillery is currently shooting H&I in a full circle around the location, as close as three hundred yards. Travel in area highly unadvised. I say again—highly unadvised."

"Lai Khe Control," Eskildsen radioed back. "I have urgent medical supplies for that location. Can you leave me an opening?"

The other end paused. Then: "Bulldog Three-Three, request approved. Will leave the north side open. Stay south of the crossroads to avoid outgoing trajectory . . . Good luck, Bulldog."

Behind, at Lai Khe, brilliant orange flashes from the muzzles of 155mm howitzers strobed against the black skyline like a distant storm. Ahead, similar strobing occurred as shells exploded in a horse-shoe around the beleaguered battalion to keep the enemy from over-running it. Eskildsen would be flying his helicopter through the north opening of the horseshoe into an area in which massive, high-explosive shells were impacting as near as *one hundred yards away.*

The force of a concussion wave from a single 155 HE round was like detonating two hundred pounds of dynamite. It left a crater six to eight feet deep and twenty feet across, more than big enough to bury a full-sized Ford. Shrapnel, dirt, rock, and other debris ejected from the crater reached four hundred yards away and at least half that dis-tance into the air. Turbulence from the explosions rattled the helicopter while it was still a good distance out.

Eskildsen set a course to the south and west to stay out of the artil-lery path. He circled downrange and approached the north opening, again with all navigation and instrument lights doused. At least the

battalion was easier to locate this time. It lay within that piece of darkness surrounded by impacting power flashes.

He dropped pitch and descended below the artillery trajectory path
to come in low and slow, looking for a red-lensed flashlight on the ground
marking the drop site. Nearby explosions buffeted the helicopter once
it entered the dragon's mouth. It was the worst turbulence he had ever
endured. It felt like speeding down a dark road at midnight through hail,
sleet, and wind while hitting potholes that slung your vehicle violently
all over the road and banged your head against the ceiling. The two crewmembers and the lieutenant in the cargo bay were all but shaken out the
doors. They grabbed and held on to anything within reach.

It was difficult to tell the difference between the black of treetops
below and the black sky above. Eskildsen depended on *feel* to fly the
chopper. Desperate eyes searched for a red signal flicker from the trees
as the chopper inched into the center of the horseshoe.

"Badger Two-Six? This is Bulldog Three-Three. Are we over your
position?"

"This is Badger Two-Six. Negative, Bulldog. Negative."

Eskildsen pulled pitch, climbed a few feet, and circled within the
arena of chaos, temporarily blinded each time a shell flashed, hammered by massive mule-kick shock waves so powerful they slammed
his shoulders into the sides of his armor plate seat and left painful
bruises. Threatening to knock the bird out of the sky, rock, dirt, pieces
of trees rained down from above and whacked and thumped the top
of the Huey, or careened off its rotor blades. Artillery shells rocketed
overhead with a rapid *Whoosh! Whoosh! Whoosh!*

Three times he circled before he caught a glimpse of red down
through the thick jungle canopy. Wilson, the crew chief, shouted through
the intercom, "I see the light, I see the light! Hold it steady here, Mr. E.
Keep it coming. Stop! Move forward. Forward . . . Steady . . ."

Confirmation came from the ground. "Bulldog, hold your position.
You're close . . ."

It was again like balancing the BB on a bowling ball all right—but this time in the middle of a cyclone. Eskildsen's only ground reference remained the ghost tree from his first flight. It was visible only momentarily during shell flashes.

Wilson sat on the floor in the bay, legs dangling outside while he lowered the box of blood and instruments, paying out the rope through his gloved hands. Samson gripped Wilson's belt to keep him from being pitched out. The lieutenant fed the rope to the crew chief.

"Okay, Mr. E," Wilson murmured through the intercom. "Hold still. We're lowering now . . . You're drifting . . . This ain't working, Mr. E. Every time a shock wave hits, we drift off position. The package keeps swinging around on the end of the rope . . . Damn it! Now it's stuck in the top of the trees. I can't get it loose!"

The Huey rocked and shuddered while the crew tugged on the rope. It was no use. The box was firmly wedged. Finally, Eskildsen ordered the rope to be thrown out with the package. At least it had been delivered, even if the guys down there had to climb for it. He lifted the helicopter away.

"Bulldog!" came an excited radio cry from below. "The package went with you!"

Sure enough, the end of the rope had somehow caught on the skid when Wilson hurled it away. The precious cargo of life-giving blood had jerked free of the trees when the chopper rose and was again dangling on its rope below the helicopter.

Eskildsen hovered while Wilson climbed out on the skid to retrieve the end of the line. Samson and the lieutenant held on to him with all their strength in the gale force turbulence. Stagnant air, dust, and smoke from the shelling resembled a brown fog in the bursting of shells. Detonated TNT stung eyes and nostrils. A tree blew up next to the Huey, its top branches raking the bottom of the bird as it fell. The jolt almost knocked the chopper out of the air. An artillery shell whipped past.

"I saw it go by!" Samson cried. "It went *under* the helicopter. The back end was glowing red. I could have almost touched it!"

Eskildsen realized he couldn't keep doing this forever, risking the lives of his crew, however desperately he wanted to help the men on the ground.

"He's got the rope!" Samson sang out. "He's got it!"

Badger 26 came up on the horn. "Bulldog, we have an alternate. We think it's a small hole in the canopy, but it's about fifty yards closer to the artillery. Please advise."

"Badger, I didn't like the last place you picked for us—but let's go for it."

Please, please God, he silently prayed. *Let me find them . . .*

Unexpectedly, a red-lensed flashlight appeared down among the trees. It was so bright that it seemed someone was shining a miniature searchlight directly at the cockpit. It flickered off, then back on again as strong as ever.

"I see it! I'm going in!" Chief Eskildsen yelled over the intercom.

Copilot Peters leaned forward in his seat, straining to see through his window. "I can't see it—but I'm glad you can."

"It's right in front of us. Do you see it?"

"I don't see it."

Was he blind?

Eskildsen hovered the chopper directly above the light. Wilson clambered out on the skid to play out the rope a second time while Samson and the lieutenant held on to him.

"Bulldog, you are over our position!" Badger exclaimed with relief. "I say again—you are over our position."

Two shells exploded nearby, one right after the other in brilliant white light. The chopper was going down this time. No way could it stay in the air.

Oh, shit! This is going to be bad!

Except something strange and surreal began to unfold. To his astonishment, Eskildsen found himself lapsing into some kind of slow-motion dream state. Engine sounds from the Huey grew muted and distant. The whip crash of explosions sounded so distant as to be virtually unnoticeable. Shock waves felt like riding over a gentle ocean swell.

Most surprising of all, he could suddenly *see*. He saw the tops of trees below, the opening in them, the horizon providing a fixed visual reference. It was like the moon suddenly shot out from behind clouds—except there were no clouds and no moon. Perhaps arty had thrown up an aerial flare to provide light at the moment he needed it most.

The light was soft, white, glowing, almost ethereal. Puzzled, even somewhat confused, he glanced back over his shoulder and clearly saw the crew in the cargo bay fused together like conjoined triplets hauntingly reminiscent of the famous photo of Marines hoisting the flag over Iwo Jima. They were lowering the blood box.

What's taking them so long? It feels like I've been hovering here for over ten minutes. Damn . . . What's taking so long?

Wilson, Samson, and the lieutenant began yelling and cheering. Badger on the ground shouted excitedly through his radio, "Bulldog, Bulldog, we have the package! Repeat, we have the package!"

Eskildsen flew his Huey free of the arena of chaos. His hands began shaking uncontrollably once they were safely outside the dragon's mouth. His entire body jerked and convulsed as suppressed emotion from the stress and strain of the night's harrowing flights broke the surface. Peters took the controls. He interrupted a long silence that lasted half the distance back to Lai Khe.

"Jim, I have no idea how you did what you did," he marveled. "We would have been dead at least six times if I had been flying. I was praying my ass off that you could see the tops of the trees every time you made an approach to hover. I never did see them. I never even saw the red light. I don't understand, Jim. I couldn't see anything. *Nothing!*"

"All I can say is those artillery guys timed it just right with the flares. I couldn't have done it without them."

Peters stared at him through a stunned silence. Finally, he gasped, "What are you talking about, Jim? It was pitch black out there. There weren't any flares."

Both critically wounded soldiers survived the night, thanks to the blood delivery made by Bulldog 33, and were safely medevac'd the next morning. CWO Jim Eskildsen was awarded a Distinguished Flying Cross for his efforts. The only way he could explain the ethereal white light was that Somebody Higher Up must have helped him.

ARMY SPECIALIST BILL MCDONALD,
Vietnam, 1967

U.S. Army Huey helicopters inserting ARVN Rangers into scrub jungle along the Saigon River across from Cu Chi encountered a buzz saw made up of more than five hundred North Vietnamese troops. Hot LZ! Enemy fire riddled the choppers, destroying one or two, while the remainder, crippled or not, wobbled back into the air and beat a hasty retreat to Phu Lai. On the ground they left about 150 ARVN Rangers desperately battling their way off the LZ.

Flying high above the din of battle, out of rifle range, a command and control (C&C) UH-1 "slick" circled the action on the ground. Unlike Huey gunships mounted with fixed machine guns and rockets, a slick was armed only with M-60 machine guns in its cargo doors. Crew chief and right door gunner Bill McDonald* leaned out his door over his pintel-mounted machine gun and looked down onto the turmoil of explosions and dueling tracers weaving spiderwebs around the oblong clearing that served as a landing zone. The full effect of the hell below escaped him, the din drowned out by the noise of the aircraft engine, the chopper's altitude, and the muffling effects of his flight helmet.

Inside the cargo bay, three South Vietnamese officers huddled around maps and a PRC-25 radio. They were in charge of action on the ground. Saying they needed to assert control over the engagement, they requested pilots ferry them down to the more neutral end of the LZ. Chatter through the intercom made it known that the plane commander didn't like the idea, but it was his duty as chauffeur to honor the officers' request. The helicopter banked and began giving up air.

McDonald turned his head to check on the left door gunner opposite him. The kid shot him back an *Aw, shit!* look. Neither of them

---

* See also Foreward and Chapter 11.

could quite believe that ARVN officers would want to join their unit in battle. It had been their experience that most ran the other way.

One of the officers, a skinny fellow with slitted eyes as dark as beads, glared at McDonald. *What the hell was the matter with this little prick?*

"We're in and out of there like grease," the pilot informed his crew over the intercom. "Kick these guys out on the ground—and then we're outa here."

Gunships had vacated the area to escort damaged slicks. That left the C&C bird to go in without cover. The pilot circled warily downwind, dropped to treetop level, and poured on the coal, *whop-whopping* in fast and low. McDonald clung to his M-60 to maintain balance and tried to keep an eye peeled for bad guys in the forest. Most of the action seemed to be occurring at the other end of the LZ, and he glimpsed nothing moving in the blur of jungle just below his feet.

The Huey flared at the first opening to hover above the grass.

It collided with a flaming wall of lead and steel as enemy around the edges opened up. Charlie must have anticipated a return flight of reinforcements and rigged up a little welcoming committee. Tracers crisscrossed the sky in bright, almost-beautiful patterns with the intruding helicopter as the focal point. Metal skin pinged as bullets ripped holes through it. Smoke from the engine, its sudden irregular beat, signified a hit on something vital.

Bucking and yawing, the injured bird skittered sideways inches above the grass, whipping the door gunners and passengers from side to side and all but flinging them out. McDonald glimpsed muzzle flashes spitting tracers from the surrounding forest. Orders were for the door gunners to hold their fire unless targets were positively identi-fied. Friendlies and enemy were so mixed together in all the confusion that it was almost impossible to tell them apart.

The Huey hit earth hard, jolting its occupants and sliding across the field on its skids. A couple of the ARVN officers looked frightened and reluctant to leave the bird, but the beady-eyed fellow unassed even before it came to a full stop. McDonald grabbed the nearest remaining

Vietnamese and tossed him out in the grass. The last man went out on his own, running like a rat deserting a burning ship.

The pilot came on the horn reporting a downed bird: *"Mayday! Mayday!"*

The engine ran rough, but the blades were still turning. McDonald checked on the other door gunner. *Okay?* They gave each other thumbs up.

He turned back to his own business. The beady-eyed ARVN had stopped on the field about twenty yards away while his comrades were racing to the trees. The guy crouched suddenly and pointed his M-16 assault rifle directly at McDonald.

What the hell . . . ?

Horrified, McDonald met the officer's traitorous gaze for a split instant before the M-16's muzzle blossomed and spat a steady stream of flame, emptying on full auto a complete magazine of 5.56mm. Impact threw him back hard against the transmission housing wall that dissected the rear part of the cargo bay. Stunned and knocked breathless, he saw streams of light entering his body from the bullets. Yet, he felt nothing beyond the initial punch. Bullets severed the radio cord to his flight helmet and left him in silence.

The Huey's rough-running engine revved as pilots struggled to get the crippled aircraft into the sky. It bounced across the field before it finally leapt off the ground, wobbling dangerously as it skimmed treetops, leaking oil and gas and smoke.

McDonald was vaguely aware of what was happening. He thought he must *surely* be dying. Smoke issued from his chest. He slapped at the flames. That was when he became mindful of the new ceramic body protector he had volunteered to test for the Army. He could hardly believe his good fortune. The new ceramic caught the high-velocity bullet before it penetrated his chest, leaving him bruised, out of breath, and in pain—but gloriously *alive!* He would have died for sure had he worn the regular-issue flak jacket.

The Huey could not stay up. It shuddered and limped through the shallow air. Tree branches slapped its skid. McDonald held on, in no condition to do much of anything else.

After making only a few hundred yards, the engine died and the awkward bird crash-landed in a small opening among the trees, skidded up against a stump, and came to a stop, wheezing like an exhausted animal. McDonald flung off his flight helmet. He could hear again the clatter and boom and roar of the nearby fight.

Recovering from shock, he scrambled from the downed bird and helped the pilots exit before the chopper burst into flame. The left door gunner remained inside. McDonald discovered him slumped on the steel floor against the web seating, suffering from multiple bullet wounds that had mangled his back from his shoulders on down. Blood splattered webbing, floor, walls, then leaked out the door and down the fuselage. Like something had been butchered. Whether he was dead or not, McDonald couldn't tell. He hoisted the kid across his shoulders and dashed with him and the two pilots to the nearby tree line to await rescue.

The pilot's *Mayday* had not gone unheeded. Other helicopters extracted the wounded and battered crew of the downed Huey.

When the Army Safety Board investigated the crash, as it is required to do, it uncovered more questions than answers. Circumstances surrounding the crash went down as one of the great mysteries of the war. In spite of the evidence, puzzled board members concluded that what happened was *impossible*.

Door gunners in flight were like silhouettes of each other, one in each door with their backs to each other and the transmission housing wall partially between them. Only one bullet struck McDonald when the ARVN emptied his magazine at him. His ceramic chest plate caught it. Seventeen bullets punctured the transmission housing wall and hit the opposite machine gunner in the back.

That was where the mystery came in.

Investigators determined from McDonald's position in his door that all seventeen bullets that riddled the other door gunner had *first* to go through him and the transmission housing. There were seventeen *exit* bullet holes from the other side of the transmission wall; there was not a single *entrance* on McDonald's side. It was like the ARVN's bullets went completely through McDonald's body without touching him. Even with the ceramic plating, the combined shock of so much lead likely would have killed him. As for why there were exit holes but no entrances? No one, least of all McDonald, could explain how that was even remotely possible.

All Specialist Bill McDonald could ever come up with was that God must have provided "spiritual armor" to save him that fateful morning along the Saigon River—for a purpose that only God knew.

MARINE COLONEL NEIL LEVIN,
Vietnam, 1966

U.S. Marine Corps aviator Colonel Neil Levin* possessed a solid personal and spiritual connection to God, whose presence he felt in the form of an imaginary angel riding his wing every time he took off on a mission. His angel took a real beating on an April morning in 1966.

He and his wingman flying twin A-4 Skyhawks refueled in Da Nang following a patrol, then took to the air en route to home base at Chu Lai. An Air Force FAC in a light spotter plane came up on the radio guard channel: "This is Spotter One. Any aircraft within fifty miles south of Da Nang . . . I have an emergency message."

Colonel Levin acknowledged: "Spotter One, this is Whiskey Kilo Six. We're twenty miles south of Da Nang at twenty thousand feet. We're armed with eight rocket pods, each carrying nineteen rockets. Plus eight hundred rounds of twenty-mike-mike cannon. What is the nature of the emergency?"

* See also Chapter 3.

"Roger that, Kilo Six. Helicopters can't get into an area to medevac wounded Marines due to extremely heavy antiaircraft fire."

"Roger. We are on top of an overcast, but will penetrate and be on our way. I'll call shortly, after we're below ceiling."

The colonel rolled out with his wingman joined tight and punched down through heavy gray clouds, heading out to sea rather than chance flying blind into ground obstacles. Shortly, the two jet fighters broke free of cloud cover over blue ocean with white-capped breakers rolling relentlessly toward brown and green coastline. The fighters streaked toward land again at an altitude of 1,200 feet below an uncomfortably low ceiling.

"Spotter One, we're crossing the beach feet dry. Give us headings to the target."

The FAC pilot provided navigation information, then further explained the nature of the target. "Three antiaircraft guns situated and camouflaged at the points of a triangle fifty yards apart in a wooded area."

Reaching the target at a maximum speed of 600 miles per hour took mere seconds. White smoke smudging out of a tree line marked the ground Marines' location and provided a point from which to triangulate the target. The enemy further betrayed himself by opening up to fill the sky with green tracers that collectively resembled a colorful spider's web.

Compressed as they were between the low ceiling and earth, the jets were forced to make low-angle and low-altitude rocket runs during which the birds would be clearly silhouetted against gray clouds. Like ducks in a shooting gallery.

"Kilo Two," Levin instructed his wingman, "take a twenty-second interval on me. Get in as close as you can before firing rockets."

Each plane was equipped with four pods of nineteen rockets to a pod. Once armed and set on *Salvo*, all nineteen rockets would release at the same time to provide a spectacular amount of firepower. However, more than one run might be required to knock out all three enemy positions.

290 CHARLES W. SASSER

Levin led the attack, roaring in at full power. He was like a super-sonic fly buzzing into the green spider's web. *Holy God . . .*

Bright tracers flickered across Levin's nose. The gunners down there weren't that good. They were leading the incoming fighters by too wide a margin and spreading the net out ahead.

Thundering above the forest, rattling leaves and flailing grass with his passage, Levin blazed away with his double 20mm cannon, chewing up trees and ground in a wide swath of destruction.

The Skyhawk shuddered slightly with the firing of one pod of rockets. Immediately, Levin pulled up and out of the run, separating his plane from the hellish spawn of death he had unleashed, lifting up and out while the brood of rockets trailing a common vapor swarmed toward their target.

Pulling Gs out of the dive bled momentum. Suddenly, Levin realized he was trapped in the middle of a green skein of tracers flashing all around his cockpit. Those gunners were getting better. He saw no way to avoid hits. The little bastards were shooting him down.

This is when and where I die, he thought.

Abruptly, to his amazement, he discovered himself *outside* his own airplane where, weightless and floating in the air, he saw himself through the glass canopy *inside* the Skyhawk. How could he be in two places at once? He was suspended in air and at the same time sitting at the airplane's controls flying through that horrific sky with tracers interlacing around him.

What the hell is going on?

Enemy rounds went right through his floating transparent body. They went through the Skyhawk's wings also, but they left jagged holes.

Action unraveling in split seconds slowed to a crawl. Time had no content for his detached spiritual form; it was as if he had all the time in the universe at his disposal. In slow motion, his life-and-death struggle lost its drama, its immediacy. Calmly, his second self, with its objective viewpoint, choreographed his corporeal self in flying the jet through the deadly labyrinth that filled the sky.

In the next instant, he felt himself sucked breathlessly back into the cockpit and inside his body again. The Skyhawk climbed and streaked out of danger. He looked back and saw his target splatter as rockets fired by both himself and his trailing wingman scored on the antiaircraft site.

Astounded and shaken by the experience, he examined his wing where he always imagined his angel rode. He half expected to see the angel hanging on out there now, smiling at him, maybe rendering a little salute of acknowledgment.

Colonel Levin and his wingman destroyed the enemy anti-aircraft site. Damages to his jet from the site forced him to make a precarious emergency landing at Da Nang, but both pilots walked away safely.

AFTERWORD

Wars are as much a part of human history as tools, clothing, and contemplating the unknown. While it might be "pretty to think" there will be no more war, as Ernest Hemingway once wrote, such a state of peace where the lion and the lamb will lie down together is not likely to come to pass, not on an earth dominated by human beings. The lion underneath his acacia tree and the lamb in his meadow do not have to bother themselves with such matters; they merely follow their biological programs. Mankind, on the other hand, must not only figure out *how* to survive while plagued with war, he must also determine *why* he should survive—and what it all means—in order to give his life purpose and meaning.

When the "times that try men's souls" are upon him, man invariably turns to God, or to what he perceives as some "Maker" beyond normal human boundaries, for explanation and understanding. This is especially true of warriors who, in whatever nation, are under the strain of combat.

"It is when they go into battle, face death, see their comrades killed, and have to grapple with the morality of killing the enemy that they search for faith with new intensity," writes author Stephen Mansfield in *The Faith of the American Soldier.*

Visitors to the secretary of Air Force at the Pentagon pass by a huge mural of an Air Force family going to church, within which appears the sentiment *Here I am, Lord. Send me.* Naval Academy cadets still pray collectively before meals. Chaplains accompany armies to war to minister to the spirits of their soldiers. Young service people away from home for the first time find that religious practices keep them connected to normal life, especially during combat when the "foxhole factor" comes into play. The foxhole factor states that the number of atheists present in a particular circumstance is inversely proportional to the number of bullets flying.

With little doubt, religious faith, prayer, and belief in a Divine God have sustained American soldiers through trying times. Soldiers under the stress of battle seek God, and often find him in surprising, unexpected, and even miraculous ways.

Professor Angelo M. Codevilla of Boston University speculated upon what it might mean should state secularism ever prohibit God from going to war with America and its soldiers. He wrote:

> There may exist a pool of young people big enough to fill America's military who combine appetite for physical challenges, tolerance for danger, a spirit of self-sacrifice, discipline, and patriotism, but who don't really care whether America is "under God" or not, who get along just fine without the Ten Commandments, are more bothered by piety than by homosexuality, and are inspired by "sensitivity" training. And perhaps the social changes forced upon the U.S. military in recent years will bring such people out of the woodwork and into uniform. Maybe America will end up with atheist foxholes. But surely these changes tell the families who now actually fill the armed forces that maybe the kinds of people who are making the rules should also be doing the fighting.

NOTES AND SOURCES

The information in this book is based on a variety of sources, the core of which is extensive taped interviews with combat soldiers from World War II to the war in Iraq. Other documents and sources obviously had to be utilized as well in relating the American story of the quest for spiritual meaning on battlefields from the French and Indian Wars to the present day in Baghdad. These varieties of sources include: official U.S. military documents and after-action reports; letters and documents preserved by museums, universities, and libraries; "living history" archives; letters and diaries made public; newspapers and periodicals; historical records; court and legal transcripts; books; and various other published accounts.

Rather than footnote, I have arranged references here by chapters for those who might like to review sources, where available. I recommend published works listed to anyone interested in further research on the topic.

FOREWORD
By Reverend Bill McDonald

INTRODUCTION
Leland Belknap From *The Deadly Brotherhood* by John C. McManus (Ballantine, 1998)

CHAPTER 1: FAITH

Paul Curtis, From *The Deadly Brotherhood* by John C. McManus (Ballantine, 1998)

Arthur Kammerer, Ibid.

NATHAN JONES

Interviews, August 1, 2006

KEVIN CRAWFORD

Interviews, August 31, 2006

TOM COTTICK

Interviews and personal letters supplied by John Cottick (son), July–September 2006

RICHARD D. "DICK" WILSON

Meridian magazine, August 14, 2006

Saints at War Archives, Harold B. Lee Library, Brigham Young University

Veterans History Project, Library of Congress

CHAPTER 2: PRISONERS OF WAR

Great Raid On Cabanatuan by William B. Breuer (John Wiley & Sons, 1994)

John McElroy, From Veterans History Project, Library of Congress

Howard Rutledge, From *In the Presence of Mine Enemies* by Howard and Phylis Rutledge (Fleming H. Revel & Co., 1973)

JAMES GAUTIER

Interviews, 2000

I Came Back From Bataan by James Donovan Gautier, Jr. (Emerald House Group, 1997)

DAN PITZER

Interview with and speech by Nick Rowe, Fort Chaffee, Arkansas (1984)

George W. Bush, Speech commending Rocky Versace, July 8, 2002

Robert K. Dornan, Medal of Honor recommendation to U.S. Congress

Five Years to Freedom by James N. Rowe (Ballantine, 1971)
Joint Personnel Recovery Center (JPRC) declassified reports, 1964–65
POW Network reports, January 27, 1997
Task Force Omega report, 1973

JAMES PAXTON

Frances Maxwell, Letter supplied to U.S. Historical Society
War Letters by Andrew Carroll (Washington Square Press, 2001)

JACK M. BUTCHER

Code Name Bright Light by George J. Veith (Free Press, 1998)
Joint Personnel Recovery Center (JPRC) declassified reports, 1971–72

JOHN MCCAIN

Faith of My Fathers by John McCain with Mark Salter (Random House, 1999)
Joint Personnel Recovery Center (JPRC) declassified reports, 1971–72
Numerous speeches and press conferences by John McCain

CHAPTER 3: PRAYER

JAMES O'NEILL

After-action reports, U.S. Army
George S. Patton letters, Library of Congress

PAUL DRINKALL

Interviews, March 10, 2006
Letter, March 22, 2006

"THE ANGEL OF HADLEY"

Hadley town Web site
History of Hadley by Sylvester Judd (H. R. Huntting & Co., 1905)
This Country of Ours by Henrietta Elizabeth Marshall (George H. Doran Co., 1917)

NEIL LEVIN

Interviews, July 11, 2006
An Angel Rode My Wing by Neil Levin (Leatherneck Publishing, 2006)
Letter from Levin, July 12, 2006

CHAPTER 4: CASUALTIES

Twenty-Four Notes That Tap Deep Emotions: The Story of the Most Famous Bugle Call, booklet by Jari Villanueva

JESUS SUAREZ DEL SOLAR

After-action reports, U.S. Marines

1st LAR (First Light Armored Reconnaissance Battalion) official command chronology

The Highway War by Seth W. B. Folsom (Potomac Books, 2006)

DAVID GRANT

Contributed by Bill McDonald, Military Writers Society of America

MIKE STROBL

Associated Press, April 9, 2004

Exceedservices.net, April 23, 2004

Military Times, April 2004

PFC Chance Phelps Web site

htttp://tulare.homelinux.net, April 27, 2007

TERRY M. JORGENSEN

Meridian magazine, March 1, 2006

Saints at War archives, Harold B. Lee Library, Brigham Young University

Veterans History Project, Library of Congress

CHAPTER 5: CULTURES

Charley Pryor, Quote from *Ship of Ghosts* by James D. Horn Fischer (Bantam, 2006)

RICHARD KILEY

Interviews, September 26, 2006

Airborne Quarterly, Summer 2006

PAUL HOLTON

Interviews, July 22, 2006

Saving Babylon by Paul Holton (Perihelion Press, 2005)

CHARLIE BROWN

Interviews, by Craig Roberts, 2001

Interviews, by Michael Sasser, December 2003)
Florida Department of Veterans Affairs
EDWARD GYOKERES
USA Weekend, March 1, 2006

CHAPTER 6: CHURCH SERVICES
Tim Sturgill, From *One*, October–November 2006
Kevin Wainwright, From *News 14 Carolina Story* website, April 30, 2006
GEORGE R. BARBER
Interviews, January 2003
O Chaplain! My Chaplain! Man of Service by Janelle T. Frese with Colonel
   Chaplain George R. Barber (Trafford, 2005)
MOLTON A. SHULER, JR.
After-action reports, U.S. Army
From letter to Helen M. Adams
War Letters by Andrew Carroll (Washington Square Press, 2001)
VIRGIL N. KOVALENKO
Historical Department Archives, Church of Jesus Christ of Latter-Day
   Saints
SYD BRISKER
Veterans History Project, Library of Congress
GEORGE WHITEFIELD RIDOUT
Raptureready.com, August 16, 2006
The Cross and the Flag: World War I Experiences by George Whitefield Ridout,
   Library of Congress (unpublished manuscript)
DELBERT KUEHL
A Bridge Too Far by Cornelius Ryan (Popular Library, 1974)
"From No Faith to Enough To Share: A Chaplain Remembers," article
   by Chuck Haga in *Minneapolis-St. Paul Star Tribune*, May 28, 2001
Oral History Project of the World War II Years
Silver Star recommendation, U.S. Army
Veterans Stories, Strikehold504th.com, September 22, 2006

CHAPTER 7: BROTHERHOOD

Quotes from Associated Press, 2004–2005

GEORGE S. RENTZ

Free Encyclopedia

Navy Cross citation

http://navysite.de/ffg/FFG46.HTM, on USS *Rentz*

Ship of Ghosts by James D. Hornfischer (Bantam, 2006)

Wikipedia

CLARA BARTON

Clara Barton Papers, Library of Congress

DESMOND T. DOSS

America Folklore Center, Library of Congress

Homeofheroes.com, December 5, 2006

Medal of Honor citation

New York Times, March 25, 2006

Patriot Post, April 8, 2006

Washington Post, March 26, 2006

U.S. Army Center for Military History

Wikipedia

DAMIEN LUTEN

Army News Service, July 17, 2003

Associated Press, numerous

"Attack on the 507th Maintenance Co.," U.S. Army release, August 15, 2006

CNN.com, March 31, 2003

CNN.com, June 18, 2003

El Paso Times, April 2003

KATU2 News, Portland, Oregon, July 15, 2003

KFOXTV.com, March 2003

MSNBC.com, April 14, 2003

Silver Star citation to Donald Ralph Walters

IndyChannel.com, March 15, 2004

"U.S. Army Official Report on 507th Maintenance Co.: An Nasiri-
    yah, Iraq"
Washington Times, July 9, 2003

EDGAR SHEPARD

Veterans History Project, Library of Congress
War Letters by Andrew Carroll (Washington Square Press, 2001)

CHAPTER 8: DOUBT

Jeremy Lussi, From *Voices from the Front* by Frank Schaeffer (Carroll &
    Graf, 2004)
"The Wall," contributed by Jim Eskildsen

JAMES WALSH

Veterans History Project, Library of Congress

WALTER BROMWICH

Veterans History Project, Library of Congress
Walter Bromwich letter to Dorothy McGibbeny

PAUL STEPPE

Veterans History Project, Library of Congress

LARRY NAUGHTON

Interviews, September 25, 2006

ARTHUR SHULTZ

A Bridge Too Far by Cornelius Ryan (Popular Library, 1974)

ROBERT GADDY

Interviews, August 12, 2006
Leatherneck magazine, February 1968
III Marine Amphibious Force Combat Information Bureau
Medal of Honor Citation for William Perkins
USMCfew.com, August 14, 2006

CHAPTER 9: WHY ME, LORD?

Ira Hayes, From *Flags of Our Fathers* by James Bradley
Vietnam History Project, Library of Congress

BOB GROSS

Interviews, August 1, 2006

HAIG KOOBATIAN

Interviews, August 18, 2006

Numerous written correspondence, 2006–2007

CHARLES MCVAY, III

Abandon Ship by Richard F. Newcomb (HarperCollins, 1958)

Associated Press reports of death, November 1968

Joint House-Senate Resolution and papers, October 12, 2000

McVay court-martial transcripts/court of inquiry, 1945–46

Oral History Project of the World War II Years

USS *Indianapolis* papers, Library of Congress

CHAPTER 10: THE UNEXPLAINED

Edgar Cayce, From *Edgar Cayce: The Sleeping Prophet* by Jess Stearn (Doubleday, 1966)

"The Past-Life Memories of Children," by David Ian Miller, Mindpowernews.com, August 3, 2006

Kevin Williams, Research conclusions on "The WDE and War," February 28, 2006

GENE BECK

Interviews, July 14, 2006

JAMES M. HUSTON

"About Past Lives, Uniontown WWII Flyer's Memories in Louisiana Boy," by Judy Kroeger, *Daily Courier*, April 15, 2004

Associated Press reports

"8-Year-Old Boy Remembers Past Life as Fighter Pilot," by Patti Dobranski, *Pittsburgh Tribune Review*, Mindpowernews.com, September 8, 2006

"The Past-Life Memories of Children," by David Ian Miller, Mindpowernews.com, August 3, 2006

"The Past-Life Memories of James Leininger," by Wes Milligan, Acadiana Profile, December 2004

USS *Enterprise* CV-6 Action Report, February 23–March 9, 1945
"USS *Enterprise* CV-6," Cv6.org, Wikipedia, September 8, 2006
"USS *Natoma Bay* CVE-62," Wikipedia

LLOYD KING

Interviews, July 18, 2006
From 'Nam with Love by Lloyd King (River Road Press, 2006)

CRAIG ROBERTS

Interviews, August 14, 2006

CHAPTER 11: PRESENCE

David Bryant, From *Voices from the Front* by Frank Schaeffer (Carroll
    & Graf, 2004)
Christian History Institute, Gospelcom.net, August 16, 2006
Civil War Christian Commission Records
Lawrence Nickell, Quote from *The Deadly Brotherhood* by John C.
    McManus (Ballantine, 1998)
The Faith of the American Soldier by Stephen Mansfield (Tarcher/
    Penguin, 2005)

SULLIVAN BALLOU

Civil War Letter, Library of Congress

JANICE HERMERDING

Contributed by Bill McDonald, Military Writers Society of
    America

GALEN KITTLESON

Interviews, 2001–2006

ROBERT H. DIRR, JR.

Contributed by Bill McDonald, Military Writers Society of America

BILL MCDONALD

Interviews, March–November 2006
A Spiritual Warrior's Journey by Bill McDonald (1st Books, 2003)

EDWARD A. PENICHE

Interviews, June 25, 2006
Congressional Record, December 14, 2005

LEONEL R. PEREZ

Interviews, April 7, 2006
Letter to author, April 20, 2006

LEONARD OWCZARZAK

Interviews, July 19, 2006

CHAPTER 12: THE BIBLE

Brice Coleman, From *Tulsa World*, December 21, 2006
Dennis A. Wright, From *Meridian* magazine, March 1, 2006

DAVY CROCKETT

Davy Crockett's Journal, Library of Congress
Exploits by Davy Crockett
Legendsofamerica.com, November 27, 2006
Talewins.com, November 27, 2006

GORDON MADSON

Americans at War: Personal Narratives of American Citizen Soldiers, U.S. Government project
Casualties, Korean War, 2nd Infantry Division Web site
"Korean War Atrocities," by Subcommittee on Korean War Atrocities, January 7, 1954
New Yorker, December 27, 1999
New Yorker, January 3, 2000
Legacy Project (Letters from Revolutionary War to Present), Washington, D.C.
U.S. Department of Veterans Affairs
War Letters by Andrew Carroll (Washington Square Press, 2001)

MARCUS "MIKE" BRUNE

Interviews, July 10, 2006

CHAPTER 13: CHAPLAINS

"A Civil Religion," by Rodney Stark, *The American Enterprise*, May 2006
The Bulletproof George Washington by David Barton (Wallbuilder, 1990)

THE FOUR CHAPLAINS

Chapel of the Four Chaplains

Florida Atlantic University Library (Jewish Heroes and Heroines in
America), January 15, 1998, vol. 7, no. 8

Immortal Chaplains Foundation

Public Law 86-656, 86th Congress, creating "Four Chaplains Medal"

Sun-Herald.com, February 3, 2005

"The True Story of the Four Chaplains," Homeofheroes.com

U.S. Conference of Catholic Bishops, Dcdiocese.org, August 1, 2006

War Letters by Andrew Carroll (Washington Square Press, 2001)

DENNIS GOODWIN

Interviews, Sergeant Cyle Anderson

"Monroe Pastor Becomes Army Chaplain" by Brad Broders, News 14
Carolina, News14charlotte.com

Voices from the Front by Frank Schaeffer (Carroll & Graf, 2004)

BRIAN KIMBALL

"Al Taqaddum Air Base," Globalsecurity.org

"Chaplain Recalls Combat Experiences," press release, Marine Corps
Recruit Depot Parris Island, September 20, 2005

Marine Corps news release on Cinelli, Woodward, Wallis, Wilson, Hensley, June 18, 2004

DAYTON KANNON

Related by brother Lawrence Kannon, June 2006

JEFF STRUECKER

"A Jeff Struecker Event," public appearances, Emanuelcc.org

Associated Press reports

"Battle of Mogadishu," Wikipedia

Captain Jeff Struecker, appearance on TV's *700 Club*

Doorway to Hell by General Ed Wheeler and Colonel Craig Roberts
(Consolidated Press, 2002)

In the Company of Heroes by Michael J. Durant (G. P. Putnam's Sons, 2003)

The Road to Unafraid by Jeff Struecker (W Publishing Group, 2006)

Specialoperations.com: Operation Restore Hope

Jeff Struecker Web site

"Struecker Puts Life on the Line for the Gospel," by Bryan Cribb, *Christian Science Monitor* October 14, 2007 (reprint)

"Terror Clarifies Soldier's Faith," by Norman Jameson, *Biblical Recorder,* September 12, 2003

3rd Ranger Battalion after-action reports

Time February 28, 1994

"U.S. Army Ranger Association October 4, 2007, as reprinted in www .jeffstruecker.com—History: Somalia," Ranger.org

DELBERT KUEHL

Ibid. Chapter 6

CHAPTER 14: DIVINE INTERVENTION

Ed Hurd, From *Military* magazine, March 2006

Ronald Reagan, From "Of Providence and Policy," by John O'Sullivan, *National Review,* December 4, 2006

"World Trade Center," *Tulsa Beacon,* August 17, 2006

LEE DAVIS

Interviews, August 8, 2006

HAIG KOOBATIAN

Ibid. chapter 9

GEORGE WASHINGTON

Fighting for a Continent: Newspaper Coverage of the English and French War for Control of North America, by David A. Copeland, from Earlyamerica.com, spring 1997

The Bulletproof George Washington, by David Barton (Wallbuilders, 2003)

The Colonial Wars 1689–1762, by Howard H. Peckham (University of Chicago Press, 1964)

ANONYMOUS

Marine Corps legend passed down from World War II

JIM ESKILDSEN

Interviews, July 21, 2006

"My Flight into the Twilight Zone," by Jim Eskildsen, October 3, 2005, (unpublished manuscript)

BILL MCDONALD

Ibid. Chapter 11

NEIL LEVIN

Ibid. Chapter 3

AFTERWORD

"The Atheist Foxhole," by Angelo M. Codevilla, *American Spectator*, February 2006

The Faith of the American Soldier, by Stephen Mansfield (Tarcher/Penguin, 2005)

GLOSSARY

AA	antiaircraft
A-gunner	assistant gunner
AO	area of operations
arty	artillery
ARVN	Army of the Republic of Vietnam
Chicom	Chinese communist
CO	commanding officer
DMZ	demilitarized zone
EOD	Explosive Ordnance Disposal
FAC	forward air controller
FO	forward observer (artillery)
FSB	fire support base
HE	high explosives
Huey	UH-1 helicopter
HMMWV (Humvee)	High Mobility Multi-Wheeled Vehicle
IED	improvised explosive device
KIA	killed in action
klick	kilometer
LCI	Landing craft (infantry)

LCT	Landing craft (tanks)
LST	landing ship (tank)
LZ	landing zone
MLR	main line of resistance
NCO	noncommissioned officer
NVA	North Vietnamese Army
POW	prisoner of war
R & R	rest and relaxation
RPG	rocket-propelled grenade
RTO	radio-telephone operator
SAM	surface-to-air missile
SAR	search and rescue
TOC	tactical operations center
VC	Viet Cong (North Vietnamese guerrilla)

INDEX